Change, Intervention and Consequence

Change, Intervention and Consequence

An Exploration of the Process of Intended Change

TOM DOUGLAS

FREE ASSOCIATION BOOKS / LONDON / NEW YORK

Published in 1997 by
Free Association Books Ltd
57 Warren Street, London W1P 5PA
and 70 Washington Square South,
New York NY 10012–1091

British Library Cataloguing in Publication Data
A CIP catalogue record for this book is available from
the British Library

ISBNs: 1 85343 376 4 hardback, 1 85343 377 2 pbk

Designed, typeset and produced for Free Association Books by
Chase Production Services, Chadlington, OX7 3LN
Printed in the EC by J W Arrowsmith, Bristol

To Shirley as ever, with fondest love
for her constant and invaluable support
and her infinite patience.

Contents

Acknowledgements

There is nothing in the world constant, but inconstancy.

Jonathan Swift

I would like to put on record my indebtedness to generations of students and colleagues in several disciplines for their help, ideas and energetic discussion of the concepts, theories and principles which were available to us in what were often frustrating attempts to extract some practical value from them which could possibly aid us in our work with the real human problems with which we were faced.

1 Introduction: Reasons for Writing this Book – its Structure and Use

This book is concerned with change.

More particularly it is concerned with the changes that human beings make, either to themselves or to others, with conscious intent.

The basis of all change processes is that they produce a difference between state A and state B, where A is the state to which change processes were applied, and B is a later state after those processes have been in operation for some greater or lesser amount of time.

This process is obvious enough not to need stating and is clearly understood by all when it occurs in the realm of physical and material things and insensate objects. For example, changes such as the application of heat to a metal bar can be measured in terms of temperature and expansion and in structure, with a great degree of accuracy. Similarly, changes which are organic can be demonstrated as being precipitated by the presence of factors like light, air, food and water.

But the behaviour of human beings – which undoubtedly does change and can be changed – offers none of this simplicity of understanding. Humans are by way of being 'biological machines' and, in so far as behaviour can be demonstrated to be caused and modified by physical entities operating within the structure of that biological machine, it appears there is some solid ground beneath our feet. The behaviour of human beings obviously can be changed by physical damage; by illness, by excesses and deficiencies of essential biochemicals, neural circuits and structures; by drugs, exercise, surgery, and so on; all of which have the essential nature of being tangible even if some of the effects they produce occupy a much less tangible form of existence.

This biological machine is also self-regulating to a degree, and possesses self-awareness, the capacity to think and to imagine, to create and to invent; in other words it has a brain and can reflect upon its own feelings and on past, present and future behaviours. This unit is thus equipped with mental and physical apparatus which form a unitary structure, with the result that incidents occurring in one sphere create effects in others. Not only are all the spheres linked, but they are essential parts of the same structure.

One final point needs to be made in this set of simplistic starting points: each biological machine is effectively unconnected to all others by any tangible (that is, physical) link. Such links as do exist are almost always to be found in the psychological aspect of individuals. They are thus relatively idiosyncratic and interpretative, and can only receive confirmation or negation of their existence and quality by the same process.

In all areas of human behaviour that do not originate in some form of physical event, and even in some that do, we have no stable base from which to calculate probabilities of occurrences. When human behaviour requires to be changed, unless it can be done by physical means in a satisfactory manner, the processes of change have to be founded upon probable explanations as to how the behaviour to be changed originally arose and how it is maintained.

Our actual understanding of the causes of behaviour and of the methods of changing it are thus of a different order of certainty to our understanding of how physical changes are brought about.

But, nevertheless, because social existence demands that certain human behaviours shall be controlled for the safety and security of all; because certain skills have to be learned and deficiencies both genetic and environmental remedied, human behaviour has always been subject to change; through learning, training, compulsion, argument, persuasion, encouragement, and so on. Gradually, as societies have become more sophisticated both in their needs and in their understanding of the human state, more and more people have become 'professional changers' – their working lives are devoted to the process of bringing about changes in others, which are essentially beneficial or at least required. There is a vast world-wide literature on the theories and practice of change processes, and on its methodologies, as well as a large army of individuals ('change agents') who practise in one form or another. So why is it necessary, at this stage of development, to examine these change processes?

As we will see in Chapter 3, I am not concerned to look at all forms of change, but only at change that can be described as 'intended' (i.e. where one or more individuals enter into a change situation with deliberate intent and with consciously defined goals of change).

Reasons for this Discussion

Simply stated, the reasons for this present discussion of intended change efforts are as follows:

(a) Because there is little evidence that it has been done before.

(b) Because the idea of the possibility and/or necessity of change has spawned an enormous industry that is fundamentally based upon an acceptance of the validity of change. Yet this has never been wholly supported, either by research data proving effectiveness, or by any thorough (i.e. unbiased) examination of the bases upon which it is founded.

(c) There appears to be considerable confusion between intended change and ideas of change based upon assisted development. The difference is crucial in that the former is basically a process which is freshly brought into being, often from outside the person or persons involved, while the latter is a process of enhancement, change or diminution of processes already in existence.

(d) Because of these factors, and those which derive from and are dependent upon them, intended change efforts tend to be much less successful than they could be. The main reason for this is that often too little cognisance is taken of what already exists in the context of the target persons, and also of their capacity to make the required changes and, more importantly, to be able to sustain them without help.

These 'reasons' need some brief elaboration, largely because there is a persistent idea that 'change' is a process that is well understood, whereas I suspect this idea is incorrect. There is an acceptance of the believed existence of understanding, which is not the same thing at all as a genuine understanding.

Reason A

Various writers have made critical comments on certain aspects of the processes of intended change; mainly in the area of the theoretical ideas which are used as the bases of practice. Of these, Andreski's scathing comments on the social sciences in general,

Eysenck's comments on the value of psychoanalytic therapeutic procedures and Popper's comments on the lack of objectivity in the theories of behaviour are some of the best known examples. My contention is that, as far as I am aware, there is little evidence that comment on change processes has been holistic in nature. For the most part, as in the examples I have just quoted, it has been aimed at a specific, and thus limited, area.

Much has been written about intervention efforts designed to bring about intentional change in human behaviour but, rather strangely, the concept of 'change' itself seems to have received little direct attention. As a consequence, it is very difficult to assess the validity of change processes because each proponent of change assumes that his or her particular version of what constitutes change is already in the public domain and thus does not require definition.

Most of the evidence, except in certain clearly defined and very limited areas, is based upon subjective opinion and hardly any upon repeatable forms of measurement from some suitably defined base. Thus there has grown up what might be called a 'change industry', which undoubtedly has beneficial objectives and strong moral standards, but which uses processes that to a large extent are accepted as articles of faith.

One of the basic aims of this book is to look at what these change processes actually are, and to place them both in the context of the natural change and developmental processes to which human beings are subjected and also in the more important context of consequence.

It cannot be allowed to escape notice that our ability to predict consequences is neither good nor accurate – especially in a social context where the variables of interaction can neither be known in their entirety nor controlled, except in absolutely unique circumstances. The most important outcomes of social intervention have often turned out to be ones which were never anticipated.

Reason B

> Laing offers a good example of the common phenomenon of how one can become the centre of a cult by holding views which correspond to what a large number of people want to hear.
>
> Andreski (1974: 147)

The literature of intended change contains numerous texts with the word 'change' in the title and in many other places. Yet, in most cases, if a search is made for the author's definition of the word (which is fundamental to his or her thesis), it will not be found – there will only be indirect references to the proposed areas of change. The assumption cannot be that none of the writers knows what he or she intends by the word 'change', which leaves only the supposition that such writers believe implicitly that the word is sufficiently well understood not to require defining.

It could be argued that the word is in common usage and in that sense it *is* understood but, like many other words in such circumstances, its very commonness has conspired to make its meaning idiosyncratic. How is it possible that a thesis about change can be delivered without some attempt to make its major term more precise? Is there a process akin to osmosis, whereby describing a particular practice will make the fundamental concept underlying that practice emerge with great clarity?

Apart from this major theme, one of the important problems of change agents lies in the area of the data they use as the basis of interventions in human situations. There is a great deal of current information about the nature and quality of data and sometimes the same process can appear to produce vast differences in results – caused probably by an infinitesimal difference in the information available at the starting point.

Given that many leaders and trend-setters in the world of change agents are and have been charismatic figures, the exact quality and nature of the data these larger-than-life characters use to propound their approaches is often overlooked. As Andreski says in the quotation at the head of this section, such individuals become the centre of a cult, and little challenge is made to the logical or factual basis of their theories. If such a challenge is made, it usually comes from outside the circle and stands to be dismissed as either professional envy or lack of factual knowledge of what is being criticised.

Laing was a good example, now largely discredited, but new examples continue to appear. An American psychologist, Jim Goodwin of Wenatchee, Washington, is one of the latest – having discovered the apparent value of the drug Prozac, he has prescribed it for all his patients.

Thus I have attempted to introduce into the discussion of the data base of intervention some consideration of the nature of that data and of the process of meaningful connections. Such material offers guidance on the degree of reliability it is possible to put upon different kinds and sources of information. I have also included brief comments on the, essentially, dually idiosyncratic process in a change relationship that occurs between change agent on one side and target on the other; both of whom are human beings, with all the eccentricities of interpretation of each other's appearance and behaviour that are possible in this situation.

Reason C

I have also tried to put the concept of 'change' into some form of context, firstly by defining intended change and secondly by showing how this fits into a mould in which unintended change and, indeed, a large element of chaotic change is a permanent and all-pervading feature. Many changes which can appear as the result of intervention may well be the result of time, and thus of change processes which were already in existence before the intervention began, or were potentially available at some stage in the individual's life.

The process of learning which takes place in childhood is a species-adaptive and developmental process which can, of course, be diverted and derailed. But nothing with that kind of biological drive is available in maturity, so learning has to be funded by other drives which can be broadly classified in terms of a highly individualistic cost/reward system.

Reason D

Because the psychological processes of change are intangible and are not readily available to be understood in the same way as physical processes; and because, in most situations, time is a considerable element and thus a cost; many changes which can be brought about do not survive removal from the sustaining and maintaining procedures in which they originated. But are sustaining and maintaining procedures any more costly of time, effort and resources than the continued relapses of achieved change, which often entails the necessity of repeated submission to yet more change processes?

The concepts of 'fade out' and the other ways in which change diminishes have been studied. However, there is a strong feeling that the odds of being able to maintain change in the face of social pressures which were probably largely responsible for producing the behaviour which required changing in the first place, may prove an impossible task. There is also the possibility that the changes which did occur were something like replacement human organs, which, in some cases, are rejected by the host body because it 'perceives' them to be foreign and its mechanisms have been designed to reject such objects.

Sustaining change may thus be ineffective if the change itself is something which is not integrated, grafted on to what previously existed; and which is, moreover, compatible with it and usable.

This book, or something like it, should have been written a long time ago. But in my case I only felt competent to attempt it after some forty years of being involved in the processes of intended change. It has quite a lot to do with perspective and a viewpoint which emerges at last from the obscuring and containing mists of involvement, allowing both the time and the opportunity to look back over the path one has travelled.

In broad terms, the four sections of the book present the main concerns of intended change and the existing supportive data emanating from various viewpoints. At the end of each section is a chapter with the sole purpose of critically examining the material presented in the section it follows, and attempting to separate and evaluate those ideas, theories and practices which appear logically valid from those which appear to have become articles of faith. It also examines why a considerable amount of obfuscation of change ideas is constantly produced by the change agents themselves. My hope in performing this process is that of discovering, if this is at all possible, what is actually based in reality; in other words, what material can offer simple factual evidence of being related to actual social existence.

Jaspers (1963: 767) wrote, 'To treat illuminating ideas as objective knowledge is a fundamental distortion of philosophy into a pseudo-science.' The fact is that a considerable amount of what is offered as a knowledge base from which methodologies of intervention are formed, falls quite clearly into the category delineated by Jaspers as 'illuminating ideas' and by Karl Popper as 'inductive theory'.

Of course there are different ways of attempting to make sense of the complexities of human behaviour. But, apart from those which are based in physical aspects of human beings where some clear and repeatable connections between cause and effect (as between syphilis and GPI) can be established, all that are actually available as the bases of such attempts are observable behavioural acts and their cumulative history. Experience has taught that, just as incidents of observable behaviour almost identical in appearance can be initiated by vastly different sources, elegant explanations which appear to fit the known facts but have no provable (i.e. replicable) validity and form, are all that can exist.

Some of the different ways of 'knowing' will be discussed here, such as empathetic approaches and tacit knowing – the latter belonging to one of the stages of the development of logical thinking and symbolic approaches, all of which have something to offer. The problem is that when change agents and the people they work with are desperate to enhance the degree of certainty about their joint enterprise, the pressure to assert that the probability of a good outcome is far greater than it actually is may be very strong. After all, the whole purpose of intended change is to bring about a situation which differs in some marked respect from that which existed prior to the change process being deployed; and, in most cases, one that is 'better' in some respect and beneficial. Thus, to employ a process in which the connection between it and the desired outcome and between it and what existed previously is largely an unknown factor, is, to say the least, not a very credible proposal and could ultimately be distressing.

If what happens as a result of change efforts could have occurred by chance, without any intervention, there is not a lot of point in that intervention. It is precisely this lack of a simple connection between effort and consequence (which can be so clearly established in the physical sciences) that causes change agents and their theorists to be obscure, or to offer false clarity, so that writers like Andreski can entitle a book 'Social Science as Sorcery'.

To establish a simpler and more fundamentally realistic connection between what is available as knowledge base, the methodologies that can be established upon it and the expectations of outcomes is also an aim of this book.

We will obviously come across some relatively inexplicable correlations like, for instance, those which operate in the relationships between change agents and targets. Here changes can sometimes be seen to be effected apparently by the nature of the 'presence' of the agent and something which may be akin to devotion or discipleship in the target individuals. But my thesis is that, even if it is not possible to understand at a rational level why some interventive procedures – direct or indirect as may be – actually work, it is essential that the correlation between cause and effect should be stated truthfully – if for no other reason than that new generations of change agents must not be pushed into thinking that this is something which can be taught or learned.

Indeed, as we shall see, the process of passing the skills of one generation of change agents on to the next exposes the logical weaknesses of the agent's position. Jaspers, writing about the mastery of natural causes for practical ends, said:

> This therapy, however, so far as it can be taught, is not derived from such knowledge alone to any major extent but remains an art that uses science as one of its instruments. The art can indeed be developed and enriched and transmitted through personal contact but it can only be learned in its technical aspects and re-applied to a limited degree.
>
> Jaspers (1963: 330)

It has often seemed to me that what we have attempted to teach in the past has been peripheral to the actual practice of intervention and, as tutors, we have made the assumption that effective change operations are an art, or a skill which may or may not be dependent upon what Jaspers called 'a mastery of natural causes for practical ends'.

If what change agents have available to them are the three factors of illuminating ideas, personal qualities and practical experience, then what should be made clear is what can truly be achieved by intervention based upon them. Such limitations as there might turn out to be, should be accepted as realistic until, if ever, the state of knowledge about behavioural causes becomes much more precise than it is now.

Terminology

A long-standing problem in the change business has always been how to name both the process and the people involved. For instance, when the 'caring' professions were seeking a model for their work and needing some kudos towards being accepted as 'professionals', the medical model was the form adopted. Thus the people who used their services became 'patients', the process was known as 'treatment' and the whole situation was regarded as a 'case'.

Later developments away from the medical ambit produced the term 'client' for the users of some of the change system, later still they became 'targets' and the change workers became 'agents'. Given that change efforts are not necessarily directed at or involve just one individual, but frequently involve a group or even a multi-group organisation, the terms 'target' and 'change agent' seem appropriate to cover the whole range of change operations.

One thing which is abundantly clear is that the process of attempting to achieve intended change is still operating from concepts and ideas which are essentially linear – hence the terminology that, because I am presenting these ideas for critical comment, I have used throughout this book. For instance, change agents, targets, intervention and consequence are all linear concepts, firmly rooted in the assumption that those who work to effect change in the behaviour of others are safely outside the change system comprised of 'targets'. Intervention implies that something is done to the selected targets and then the agent withdraws to a previous position.

While the whole line of thinking about change systems (which owes a great deal to the work of Bateson) may be extremely difficult to grasp, and the adaptations designed to meet the need for a reduction in that complexity usually have an unacceptable degree of simplistic mechanics about them, there are factors relating to being part of change systems, rather than separate from them, which could have been used to modify the very polarised 'them and us' situation which appears to be the norm.

Bateson (1973) has often stated that the pragmatisation of ideas in order to use them as the basis for activity results almost in their destruction, or at best, in their diminution. But ideas have to form the basis of action, and involve what many writers have described as an acceptable sacrifice of purity, clarity and quality for the sake of producing usable techniques.

There is no doubt that the concept of 'target' so beloved of 'change agents' tends to signify a singling out of individuals and groups for the application, even if co-operatively, of intended change efforts. It is equally clear that such a reduction to target status may happen to only one particular aspect of that individual or group, rather than to either as a totality – let alone to all the network of relationships and contexts which maintain that individual or group in existence. Once any individual enters into this situation with intent to change it in some way, that individual and his or her supporting and maintaining networks become part of the 'target's' networks also and, likewise, the targets of the intervenor.

The complexity of these engagements is incredibly difficult to describe; language is barely adequate to the task; and I would suggest that this is part of the problem of the slow adaptation of cybernetic ideas to all forms of the 'change' industry – it is much easier to use harder, clearer more separate models – for, after all, the usual concepts of professionalism and of offering a service are almost incompatible with being a part of the system one is trying to change.

Perhaps the closest we can expect change agents to come to these concepts in practice is that they should become more distinctly aware, not just of involvement at a different kind of level from that usually employed, but of the whole contextual complexity they enter into.

But there are other sides to this matter which are also significant, besides finding an all-inclusive terminology. Words, particularly names, not only define the objects to which they are applied, they also define to a considerable degree some of the attitudes to that object of the individual who uses them. What emerges clearly from the nomenclature of change systems – and this despite ceaseless protestations of not being judgemental, or directive or coercive on the part of those in the change business – is the fact that change is effected by one individual inducing it in others. In other words, it is an external influence situation for the 'changee'.

Without doubt there are many change situations where this is not just verbally correct but also true of the actions involved. The US probation service once bore the title 'Corrections'. with the factual recognition that the behaviour and thinking of those who passed through its hands were to be compulsorily adjusted to be more in line with what was considered acceptable by society. This is but one example where society, through the agencies it employs, attempts legally to adjust the behaviour of some of its citizens to acceptable norms – without the consent, necessarily, of those being adjusted but supposedly with the consent of those empowered by the state to make such decisions, ostensibly on behalf of the whole society.

Whereas the aim of effecting change in behaviour is common to all these situations, the methods by which it is brought about cover a enormous range of human activities. But if what we know about the lasting effects of induced change has any clear message, it is that only two forms of sustained change exist. One occurs when the controlling pressure is constant, unrelenting and inescapable and the second occurs when the individual or system accepts and integrates the change factors so that they are no longer wholly or even partially an outside influence.

Another problem occurs in quite a large number of social work situations, for instance when there is a combination of roles such as change agent, law enforcement, supervisor, and so on. This problem has been discussed many times but there is no satisfactory solution. If the agent carries the authority of some part of the legal system as part of his or her contact with target individuals, then that part of that worker's role which is concerned with effecting beneficial change on a non-legal basis cannot be separated from the former without denial and rejection of the legal role. Indeed, even without a logically based right of intervention, the process of working to effect change can be fraught with many perceptible differences that, even when the worker is mandated to interfere by an individual, can cause considerable difficulties.

Of course, people use difference to their advantage, and differences in knowledge, experience, understanding are the central stuff of change efforts but what cannot be excluded is the fact that once an individual enters the ambit of others in order to effect change, legally or otherwise, that individual becomes an integral part of the system he or she is hoping to change.

I have no wish to attempt to create even more terms to define those involved with the processes of change, so, because I am attempting to present what are the current practices of intended change and then to comment upon them critically, I have chosen to use the terms agent and target as each can be held to stand for several different kinds of approaches; although biased, they are at least generic.

This book is also essentially about understanding.

- To change anything, living or inanimate, it is necessary to try to understand the nature, structure and potential of that thing or organism if the process of change is to be constructive and beneficial rather than damaging. The quality, quantity and nature of that understanding are the fundamental limiting factors on the effectiveness of the change processes.

- It is more than possible that the levels of understanding achieved by some change agents greatly surpass their ability to initiate change processes, which are based in theoretical assumptions about the sources of behaviour and which are fallaciously believed to be explicit.

- The causes of human behaviour are seldom explicit.

- The processes of intended change should be consonant in nature, quality and quantity with the available level of understanding.

- The processes which create an imbalance in this equation between change processes and understanding in favour of enlarging the former need to be better understood.

Part One:
The Nature of Change

2 The Universal Nature of Change

All is flux, nothing is stationary.

Heracleitus (513 bc)

'Change' is scientific, 'progress' is ethical; change is indubitable whereas progress is a matter of controversy.

Bertrand Russell (1950)

It has been said that chaos, not order, is the primary state. Thus the major thesis of this chapter is that any change effort cannot start from a position of a clear field. However slow it may be, all individuals, groups and organisations are in a process of constant change – even if that change is one of decay. All change efforts need to fit into those existing change patterns, whether to stop, redirect, add to or whatever, if they are to connect in any meaningful way with their targets. The process of linking the change elements with the state of constant change will be considered here.

One of the main reasons why the discussion about change has never been satisfactorily undertaken is that there is a lack of factual evidence, which is complicated further by the fact that those who might be expected to partake in such a discussion do not speak the same language and do not abide by the same rules.

A debate, however, merits to be called scientific only in so far as it can be settled by appeal to factual evidence – which means that, firstly, the case must be stated with sufficient clarity for its logical structure to be transparent, and, secondly, there must be a measure of agreement about what kind of evidence counts for or against the thesis. But first of all the debatees must be able to understand one another.

Andreski (1974: 87)

Some of the most disconcerting facts about the activities of change agents relate to two areas. Firstly, the apparent acceptance by them of a universal and acceptable understanding of what change means and, secondly, the seeming acceptance that intended change efforts are directed at individuals and situations regarded largely, if not wholly, as static.

The English language contains many hundreds of words which are concerned with some aspect of the movement or transformation of objects, individuals and situations from one state to another. In other words they are concerned with the creation of difference; an altered state. Indeed it would be peculiar if this were not so, for there can be no more universal experience for human beings than that of change – a fact which has been recognised at all stages of human development.

But the recognition of change as a universal factor of human existence is often related almost wholly to the idea of 'natural' change. We are surrounded by patterns of growth and decay; by factors which are changed by exposure to natural elements, to the processes of birth and death – which are universal experiences – and the differences that some of them show are often related to a perceptual time-scale. For instance, rock changes and steel decays, but over a time-scale in a natural state which is infinitely longer than the time it takes for human tissues and some vegetable matter to change.

This very universality of change seems to produce an acceptance by human beings, especially where the time-scale involved is very long, that change does not actually occur. Indeed, as we shall see later, the time-scale of natural change produces very interesting effects in relation to the time-scale of the life expectancy of human beings when we come to consider aspects of stability and equilibrium.

Thus, when change agents assume that everyone understands the processes of change they are right, but that is not really the point at issue because that understanding may not only be idiosyncratic it may also be essentially qualified by an individualistic time-scale. So it becomes essential to seek rational and explicit statements about change efforts in terms of why change is deemed necessary; what is to be changed from what state to what new or different state; how is the change to be effected; what are the expected outcomes in terms of, say, benefit and permanence; and over what time-scale these changes will occur.

The question of why change may be considered necessary will be considered in Chapter 11, but the essentials may be stated here. Change is required because, in the first instance, an individual may be dissatisfied with him or herself in some aspect of his or her life and decide that alterations would be beneficial, either self-performed or with the help of others.

Then there are other individuals who consider that they have a mission to change others, supposedly for the benefit of those others. Of course human societies are dependent for their continued existence upon a degree of consensus and conformity from their citizens, and so the state believes it has a right and a duty to bring about changes in some of its citizens, through various agencies, for the sake of the survival and the safety and comfort of the majority. This duty of expecting, and probably of enforcing, compliance and a degree of uniformity filters down from the state and its agencies to all forms and divisions of organisation within it and the instruments of enforcement become many and various.

Without doubt, therefore, we are constantly surrounded by forms of change which would appear to fall into two major categories; 'natural', that is change which occurs because it is a natural and intrinsic quality of things and organisms; and 'intended' change which is change conceived by some human beings and effected by them or on their behalf on other human beings. The point of maximum interest about this dichotomy is simply that the first form would continue to exist if every human being was eliminated; whereas the second is initiated and effected by human beings in the *context* of the former.

All organisms grow and thus change. The sequence of growth stages is pre-ordained but can be disrupted; the material upon which the stages operate can be deficient; environmental and other factors can frustrate and impair; but, all in all, the sequence of growth is genetically determined. Because interference with the outcomes of these built-in sequences is possible, intended change can be directed at them in order to facilitate or maximise development. Of course it can also be directed to produce deteriorating results. Thus the process of maturation in human beings can be facilitated by a nurturing environment, and by appropriate stimulation at the right times, to maximise the genetically defined potential. It can equally well be diminished, frustrated and left undeveloped by inadequate or inappropriate stimulation, or stimulation applied at the wrong time, omitted or even applied in the wrong areas.

There is thus a natural sequence which may have different degrees of developmental potential that is the 'given' for each individual, and on it play the environmental and stimulus factors which initiate and enable the those developmental sequences. These may also be maximally or deficiently available.

Added to this is the factor of intelligence and the awareness of the processes of development, which implies, in brief, that each individual can, if circumstances permit, intervene in some part of the developmental processes. Once again, that intervention, as with the genetic and environmental factors, may be appropriate or deficient.

Thus the developmental sequence of human beings, however it has been set by genetic and environmental influences, is susceptible to change efforts either to maximise what already exists or to attempt to counter the effects of existing deficiencies of potential or of limitation.

In some senses, changes which are effected when the natural development sequences stabilise at maturity are a continuation of this process of the deliberate interference with the product of genetics and environment. The process is one of learning; the adaptation of different forms of environmental stimulation to the genetic potential, the development of control factors and the avoidance of stimulating factors which produce unwanted outcomes. But, whereas the process of learning – making the most of what is available when the maturation process is still under way – is quite acceptable, and most societies have some form of training process for their developing young, interfering with mature and stable adult behaviour patterns (apart from the use of standard methods of punishment) is regarded with some suspicion.

Many people may well be very dissatisfied with themselves as they are or have become and may wish that they were different, but they are most unlikely to regard intervention to make changes as possible unless that dissatisfaction is very deep and its consequences extremely traumatic – perhaps connected with a state of health or with physical appearance. The concentration by psychoanalysis on the unconscious removed much of the concept that human beings were totally in control of their behaviour and thus could be held to be responsible for it. So the reluctance to regard deliberate interventive change as possible, coupled with the unconscious motivation thesis, provided argument, explanation and excuse for socially unsatisfactory behaviour patterns. It is for this reason that most interventive changes are still directed at individuals, groups and organisations at the behest of some person or authority other than the recipients of the change efforts.

It should be remembered that change efforts are directed in other ways than to enhance; they may also be used to stop, alter the direction, intensity or frequency of occurrence and to diminish selected behaviour patterns. But, whatever change is intended, there are certain factors which must now be considered.

Although, as we shall discuss later, stability is a time-related concept, it is certain that change implies some modification of the existing situation, stable or not. One factor which is common knowledge is that change, of any sort, has implications of threat. The reasons are not hard to find and involve the idea of the investment of energy as a cost, and of the presence of ignorance and of anxiety. The difference between public conformity, that is appearing to be in line with the prevailing practice, and private acceptance is primarily that, in the latter case, the changes required are accepted as necessary, desirable and, above all, worth whatever costs they might entail.

The components of the threat of impending change start with the reluctance to accept that interference with the 'natural' state of an individual, group or organisation is a valid option. This may be compounded by the fact that there are relatively few statistics commonly available, or understood, to reassure individuals threatened with change that the processes of intended change can actually work. The effective treatment of abnormal states which grossly diminish the quality of life are a case in point. Although there are records of success in these areas, the ones which are most acceptable appear to be those where the changes are effected by the use of drugs or other physically intrusive methods.

Maybe the alterations in behaviour brought about by medication or surgery are seen as requiring less expenditure of energy than other forms of interventive change, and thus less costly and more immediately rewarding. There is also the fact that this type of treatment has a long and reasonably well-tolerated history. But, even so, drugs and surgery have their costs too – in side-effects and other consequences. The main component of the threat involved in change, however, seems to be the fear of the relatively unknown. When heart bypass operations were a unique surgical performance, patients were in near-death circumstances before they were recommended. They were then accepted on the basis that if the patient died in treatment it only brought forward by a short period what was inevitable anyway. Now, double and triple bypass operations are routine and patients are offered such treatment and accept it with much greater alacrity than previously. Two things have changed: firstly, there is a well-publicised success rate; secondly, a major contributory factor to that success rate is the enormous development in the skill of the cardiac teams by virtue of the amount of practice and cumulative knowledge that is now available.

Individuals bring about many changes in their own behaviour patterns by a conscious effort of will. But even here threat exists – the fear of the unknown, the costs in terms of energy and time and the uncertainty of a successful outcome. While some very effective changes can be brought about by increases in relevant information, there is no necessary correlation between acquiring such information and being able to use it to bring about change. It is also necessary to commit energy and the correct application of that knowledge to the situation in order to eventually secure change.

Despite all the foregoing, many individuals do seek to change themselves and many seek the help and advice of others about how to proceed.

Natural Change as an Indicator

Change is universal. At the risk of appearing to state the obvious, it is demonstrated by the alteration of a particular state between two sequential points of time. Because everyone accepts this, change is frequently not noticed because no attempt was made (indeed there is often no apparent necessity) to note clearly any one position in the change sequence. Thus change becomes a matter of memory and of opinion instead of a relatively unassailable fact, hence subject to disagreement. Those who are constantly together are much less likely to see changes that occur in each other than those who visit only infrequently. The reason for this is that most personal changes, but not all, are gradual and the contrast between one sighting and the next may be so small that the essential image each possesses of the other is not falsified, thus no attention is drawn to the change. In this case, the continuity of image remains unbroken by the minimal change but, although the statement about change having to be recorded between two points in time is generally true, it is also true that if the perceptions in time are made by someone who has been absent during that period, the retained image and the current one are much more likely to appear discrepant.

When we come to consider the data bases of change efforts, change becomes a very important indicator. Indeed in itself change is indicative of change, but all the problems of recognition mentioned above complicate the issue. Some changes which are essential indicators tend to follow one another, or to appear in sequences or relatively set relationships to one another, and form recognisable patterns which are associated with particular kinds of change. They become, in fact, the criteria of diagnosis – both of medical entities and, with less certainty, social ones.

Thus, changes in previously well-established behavioural patterns are usually evidence to indicate that other less visible changes have occurred. That there are problems here goes without saying. For instance, changes in behaviour may be the result of a deliberate effort of will on the part of an individual or a group, but they may equally be scarcely conscious – the result of a response to changed perceptions, situations or people. The fact that both may produce changes in the patterns of behaviour which are remarkably similar in appearance is part of the complexity which faces change agents, who may want or need to modify or support those patterns.

A group of residents in a hostel had a reputation for being hostile, aggressive, violent and disruptive. They caused damage to property, abused staff, flouted most of the rules and in general behaved very badly – being the main cause of several staff leaving for quieter work elsewhere. The local authority brought in a counsellor, a psychologist, to explore the causes of this behaviour and to advise on the future, if any, of the hostel. She managed to talk to most of the residents and, without being threatening, pointed out the consequences of their behaviour should it continue unabated. Within a matter of days the general standard of behaviour within the hostel improved, not a great deal, but enough for the staff to record a change for the better.

But what actually happened? There were several factors during that period which could have been responsible for the change: the advent of the psychologist; the departure of one long-standing resident; an article in the local paper widely read in the hostel about the possible closure of some of the local authority's facilities, which mentioned this particular hostel by name; the expectation by the staff that change might come about because of the presence of the psychologist; and there would certainly have been others. The change in behaviour marked some change in the attitudes of the residents, but for those who wished to support and encourage those change factors, discovering which were the promoting elements was almost impossible.

Change in behavioural patterns as an indicator of other changes, with the subsequent problem of discovering what those visible changes actually represent, is demonstrated in the following incident.

A businessman had received treatment for depression in the local psychiatric unit and was to be discharged back to his home. The psychiatrist was concerned that the man's sleep patterns, inevitably disturbed by the bout of depression, were not yet re-established in 'normal' limits and requested his social worker to visit the man at home every morning at breakfast time to discover how he had slept and to record changes, and also to ensure that he was taking his prescribed medication.

This was duly done and a somewhat bizarre sequence of events was revealed. The man, impressed by the concern about his sleeping patterns, made strenuous efforts to sleep. He took his tablets religiously and obeyed all the instructions he had been given about preparing for bed in terms of food intake, excitement, and so forth, but still remained sleepless and anxiously awake most of the night. In desperation he increased his medication of his own volition, but with no effect. Eventually the social worker reported that a bottle of whisky plus three times the prescribed dose of pills left the man still wide awake apart from a few minutes during the night. The reports of sleeplessness were confirmed by the man's wife, who was becoming sleepless herself with worry about her husband's distressing inability to sleep.

Finally the social worker went back to the original case notes to see if there was anything that had been overlooked. As a result of this scan he asked the man what his sleep patterns had been before the onset of the depression, some long time before. He then discovered that the man, now in his late forties, had never slept more than two hours in any one night for nearly thirty years, until the depression had destroyed even that pattern.

The problem had arisen because the man had assumed that the psychiatrist was telling him that after treatment he should sleep at least six hours a night; the psychiatrist had not checked the man's normal sleep patterns, that is those which pre-dated the depression, and so believed that what he saw in the ward was the pattern set up by the depression; and between these omissions and errors, they were working to restore a change which had never happened.

When the pressure to sleep longer hours was removed, the man reverted to his previous sleep pattern, lost most of his anxiety and progressed reasonably well.

Any analysis of this situation, ignoring the careless mistakes which were made, would indicate clearly that changes as an indicator of processes taking place in an individual have to be genuine changes. What psychiatrists call the 'pre-morbid personality' is the bench-mark against which changes developed by either damage or disturbance can be measured. In this case the bench-mark was missing and the apparent change was related to a preconceived standard which was in fact inappropriate.

But the salient feature of change is still the acceptance of the need to change and the capacity to effect it, whether the effort comes mainly from others or from oneself. Without some such acceptance, change efforts tend to become an exercise in conformity under some perceived pressure.

A further factor in the fear of change is that change may make an individual or a group too different from those in the same milieu. This indeed often happened with children who were removed from family situations and processed through a training programme which inculcated not only new behaviour patterns but also different standards and values. When such children were returned to their families they were frequently rejected because the changes had made them unacceptable. Alternatively, the children reverted to their previous behaviour patterns with great rapidity in order to become accepted by the milieu in which they would now spend most of their time.

This example has often been quoted as implying that great change (e.g. from criminal to non-criminal behaviour) cannot be durable unless the surrounding network is supportive of that change. This would mean at least changing that part of a child's network which was most influential, or replacing it with one which was already supportive. Most of the arguments for residential care rest on this line of reasoning.

But an alternative approach is to consider that the change process should not be located in individuals at all, but instead should include at least cognisance of, if not involvement with, the network of which the individual is part. The extreme of this view would also include in this network the change agent and the systems in which he or she was embedded. It is logical to argue that, whereas a change agent was an unknown before engagement with a client or target group, after the engagement has been started he or she is not only known to the target but is actively involved in the situation, and indeed is an essential part of it.

Interdependence of System and Network

What emerges from following this path to its logical conclusion is the enormous complexity of interdependent 'people systems' and influences which must exist. The individual who is presented as the sick member in, say, a family group, is often essentially only a product of the interaction of the family or group members. As such, he or she is but the first step in the realisation of all the further complications and processes of influence which attach to each individual, and their connections with other groups. Indeed the process does not stop there. At this level it is not only the present and the immediate past which may direct the connections of influence; also in existence are connections and influences from the more distant past, and even those which may be anticipatory future connections.

But, as Jaspers (1963) and others have said, while the probable presence of such ramifications of influence systems can be admitted, they cannot conceivably be taken into consideration as a whole. Thus, changes have to be effected in the knowledge that there are many unknown and probably inimical factors in existence. But judgements have to be made and, as I hope to show, they have the possibility of being more effective if they are not only related to what is known to be possible, but also to some extent are made flexible enough to ensure against the emergence of features and influences which were previously unknown.

One factor of this matter of unknown influences is quite simply that when change is introduced it may not just influence those factors for which it was set in motion, and which were reasonably understood, but it may also cause a precipitation of much that was hidden. There is a common enough example of this in therapy when individuals are given the freedom to unburden themselves about particular areas of a problem and the cathartic process pulls into expression an amazing amount of material, related and unrelated to the matter in hand, which was never foreseen.

Finally there is a need to clarify some of the terms which surround the idea of change. For instance, the terms 'evolution' and, particularly, 'development' are often used in confusing ways.

- *Evolution* is species related change which occurs over generations by virtue of genetic mutations. Survival characteristics are passed on through generations, whereas non-survival characteristics tend to disappear. If the environment changes dramatically, different characteristics become important and replace those which were previously survival oriented.

- *Development* has a connotation of programming. For instance the maturation process of the human child appears to have well-defined stages which are lineally sequential. Such a sequence applies to all living things. As we have already noted, this kind of sequence may be influenced by deficient programming or by adverse environmental factors such that the genetic potential to advance from one stage to the next is not able to be realised or is frustrated. In this sense, *development* and *growth* are terms defining the same process. But development is also used to define change which is not genetically programmed but is the conscious enlargement of consciously selected targets. Thus an individual may choose to improve his or her musculature and is then said to be *developing* his or her physique.

3 The Concepts and Practice of Intended Change

However, all the evidence so far suggests that while the traditional methods are almost completely ineffective, modern psychology holds a promise that effective methods can be worked out for manipulating attitudes and behaviours in a direction favourable to the safety of society.

Eysenck and Eysenck (1981: 205)

The purpose of introducing intended change here is primarily to show that the main theme of this book is *change*; but change which is consciously and deliberately introduced into the lives of individuals, either by themselves or by others, with the express intent of procuring some relatively defined and probably desirable outcome. Thus it follows that I will be looking at three distinct parts of the process of intended change:

1. some kind of recognition that change is either desirable or necessary;

2. in order to secure that change, some form of intervention in the current behaviour of the individual or individuals is essential;

3. any or all interventions will produce both those consequences which were intended and those which were not.

It is essential in this thesis that the process of intended change should be clearly understood to be a deliberate attempt to alter the pre-existing state of the individual or individuals; and that the factors which this process has in common with change efforts in organisations and other institutions will be drawn later, as part of the critical examination of the claimed effects of intended change.

The Eysencks, in the quotation at the head of this chapter, were discussing the rehabilitation of criminals. Rehabilitation is a form of intended change often applied to people who have little or no genuine interest in the process. The Eysencks' comments would indicate that they believed the traditional forms of intended change (i.e. rehabilitation) were ineffective, but that 'modern' psychology (by which they presumably meant a Behavioural approach) held out some promise of success.

As I hope to show, this demand for clarity is easy to make but incredibly difficult to sustain in practice. Thus it is essential that we should start our exploration of intended change efforts with an attempt to understand the nature of 'intent' and of its relationship to action and eventually to consequence; and, in the process, open up possible avenues of exploration of claims that there can be a known, clear and predictable link between intent and outcome in the processes of generally intended change.

> No man can be wholly comprehended and it is not possible to make a final and total judgment upon him. In practice judgments of this sort are unavoidable because decisions must be taken when dealing with persons and in this situation, in relationships of authority and responsibility, they are valid enough but inefficient in so far as they are based on knowledge alone. We can never strike the balance of a man and sum him up as we simply know him to be. It is prejudicial to review a man as an object and think scientific enquiry can treat him as a whole.
>
> Jaspers (1963: 767)

Very simply, the stress is on intended change because intent implies goals and outcomes which it is desired should be achieved. Often enough, indeed, the change agent expresses the form of the intended change he or she wishes to pursue in terms of its expected outcome. Thus there is an expected, direct causal relationship between change efforts and outcome – or at least there should be if the change processes were actually effective.

Because so much change is constantly occurring, the outcome of intended change efforts must be clearly related in a direct causal sequence, otherwise it is more than likely that the effects achieved and claimed as a result of intervention may just as likely have occurred without intervention.

In statistical terms, it is necessary for a change agent to show that his or her intervention to secure any intended change in the target individual or group occurs with a probability higher than chance, so that there is some probability that the change and the intervention may be causally linked.

As change efforts are seldom simple, and always time-limited, the effects also have to be seen in the context of the passage of time when a multitude of unintended effects may also have a bearing upon the outcome and, in most circumstances, can neither be detected nor isolated.

This is not to say that unintended consequences may not be beneficial, for frequently they are. The point being made is, that beneficial or not, they are not part of the *intended* change process and even though they may have been precipitated by the intended change efforts they cannot be claimed to be part of it without some distortion of definition.

Which leads directly to some consideration of the nature of intention. It must be obvious that intention, in our case to effect change in others, is an extremely variable process. It can be precise, as in the intent to change a stammer to a more fluent form of speech; it can be vague, as in the intent to improve an individual's quality of life; it may exist within the change agent with great intensity, or be merely a notion that something should be done.

Change efforts are made by virtually all human beings but it is not this universal phenomenon which concerns us here. Such general behaviour has not arrogated to itself the status of professional expertise. However, where change agents are to be considered as experts (i.e. offering a service which is beyond the ability of the untrained person to apply), it behoves such professionals to specify the nature of the difference between their approach and the ordinary person's, and, more explicitly, to show that there is a positive relationship between their professional expertise and their effectiveness in producing changes which is greater than could be either expected by chance or produced by the uninitiated.

Indeed, even more should be expected of change agents who claim professional status and operate in the public domain: there should be a clear, positive relationship between their stated intended outcome and what actually occurs. This would imply an understanding of the mechanisms of the production of behaviour and an even greater understanding of how either such mechanisms or their products can be influenced.

It is part of the aim of this book to show that these relationships, in the current practices of intended change, are in no way as good as they are often assumed to be. In fact the relationships and the knowledge upon which change efforts are promulgated are often assumed and stated to be precise when such claims are inherently spurious. Given that the outcome of any such procedure without the operation of chance or phenomenal luck, can only be as good as, or even worse than, the quality of the information upon which it is based, this is quite a serious matter.

One other factor that needs to be stated here and considered in some detail later is the nature of causal relationships. Asking for clarity between intent and outcome in intended change processes is to make a very high level demand. A simple statement of intent–action–outcome is never actually simple at all. Jaspers (1963: 451), discussing causal relationships in therapy, wrote: 'However, in itself this one-track relationship between cause and effect is completely obscure. Between the two lie an infinite number of intermediary events.'

If 'completely obscure' is the way to describe the events which lie between intent and action, and between action and consequence, then claims for a degree of precision in the process of intended change do need careful scrutiny. Even in the apparently simplest of intended change efforts, that 'simplicity' is misleading. It is dependent upon many obscure factors, ranging from hidden influences upon perception and assessment of data, to different but equally hidden understandings between change agent and target of what is involved.

As we shall discuss later, there are two main approaches available to change agents to help them to introduce an element of precision into the obscurities of translating intention into consequence. These are: (1) 'explanations' of human behaviour which assert theoretical meaningful connections between, for instance, genetic endowment and behaviour, or between environment and behaviour; and (2) many collected and analysed records of observed human behaviour over long periods of time. The former are by nature unprovable; the latter are either infinitely general or essentially specific, by virtue of being by nature statistical.

A further consideration must be that efforts to change individuals need not necessarily be employed directly towards that individual (i.e. in terms of increasing his or her information, insight, learning, skills, etc.), but may equally be aimed at the situation in which that individual exists.

Thus we can assume that intended change can take two major forms: (1) direct intervention, that is with the individual or system as target; or (2) indirect, in which the target becomes the environment or situation in which the individual or system is embedded.

The ways in which attempts are made to change individuals directly are many and various, as we shall see, and have in common the principal difficulty of actually reaching an effective understanding of what is to be changed and, more importantly, how what is to be changed was created and is sustained. The ways of changing situations and environments in which individuals and systems are embedded seem on the surface to offer a much simpler and more practical approach; if only for the fact that environments are largely material and situations, though often complex, have histories for which some factual record exists.

Even in environments, however, there is the complication of idiosyncratic perception. While bricks, walls, rooms and so forth, may appear to an uninvolved onlooker to be just that, to the people who live and work inside them they have associations which may make bricks and walls hateful, delightful, and so on, throughout the gamut of human reaction, according to circumstances and experience. They may even generate feelings that change according to other factors, including events which are not part of this particular environment.

So there is a possibility that the changes intended in an individual may be procured by changing his or her environment; there is also the possibility of procuring change by activating a different perception of the same environment, which may be considered as belonging to either or both of the main categories of change events.

While there is little doubt that changing the environment or situation may present fewer problems of lack of knowledge and understanding of it as a target, there may, however, be an even bigger fall-out of unexpected consequences, due to the fact that the relationship of an individual to his or her environment has only fairly crude parameters of understanding attached to it as a cause of long-term effects.

Let us illustrate this conception and analysis of intended change by means of an example of conscious and deliberate intervention in the lives of the members of a family, and note the consequences. Given that the whole of this example lies in the past, the advantage of being able to look at everything in sequence should serve to show the three main parts of the process: (1) the realisation that change was required and necessary; (2) that deliberate and directed intervention was necessary to secure that change; and (3) that such intervention produced consequences, some of which were consonant with the original intention to change and others which were largely unforeseen. However, we will, in the analysis of this story, tend to concentrate more for the moment on the nature of the intent of the several change agents and, even more specifically, upon the nature of the information which was available to them at the time when decisions were made.

Of course, much of the incidental and important detail cannot be included, even in one history of a family; the following, therefore, is a brief summary of some intended change efforts directed at alleviating suffering.

Some years ago, a family of four (mother, father, son and daughter) came to the notice of the social work department in a seaside town because the mother, Mrs Jones, had been referred by her GP to the local psychiatrist. He had requested that a visit to the family should be made and a case history compiled. The initial diagnosis of Mrs Jones' problem was one of depression and the psychiatrist believed this was reactive to the conditions prevailing in the family. What he had ascertained of those conditions from the case history and from the brief interviews that he had had with Mrs Jones led him to believe that not only was she being systematically humiliated but physically ill-treated as well.

In appearance, Mrs Jones was a thin, lank individual with a stoop and a very mournful expression. She was 47 years old. In brief, what the social worker discovered was an angry bullying husband who worked for the local authority transport services; a teenage boy who supported his father and whose behaviour at school and at home was described as truculent and at times violent; and a girl of 11 who was meek, given to sulking and not very bright.

Other matters which were revealed included the fact that Mr Jones, who was the same age as his wife, was a heavy drinker, had a violent temper, blamed his wife for everything that went wrong both at home and at work and employed physical violence to all three members of the family to get his way.

The psychiatrist requested social work help to try to modify the family interaction problems, meanwhile prescribing anti-depressants for Mrs Jones and requiring her to attend outpatient appointments. For a while things improved and then the original pattern of interaction reasserted itself. Bad temper, bad behaviour and violence became everyday occurrences and Mrs Jones was back once more in a depressed state.

This process of occasional referral for treatment and periods of apparent peace went on for a time, with no apparent change in the routine – a fact which later proved to be quite significant as no change meant no deterioration as well as no improvement. Eventually, coming home late one night and very drunk, a quarrel between husband and wife ended when he hurled her down the stairs of the house. Mrs Jones was admitted to casualty and found to have severe bruising but otherwise no major physical damage.

The psychiatrist visited her in the general hospital and then admitted her to his own unit.

After much consultation and discussion, the psychiatrist, nurses and social workers decided that Mrs Jones' life would be in danger if she returned to her husband, and they counselled her that she should leave home and establish a new life for herself elsewhere. At first she was extremely reluctant to make this move, despite her disclosure that being thrown downstairs was only the last in a long line of violent incidents – including joint attacks by father and son together.

Eventually Mrs Jones was found accommodation some distance away from her home. Mr Jones made no objection to this removal, indicating that he was glad to be rid of his wife's miserable presence.

For some weeks all appeared to be well. Mrs Jones seemed to be happier when removed from her family, and anti-depressant treatment was discontinued. Social work supervision continued for several months and then was withdrawn.

Some eighteen months after leaving her home, Mrs Jones killed herself. When the family was visited, social workers discovered that Mr Jones had lost his job, was drinking very heavily and was constantly in a very poor state of health; the boy, who had been going to join the Royal Navy, was in prison for a series of offences including assault, burglary and other violent and abusive behaviour; and the girl had run away from home some time before and was believed to be earning her living as a prostitute.

The total period of time which had elapsed from the first psychiatric referral to Mrs Jones' death was just under five years.

Of course there is much missing from this bald statement of events, and indeed much that was never known about this family and much that never could have been known. But what there is will suffice to highlight the main factors about the intended change efforts, the interventions and, above all, the consequences which occurred.

1. Intended change efforts arose because Mrs Jones visited her GP on several occasions with complaints which led him to make a tentative diagnosis of depression and, when his own efforts to do something about this seemed to make little difference to her state, he sent her to see the psychiatrist. Given the information the psychiatrist was able to collect, the diagnosis was confirmed, and, given also the known fact that she was a very submissive personality, the humiliation, violence and rejection which this woman

suffered was, in his opinion, sufficient cause. His main concerns became the need (a) to alleviate her depression with medication and psychotherapy and (b) to attempt to alter some of the circumstances which he believed to be causal. He did not, therefore, pursue the possibility that these circumstances may have been precipitative rather then causal, or that Mrs Jones may have been suffering from endogenous depression.

2. By regarding Mrs Jones' state as a medical matter, the concentration of the intended change sequences was directed at her depressive condition in the initial stages. Ultimately the total situation of the family was seen as the essential focus of intervention, but the action taken was to remove Mrs Jones from it. As a result, the actual focus was still Mrs Jones, though the effect on the remaining family members, and on her as well, was eventually catastrophic. The action taken is illustrative of two major areas of intervention – with a person or persons directly, or with the situation. Of the two, changing the situation offers more easily achieved ends but, as was instanced in this case, because even less tends to be known about how individuals are 'anchored' in their situations, even more dramatic unforeseen consequences are liable to ensue.

3. The 'equilibrium' state of the family was overlooked by virtue of the fact that part of its stability proceeded from what the social worker and the doctors perceived as unacceptable behaviour. Mrs Jones had not directly complained about her husband's treatment of her until the psychiatrist and the social worker started looking for reasons for her depressed and dejected state. They could not condone Mr Jones' brutal behaviour, but neither did they concern themselves enough with how it had grown up nor with what satisfactions existed for Mrs Jones in her apparent acceptance of that behaviour.

It is arguable that the collapse of the family on her departure demonstrated the existence of considerably greater dependence of each family member on the others, in terms of their performing a familiar role, than was discovered during the change efforts. The balance of satisfactions was definitely tilted when Mrs Jones was referred for psychiatric treatment.

The family structure could tolerate short periods away from home because the return of the status quo was always imminent. However odd and unbelievable the balance in the family might seem to outsiders, it had actually existed for some considerable time, and it is not very likely in the light of subsequent events that the family on their own could have devised a different modus operandi.

This latter statement is not entirely true because each time that Mrs Jones was away from home some small degree of change in the pattern of family life must have occurred. With hindsight it is easy to be critical of what was done in this case, but there is always the possibility that the same thing, or something very similar, might have occurred in any event even without the impetus given by outside intervention. The children were growing up and would no doubt have fed their own contribution into the family configuration, forcing in some element of change. There is no way of assessing what this might have been without the introduction of an unacceptable level of speculation.

4. A common comment by social workers, doctors and others upon a situation like that of the Jones family usually contains two elements – one relating to the lack of time available and the other to the amount and quality of the information which was available.

There comes a point when decisions have to be taken as something has to be done, and the possibility of being in a position at that moment to know everything that is relevant about the individuals and their situation is non-existent. It is a common experience of all change agents to discover that the information upon which they have acted related only to a fairly specific area of an individual's or group's very complex existence. It may, at the time, have seemed to be vitally important, even dangerous, urgent or crucial information, but nevertheless it cannot be the totality of what is involved, and often is not even the most important part.

Some writers argue that when change agents become involved in a situation, not only do they translate the information which is available to them in ways which relate to their training, beliefs, theoretical and ideological backgrounds but they also, merely by being part of the situation, influence in numerous and often disregarded ways what is being presented to them.

Knowing this, there is the possibility that constant monitoring of a change situation may start to reveal other factors of influence which were previously hidden, and changes to the intervention process can be made – adaptations which allow for this access of different information. But the element of time and a lack of resources frequently mitigate against such a possibility: all of which would tend to indicate that change agents are attempting to bring about changes which have a poor feasibility in the current state of knowledge and ability. This may stem from professional arrogance or from pressures from society to produce results. The parameters of what is possible need to be much more clearly defined, and the nature of change agents' performance much more adapted to the reality that exists than to a faith in what might be possible.

The intentions of the change agents in the Jones family affair were without doubt sincerely and humanely directed, but, as we saw, the outcome of interventions based on those intentions was not at all what was expected, except for very short periods of time. It is in this area of consequence that a considerable number of the problems of interventions arise. Change efforts are often very successful in the short term because they have been designed to deal with specific, and therefore limited, situations. What then appears to happen, however, is that the successful change precipitates other changes which, if they were foreseen, were discounted but which more usually are not foreseen – at least in the way they eventually manifest themselves. Thus what may have been seen as a single enterprise has a habit of spawning many others.

Mrs Jones' situation serves to highlight the various themes of this book, for instance the concept of change. Mrs Jones was the individual member of the family who, having presented herself to her doctor with some minor complaint, was eventually thought to be suffering from depression and passed on to the psychiatrist. Most of the change efforts were, as a consequence, directed at her because she was deemed to be ill. The causes of her depression, while noted as probably being reactive to a punishing domestic situation, were also mainly regarded as treatable by the administration of drugs. Any attempts that were made to redefine the family situation with respect to Mrs Jones were met with disclaimers of responsibility and some hostility by Mr Jones.

As a result, the ultimate solution appeared to be to break up the family unit in order to protect Mrs Jones from its apparently malign influences. But changes had been going on in the Jones family for many years, all of which had occurred without any evidence that they had been destroying the family unit. For one thing, every member of the family had been growing older and while this may have meant some behavioural deterioration for the adults, the children were fast approaching the time when they would have left home and the unit would have changed drastically. But in a sense this change would have been a 'natural' progression, and thus expected and in some ways prepared for.

The change which did come was the unexpected loss of a member, and the family could neither have anticipated this loss, nor the way in which it occurred. Whatever balance existed in the family unit – and there must have been quite a strong one which had existed and developed in its own idiosyncratic way for over twenty years – was suddenly subject to an intolerable pressure imposed from without, and with a time-scale which did not give the family leeway to re-establish a new equilibrium, especially without help. The nature of the individual, in this case Mrs Jones, was taken as the prime target of intervention and, as a result of resistance, the network of support systems, which, with hindsight obviously existed, was not only ignored but violently torn asunder by the removal of a key member.

The quality of the information upon which fundamental interventive actions were taken was thus essentially skewed in favour of what was clinically available. As a result, the forms of intervention were set on a particular path which regarded Mrs Jones as the 'patient' and were ultimately designed to protect her from what the change agents considered to be intolerable and depressing circumstances. The almost inevitable consequences of such specifically aligned intervention were therefore not only unforeseen, but far in excess of anything that what might have been expected. Indeed the relapse factor which affected all members of the family showed, as nothing else could, the heavy interdependence which had previously existed between them.

The change agents in this case: the GP, the psychiatrist and the mental health social worker, had directly imposed their own understanding of the situation on at least one member of the family, and indirectly on the others. Because of their status in the community, their legal responsibilities and the nature of Mrs Jones as a relatively submissive person, she was easily persuaded that they were acting in her best interests; as indeed I believe they were.

Thus all the factors of intended change which will be discussed in this book are to be found in a relatively ordinary sequence which produced some extraordinary consequences. Of course it can be argued that change agents have to make decisions based upon what evidence is available to them, and usually have little time to pursue enquiries which might reveal different and more important factors than those which lie so obviously on the surface, and which are interpreted in terms of the agent's views of what is tolerable and acceptable. There is the compulsion to do something and, as many writers have noted, just to do something, anything, which often produces a salutary change in the circumstances of target individuals. Usually this sort of change is attributed to a fairly large increase in the amount of attention and interest which the change agent brings about simply by being there.

The language of 'change agent' and of 'target' or 'client' implies an attitude of power and direction which in turn implies a mind-set that will interpret whatever information is available in terms of the need to do something to the individual or group in focus. Allied to the relative ineffectiveness of many of the actions which can be taken by change agents, this can generate a rather dangerous situation. On the one hand, the pressures of society for something to be done to some of its citizens – which often includes the added pressure of legal responsibility and obligation – and, on the other, a paucity of genuine person-centred information and a limited number of available actions.

Some greater accuracy of fit between the contending pressures must ultimately be of great benefit to individuals, groups and organisations, and can only be hindered in its development by what amounts to a refusal on the part of change agents to assess accurately their skills and resources and those of the people into whose lives they intrude.

4 The Forms of Intended Change

The word 'change' produces emotional reactions. It is not a neutral word. To many people it is threatening. It conjures up visions of a revolutionary, a dissatisfied idealist, a trouble-maker a malcontent. Nicer words referring to the process of changing people are education, training, guidance, indoctrination, therapy

Cartwright (1951: 381)

It is essential that we should now attempt to be more explicit about 'intended' change. Given the fact that change of many varieties is constantly occurring, and that the time-scales in which these changes are occurring range from very small intervals to very large, then intended change has to fit into and operate within, not a static system but a dynamic one. As we shall see later, the implications of this are complex. By selecting a process in a particular area of an individual's behaviour patterns and then proceeding, by whatever method that is chosen, to attempt to change it, there is a great possibility that the very processes of selection will imbue the chosen area with an aura of isolation. In fact, all behavioural systems are interdependent and the many, and usually unforeseen, networks which maintain the area of behaviour selected for change also support others. Indeed the area of behaviour selected may be a maintaining factor of some importance to other patterns.

In short, the same kind of fallacy that supports the concept of an independent individual underlies the separation of an area of behaviour to which special attention can be given without affecting other areas. Nevertheless, changes do have to be made and in our current state of knowledge about the complex supportive networks which exist both within an individual and in his or her milieu, the only reasonable possibility is that change agents should be fully aware that separation of 'target' areas is a device, and that separation does not in fact exist in the reality of the individual person.

If we now look at the processes which are open to change agents, some further clarification of what intended change actually implies may evolve.

We must start from a 'need to know' basis – in this case what it is that requires or needs to be changed – and straight away we find ourselves in a very complex situation.

The basic material with which a change agent operates is the individual and his or her behaviours. The problem is immediately apparent whether we regard individuals as biological machines or have some different concept of them – there is no blueprint of how they are constructed or, more importantly, how they work. Added to this is the fact that sentient human beings have the ability to control and direct some of their behaviour patterns to their own intents and while we may discover general patterns (e.g. that all behaviour is purposeful, or that it is based on a cost/reward style of analysis) the basis of value, which is the crucial issue in such behaviours, is largely individual; and is almost wholly unknowable in the sense that we are unable to prove that it exists, except by inference.

It is characteristic of change efforts that some patterns of behaviour of an individual, group or organisation are selected to be changed. But the basic requirement of any change effort – to discover what produces the behaviour in question – is usually not readily available. The pattern to be changed can be isolated easily enough but to find out what maintains it and what should then become the essential target of change efforts is not. One of the main reasons for this difficulty is that the maintenance and support factors may well be unknowable – guessed at maybe, but hardly ever known beyond any reasonable doubt. A second factor is that there is no doubt that behaviour of an apparently similar nature can be arrived at from influences that are not even remotely similar, and from wholly different, complex interactions of factors.

It is after consideration of these primary problems that change agents divide into one of two major groups:

- The first accept that the 'need to know' in terms of the causes of behaviour cannot be met by any readily verifiable factual data. They operate, therefore, from some form of explanatory theory which cannot be factually based, but which can seem to fulfil the purpose of a guide by fitting, with some degree of elegance, the observed behaviour patterns and the changes which occur in them.

- The second group are much more pragmatic in that they remain in the area of reality as they see it, and not that of speculation.

Thus they accept that they cannot know what produces and sustains behaviour patterns, but they can observe them and they believe that, by a conscious effort of will, they can be modified.

Obviously looking at what changes behaviour by a simple accident of circumstance has led to an accumulation of ideas about change, which may then be used to introduce change deliberately. It is clear that changes in ordinary circumstances, such as getting help, support, love, information, understanding, and many other examples, happen without intent and their consequences can be clearly seen. From the observation of circumstantial change, two patterns of some consequence can be seen to emerge. The first changes a pattern which already exists and the second introduces a new and completely different element into the individual's existence.

For instance, if I want to take up archery I start from a situation of apparently having no skill in this particular sport. In fact, obvious as this appears, it is not wholly true because I already have some well-adapted skills of a muscular nature which need only to be adapted to a different process, and I have reasonable eyesight and some ability to judge distances and so on. But ignoring these quibbles for the moment, in order to become an archer I have to learn new skills; new in the sense that I did not already possess them. This is the second kind of change noted above – which involves acquiring something not previously possessed.

But when I become a competent archer, if I wish to enter competitions, I may well discover that in order to reach the required level of skill I will have to modify or even eliminate some of the habits I have just acquired. The first process of change will now need to be implemented and something that already exists will need to be modified, re-directed or improved.

Now we have two dichotomies in change efforts: (1) those which are directed at causative and supportive factors of behavioural patterns; and those which are directed at the known and visible behaviour patterns to change outcomes; (2) those which are directed at patterns which already exist; and those which introduce new and different elements into the behavioural matrix.

It seems appropriate to borrow the concepts of analogue and digital difference to describe the last pair of this foursome. Wilden's (1980) description suggests analogue differences are differences in the same system (i.e. differences of magnitude, frequency and patterns etc.), whereas digital differences are those which comprise new elements, distinct and discrete. Thus analogue changes would be alterations of existing factors which do not change their essential character, like the skill of archery described above. They could be positive or negative but they would exist in an unbroken line from one state to the next.

On the other hand, a digital change would be one which was effected by the importation into the target system of some factor which is different in kind from that system and its elements, having definable boundaries which mark it off from the host system. The analogy is not exact but it will suffice.

Cartwright (1966), in a paper about achieving change in people, states that the continued existence of society will eventually depend upon our learning how to change the way people behave to one another and then goes on to ask a fundamental question. 'How', he says, 'can we change people so that they neither restrict the freedom nor limit the potentialities for growth of others; so that they accept and respect people of different religion, nationality, color or political opinion ...?' He then asserts that there are some semantic obstacles to the use of the word 'change'.

What Cartwright was proposing as the answer to the question, 'How is change to be produced?' was what he called 'social technology'. This, it would seem, is a form of digital change (i.e. change which is based on intervention from someone outside the target area); it should therefore be instructive to look briefly at Cartwright's conception of change.

In his paper he was preparing the ground for offering group work as a very acceptable 'social technology', to be used in the achievement of change. During this process he raised a number of very interesting questions, for most of which he did not provide answers! This is in essence what occurs in a large number of papers about 'social technology', a fact which will be discussed in the next section. For instance, he asks whether the social sciences have any 'particularly useful knowledge' which can be used to deal with social problems; he suggests that 'social technology' might be used in ways similar to the physical sciences and that there might be 'scientifically based principles' useful for guiding programmes of social change.

Many of the questions raised, directly and indirectly, are still pertinent several decades later, but it is significant that there are no more answers now than there were when Cartwright wrote his paper. This has not stopped change agents, however, from believing that a sound knowledge base for change efforts actually exists, despite the simple fact that in reality there are only a very limited number of forms of interventive methods. Where proliferation occurs is in the number of techniques developed on the foundation of these basic forms, and an even greater proliferation occurs in the specificity of the problems to which they are applied.

The approach defined by Cartwright – the use of groups – is an indirect approach in principle, but one which can contain influence efforts directed explicitly at the individual member; it is also agent-controlled in that it is the group leader or enabler who sets the initial agenda by both recognising and defining the area of change and the methods by which the change is to be effected. This is true even for so-called self-help groups, whatever they develop into later.

But one fact which emerged clearly from the Cartwright paper was his clear belief that unless change agents tackled the network of group influences which held an individual in his or her social position, there was little chance that enduring change would occur.

Perhaps the most important form of intended change for an individual must generate an awareness of the bonds of those networks – a first step in making it possible to choose whether he or she will need to continue to accept them.

To the two dichotomies already noted in the forms of intended change we need to add two more, which relate to the directions of the change effort and to the agent. In the first case, although I would maintain that in whatever context change efforts occur the ultimate target is the individual, the process can be either direct, that is applied directly to that individual; or indirect, that is mediated by others or by other circumstances.

The first is simple and obvious enough and, as we shall see later when discussing methods of intervention, covers the mass of face-to-face situations between agent and target, whatever techniques the former employs in such situations. Indirect change efforts are essentially those which are applied to the milieu in which the target individual exists. Much group work is of this nature, in that the individuals who comprise the group learn about themselves through observing the responses they provoke in others; they see behaviours which they can emulate to their advantage; and feel supported and rewarded when they attempt to make approved changes in their behaviour.

Of course there is some degree of overlap and of merging of these forms of intended change, and this is equally true of the dichotomy which is the self/other as agent form.

It must be obvious that many individuals seek to change aspects of their behaviour or image for reasons which are immensely varied but are linked by a common factor. The individual has a perception that achievement of the change would serve to bring about increases in satisfaction or other benefits. This may prove to be untrue in the final outcome, but the cardinal point is that, at the juncture when change efforts begin, the individual is convinced that the outcome (reward) will be worth the effort (cost) of achieving it.

I said earlier that all change efforts were ultimately directed at changing individuals, for the simple reason that all social organisations are comprised of individuals – they form the sole irreducible unit. Whatever the conformity pressures may be; however irresistible the calls of loyalty or the fear of being isolated may be; each individual has, however little he or she appreciates it, the freedom to choose whether to submit, resist, seek alternatives, opt out, and so on. The apparent consequences of choice are an enormous factor in change efforts; and once again it is necessary to state that no choice exists where the alternatives are not truly understood, and the perceptions of the possible consequences of choice are thus likely to be erroneous.

Many people have responded to peer group pressure against their better judgement; swayed and persuaded by the possibility of being rejected for being difficult and unhelpful; coerced by people whom they have regarded as having the authority and competence to be better informed; only later to realise that their own ideas would have been better or more appropriate. We shall come across this again in greater detail when considering the change agent as a member of that class of people who 'are supposed to know', and the effect that this perception has on their relations with their clients.

- There are many situations when individuals realise that some change in their behaviour is necessary; but knowing that change is needed is not at all the same as being able to bring it about, or even of knowing how. The help of others who not only know, or are supposed to know, the forms of intended change but also have the pragmatic skills, may be needed to effect such changes.

- There are also many situations where the target individual may be wholly unaware that his or her behaviour is in some measure unacceptable to others in the community. Then those who either have the power or the responsibility to act on behalf of that community may have a statutory and/or moral obligation to offer to make changes in the behaviour of the 'offending' person.

- Finally there are individuals who know their behaviour is unacceptable to a part, even a very large part, of society but who have no intention of bringing about any form of change in it. In these cases, the description of the behaviour as 'unacceptable' is usually made by the wider society, and there may be legislation prohibiting it, but to the individual his or her behaviour is not only acceptable but may be immensely satisfying. Change efforts directed at such individuals are thus usually founded in the desire of the society to maintain some degree of conformity to its rules, rather than in desire to change on the part of the individual.

The common element in these three situations is that the change agent is ostensibly a person or persons other than the target individual.

But almost immediately we must enter a caveat about the last statement.

Having declared that the ultimate target of all change effort is the individual, however approached, it follows quite logically that unless that target individual does change, the whole change effort is lost. Whether the individual target is inspired, compelled by pressure or fear to change, persuaded, trained or whatever, he or she must make the change. So, in one sense, all approaches by others must rest for their success in initiating and maintaining the individual in a process of self-change. Put another way, this would imply that all change requires the co-operation of the individual, however obtained.

At this point it is instructive to look at the processes of self-change and to note that, like many human behaviour patterns, what appears to the observer can have sprung from very different causes. Effective, that is durable, change has to be change which continues when the inspiring influences withdraw; or it has to be change which exists for that period of time required to suit the purpose for which it was initiated. In most cases, such change can only take place if the target of the change process not only accepts that it is necessary, but also believes that it is possible to achieve; that the known costs do not exceed the expected benefits; and that it will comprise something that the individual can maintain without help after the initial stages.

Without the desire to change, compliance with and conformity to change efforts become mere survival techniques and, like all behavioural patterns which have survival as their main objective, they expire when they are successful and behaviour patterns which existed prior to the need for the survival exercise reassert themselves. It is not beyond the bounds of possibility that, by employing compliant or conforming tactics in order to survive, an individual may discover a willingness to accept them as beneficial, but this requires a large shift in the perception of the rewards available through adoption of the practices; and perhaps also a similar shift in the patterns and networks which necessitated, supported and maintained the old patterns.

Given the forms of intended change which have been discussed here, it remains only to show how these forms contain the major approaches of change agents.

For instance, the search for causal explanations produces a deterministic approach. If what is happening now is actually produced by moulding and limiting factors which were established in the past, then intended change can be applied in two large areas – to reveal the historic causes of current behaviour and to control the emission of the behaviour patterns which result. Whether those historic controlling features are regarded as genetic, or learned, or both probably sets the main differences in approaches to past or current behaviour patterns. What has been learned can usually be unlearned, providing the constitutional factors are of such a nature that re-learning is at least a possibility.

So these approaches use analogue changes; that is, changes of magnitude of the emitted behaviour along such axes as intensity, frequency, occurrence, pattern distribution, and so on. In other words the *manifestations* of a behavioural pattern are changed although the essential *nature* of the pattern is not. For example, a pattern of consistent and destructive quarrelling is turned into a pattern of quarrelling which, while still serving to release frustration and tension by the expenditure of energy, is no longer destructive or physically damaging.

Direct and indirect approaches to change targets do not comprise such a simple dichotomy as would at first appear. Direct approaches have the connotation of being confrontational; and indirect approaches of being more subtle; with a much greater emphasis on leaving the target individual free to choose and to absorb ideas, patterns, and so on, without apparent conscious consideration of what is actually happening. The most subtle forms of indoctrination and propaganda employ this method because it tends to bypass the conscious awareness of the individual. If the target does not realise what is happening, even though he or she may have been told, conscious resistance cannot take place because no choice is seen to be available. The ethics of such procedures then become a matter of considerable concern since the possibility of undue influence is always present.

The fact of the difference between the self as agent and the other as agent is extremely important and warrants closer consideration which I hope to put forward later. David Reisman (1950) suggested that individuals were either predominantly self-directed or other-directed. While this statement might be hugely simplistic, it does give some clue to the fact that what might be the case is that all intended change efforts have ultimately to find a way through to and support the self-directing side of the change targets, however weak or strong that may be in each case.

Models of Individual Change

As I have stated earlier, very few 'theories' of change have actually been produced, largely, I suspect, because of the common and universal nature of the concept. However, of those which have been offered, most appear to have arisen when consideration has been given to how to provide an explanation for the process of change of the individual in group situations. Like all such conceptual presentations of change these also have two factors in common: (1) they all have a simplistic nature; and (2) they involve the coining of an elaborate but fundamentally unnecessary jargon. However, they do all try to encapsulate the problem of individual choice.

Individual change, as we shall see, is constantly related to the idea of choice. Consider the idea that, if an individual's choice of behaviour is limited not so much by the constriction of that individual's abilities but simply by the fact that he or she is wholly unaware that anything different is available, then the exposure of alternatives to that individual could make change not only possible but desirable. Of course there are several problems inherent in this process, which can be simply stated as relating to the perception of the need to change and the costs and rewards of so doing.

- In the first instance, most people have only a poor idea of what kind of position they are already in – their self-image usually being at variance with others' perception of them. So, initially, change agents have to concentrate on bringing that image up to date and discovering and exposing the bonds which hold it in place.

- The next stage is to demonstrate in the selected target areas, the kind of changes that are available and the probable rewards of adopting them. The individual now has a choice which did not previously exist.

- If he or she should adopt the changes on offer, on the basis of clearly understanding what they are in his or her own terms, and their probable consequences, then the third step is that the individual should be helped to integrate these changes into his or her behaviour patterns so that they become, in time, as essential a part of those patterns as the previous static behaviour.

Lewin (1951) described this process most succinctly as 'unfreezing, movement or change, and re-freezing'. He believed that the original impetus to consider change developed from tension in the individual, aware that in their contact with others something was either wrong or deficient about their perceptions and/or behaviour.

Jenkins (1964) posited a similar sequence in four stages in a group: security, disequilibrium, challenge and discovery. Interestingly this thesis, which postulates that change can only take place when there exists a very delicate balance between the individual's perception of security and disequilibrium, has been somewhat corroborated by the Chaos theorists. In their language they offer the idea that change takes place in nature 'at the edge of chaos'. The threat and cost of change can be considered as an acceptable risk because there is a substantial support system which will not be engulfed by the ensuing change (see Langton [1994] in Chapter 9).

Rogers (1961) described the change process as arising from the general disposition of people to grow and change. However, while this is indisputable in terms of the universal pattern of change of everything, it is not and cannot be entirely true in Rogers' terms of beneficial growth and change.

His emphasis was that individuals in a group should initially be free to be themselves and only when contradictions in an individual's current experience in the group were recognised as such, could change begin to occur as a 'natural' process. The emphasis is thus on the freedom of the individual to 'own' his or her current self and to make such changes as he or she chooses, based on personal perception of the choices available.

Hampden-Turner (1966, 1970) developed a cyclical model in which the individual risked (i.e. exposed) part of his or her competence to others. This investment produced a response, which, as feedback, could be integrated or rejected and thus naturally altered his or her quality of cognition; clarity of identity; and level of self-esteem. (Hampden-Turner's cycle may produce negative as well as positive effects.)

All four of these models are concerned with the discovery of the need to change, and with the choice which then becomes apparent.

Without realistic, that is 'understood', choice, no change is possible. While some obvious truths reside in these models, especially that concerned with the individual's acceptance of change as the one fundamental essential, their simplistic nature has tended to encourage change agents to believe that the processes of change are easily started, and that the myriad processes of contamination, evasion, resistance and intellectualisation cannot really affect outcomes because the experiential nature of the process is held to bypass rational thinking.

Vinter (1974) believed that behaviour which was socially induced through learning was amenable to change as it was exhibited in the context of specific social situations. He was in fact saying that behaviour which has been learned can be un-learned by exposing alternatives that exist, thus new learning can take place, and new ways of behaving can be acquired. Ultimately, most of the forms of intended change set up new, or at least different, perceptions for the individual of what is possible, but unless that individual chooses to act on this new information and employ new behaviour patterns and skills, the change may remain merely one of perception. In that case, the possibilities will have altered, but the actual target behaviour will not.

Intended change can therefore be directed at modifying what already exists, at adding to that state or perhaps subtracting from it. But all change has to be within the capacity of the organism to achieve, otherwise it is destructive, taking away what previously existed without replacing it with compatible new patterns.

As there is a great deal of emphasis placed upon equilibrium states in the process of intended change, the examination of these states is important.

It is possible to show that stability, equilibrium, and so on are perceptions that are products of the time-span in which they are set. If a time-scale is large enough, even quite long periods of stability can be seen to be merely pauses; hiatuses in a process of constant change. This issue has to be examined because the definition of 'stable' is misused. Given that change is a constant factor, a stable state would be a contradiction. Thus 'stability' has to be a question of degree, and may well need to be defined in a way that shows the integrity of a system, while also containing sufficient flexibility to absorb change elements; what the Chaos theorists refer to as the 'boundary of chaos' – an area where change can take place without the total destruction of the original system.

5 Internally and Externally Organised Change

In India two amusing figures are used to characterise the two principal types of religious attitude. One is 'the way of the kitten'; the other, 'the way of the monkey'. When a kitten cries 'miaow', its mother, coming, takes it by the scruff and carries it to safety; but as anyone who has ever travelled in India will have observed, when a band of monkeys come scampering down from a tree across the road, the babies riding on their mothers' backs are hanging on by themselves.

Campbell (1973: 126)

This chapter examines another basic dichotomy in the change processes; and the possible consequences of their being opposed' or being in a state of co-operation. Individuals, groups and organisations frequently become aware that, for advantage, gain or survival, there is some need to effect change. They are then faced with the prospect of either attempting to bring about what they see as necessary change by self-effort or to request assistance from outside with the process.

The polar opposite occurs when those outside the individual, group or organisation become aware that change is necessary or desirable and insist that it be brought about. The processes of resistance, co-operation, acceptance, security and conformity will be considered here in relationship to the imposition of change; and those of potential, method and ability will be considered in relation to both forms of change. All these factors are crucial when we consider the desirability of intervention to create change.

If the individual is the essential target of all change efforts, as I have suggested, the dichotomy of external and internal change takes on a rather different significance. If also, as I shall argue later, effective change (that is, by definition, change which is integrated by the individual and does not require continual reinforcement) can only take place at the individual level and with, in most cases, the consent of that individual; it follows that external change efforts have to activate internal acceptance of change.

In *The Lonely Crowd* (1950), David Reisman expounded the idea that individuals by character, personality, social and cultural influences were either inner or outer directed. By this he meant that there was a distinct difference between those who readily accepted direction and guidance from others and those whose own inner cogitations and deliberations formed the main basis for their actions.

This apparently simple dichotomy is not as straightforward as it seems. For instance, if the outer directed and the inner directed are the poles of a continuum, as seems likely, there must inevitably be various points along that continuum which are combinations of the two, with different weightings. As little of any human behaviour conforms to the purity of the defined modes of theoreticians, we must take this into account and refer instead to the dominance in an individual of one or other of the two defined modes. But even this is not entirely satisfactory, for individuals are seldom entirely consistent over time. So, although it may be true to say that an individual frequently produces behaviour which is largely guided, directed and influenced by others, we have to take cognisance of the individual's perception and understanding of the situations in which he or she exists. The dominance of one mode of behaviour may thus be a statistical fact based on frequency of occurrence rather than a factor of personality.

A lot may depend upon the passive nature of an individual, but even passive people have been known to become thoroughly and aggressively independent when they have seen the outside direction, that they have been accustomed to accepting, as having qualities of being massively interfering, probably harmful or dangerous, and lacking in some special quality of understanding about a specific area of existence well known to the individual.

There are change efforts which are effective without consent or the integrating process being present. These are the irresistible intrusions such as, for instance, in the case of the administration of drugs, tranquillisers, stimulants, psychotropic substances, and so forth. These are all biochemical changes, and there is little recorded evidence that they can be resisted by an effort of will, though some abnormal resistances to their administration have been noted.

Thus when we now consider the events of the externally or internally directed change, we are compelled to recognise that internal change is the fundamental issue – whether the impetus to make the change comes from outside the individual or is internally inspired.

Self-directed Intended Change

Like all forms of intended change, that which has its source within the individual has to start from a recognition that some form of change is desirable or even necessary. But this must also be followed by a perception that the required change falls within the bounds of what can be achieved, either with or without help.

This immediately highlights the fact that most human beings believe that change, desirable or not, beneficial or not, is actually possible. Given that progressive, developmental and insidious changes are taking place constantly, such an assumption may well appear to be warranted. But progressive, in the sense of continuous, change and intended change are not even similar. So is the assumption that change is possible in all cases justified? Let us look at a special case.

To the general public, the individual dubbed a 'psychopath' is one who produces behaviour which is significantly different from that of the 'normal' person and which, given even minimal consideration, has the makings of a some very frightening possibilities. Thus 'psychopath' has become a term of abuse directed at individuals whose behaviour – usually of a criminal nature, often including indiscriminate violence – is appallingly cruel and mindless, and for which the perpetrators appear to display little or no remorse and which they repeat continually.

Certain aspects of this public image, which is usually expressed with some loathing, horror, a great deal of fear and little understanding, coincide with the clinical description of the personality disorder variously known as 'moral insanity' or, in Kurt Schneider's terms, as the 'affectionless' or 'unfeeling' psychopath.

They strike us as strange creatures, highly exceptional in many ways; their destructive drives are unaccompanied by any sensitivity for what is right, they are insensible to the love of family or friends, they show a natural cruelty alongside isolated displays of feeling that seems strange in the context (e.g. a love of flowers), they have no social impulses, dislike work, are indifferent to others' and their own future, enjoy crime as such and their self-assurance and belief in their own powers is unshakeable. They are completely ineducable and impervious to influence.

Jaspers (1963: 441)

Psychopathic personality is defined as arising from abnormal variations in the quality of an individual's personality; possessing in much greater or much lesser degree the normal instinctual and emotional dispositions and drives.

Once again we are faced with an extreme polarity – psychopathic personalities at one end and 'normal' human beings at the other – when in fact this is another spectrum situation, with each individual having various aspects of their personality on a scale somewhere between the poles and liable to vary that position in different social situations. Nevertheless, the salient point to derive from the clinical definition of the affectionless psychopath is that, because there is no recognition on the part of the individual that what he or she is doing is unacceptable, there is no intention to effect change.

Some attempts have been made by, for instance, Maxwell Jones and others to bring about changes in the behaviour of such individuals, when the intelligence available was of a reasonably high standard, by inculcating a process of rational control – inserted between the impulse to act and the execution of that action.

The recognition that there is a need for change is most often driven by an individual's experience of crisis or stress. After the period of socialisation and maturation, individual change and adaptation becomes an insidious process which is largely accepted and ignored. As a result it becomes invisible to the individual, and in his or her consciousness this registers as having become a stable person whose main attributes, characteristics, behaviours, attitudes, opinions, and so on, are reasonably well known and constitute the individual's self-image. The fact that in many individuals this stability, though genuine, is more apparent than real is demonstrated by its disturbance.

A stable personality is one in which the individual is adapted to function within known and experienced social parameters. It is maintained in terms of self-perception and self-esteem by the individual being aware of the feedback and approbation of those of importance in his or her social milieu and there is a tendency to ignore or avoid people and situations where that self-image may be challenged.

Human beings, despite their assertions of independence, are essentially social beings – very dependent upon others for existence in social, physical and emotional terms. The status of isolates – those who are being punished; those who choose separation, or those who are deficient in some form of learned social skills – often quite clearly demonstrates this dependence. But even isolates, if they have some experience of society, can have social contacts in imagination and in memory.

It is frequently a shock to this stable pattern, in the form of an unexpected contact or situation, which triggers recognition by the individual of some possible deficiency in his or her self system. The shock may or may not be pleasurable, and the outcome may not necessarily be a desire to effect change in oneself, but rather in others. Bearing in mind that a stable person may be well adjusted to an abnormal situation, and that changes in the situation or removal to another will trigger the perception of a maladaptive style, then most factors which, singly or cumulatively, can constitute stress can also act as triggers for recognition.

The recognition of a deficiency in adaptation may rise from a consideration of how achievement and other drives may be met. Indubitably individuals who are seeking to impress, who require the support of others, or are endeavouring to satisfy ambition, will all make changes to themselves, their behaviour and appearance in order to gain their ends. Some such changes will be long term, others very transient and safely abandoned when the end is achieved and the experience added to the individual's repertoire of adaptations.

Recognition of the need to change may be due, therefore, to what may be called the 'highlighting' by circumstances of certain deficiencies of current behaviour. These may be deficiencies due to altered circumstances, that is external change; they may also be genetic endowment deficiencies; or those which occurred in socialisation. The essential point is that, for whatever reasons they appear to an individual who may never have previously suspected they could or would exist, they are essential to the next step which is a decision-making process: what, if anything, to do about the revelation.

The idea that individuals can be confronted by the need to change is one of the main drives behind a considerable number of group approaches. When an individual perceives that some aspect of his or her self is incompatible with certain areas of their current existence, the decisions that will be made depend to a large extent upon several factors. The first of these may well be whether the individual is prepared to accept what appears to be needed – that is, that in order to proceed efficiently, some change in aspects of their performance as an individual is required. Indeed, the individual may choose to disregard this information – he or she may accept that the deficiency exists, but choose to believe that its cause lies in others or in external circumstances. And finally there is always the possibility that the individual may be wholly unaware that a deficiency of any kind exists.

This blindness and disregard can be exposed by others, but may well be a painful process and one which generates far more heat than light. In a group situation, where the individual members have had experience of one another for long enough to have developed some level of belief in the fairness and trustworthiness of one another, confrontation of individuals with their deficiencies can take place with the maximum possibility that not only recognition will occur, but also acceptance plus some move to act on what has been highlighted; with the support and consideration of the other group members.

We will look at this process in greater detail later, but suffice it to say here that what is claimed to be one of the most important factors for success in group confrontation, after the issue of trust is established, is number. Consider: if one person confronts another about some aspect of their behaviour it can quite easily be considered to be a hostile act, and thus be responded to with anger and rejection; but if a number of people say the same thing about an individual, in roughly the same terms and at the same time, anger may still be the response, but disbelief in the accuracy of the comments is much less likely – unless the individual has some extremely desperate need to protect, and rejects those comments. In such a situation, it is most likely that the individual concerned will leave the group, if this is possible.

It may be that the reason for non-acceptance of a confrontational comment is that the individual, like the affectionless psychopath, is constitutionally incapable of assessing his or her behaviour in any terms other than his or her own.

Accepting that some people cannot induce self-change because they are apparently congenitally incapable of assessing the need for it, the next stage for the self-inspired change agent to deal with concerns the magnitude of the required change and, more importantly, whether the capacity exists to bring it about. All human beings have some sense of their capacities, though the estimates are frequently quite grossly over- or under-estimated and are affected by experience; by illness, especially of a depressive nature; by intelligence; by the opinion of others; and by several other factors as well.

The difference between externally and internally organised change can thus be seen to resolve itself into several relatively distinct forms. If we assume that effective change can only come about by the co-operation of the target and by the integration of changes, then externally organised change is different from internally organised change only in that the former is an adjunct of some kind to the latter. This can be demonstrated quite clearly by proposing a series of questions about the organisation of change efforts, and by a careful consideration of the answers.

1. Who or what decided initially that there was a need for the target (individual, group or organisation) to change?

There are only three possible answers to this question but, where each answer holds true, the change efforts and outcomes may be remarkably different. They are:

(a) Some person or agency different to the target and having or assuming the power to make a suggestion or order that change is needed.

(b) Some such agency operating in mutual agreement with the target that change is needed.

(c) The target making a decision about itself that change is necessary.

In (a), the agency or person in question may be agents of the law with the authority of the state to require change in clearly defined and specific circumstances; or others basing their requests for change on professional opinion, like doctors; or others with the authority of interested and involved people, like parents, friends and loved ones. This situation has the problem embedded within it that the target may refuse to accept that the suggested change is needed. The other two situations do not initially have this problem because in one case, some, and in the other, all, of the move to change comes from the target.

2. Does the target accept and understand that change is needed?

If the answer to this is negative, depending on the degree of authority the agency suggesting the change has to compel compliance, the question becomes what legitimate forms that compulsion can take. At one end of the spectrum are the forms of force, both physical and psychological; next come the forms of coercion and persuasion; then the processes of increasing the amount of information available and the application of rational argument; also the presentation of the possible consequences of refusal, not as a form of threat but as additional information. All these processes can be used at different levels of power to produce a positive and affirmative answer to this question.

3. Does the target, having accepted that change is to be brought about, know how this is to be done and in what sort of area?

Many people and organisations may know that there is some need for them to change, and indeed be quite keen for those changes to be made. But knowing that change is necessary does not automatically imply that they know where change is to take place or how to effect it.

There are many common examples of individuals and groups freely entering into change situations knowing that 'something' had to change and then being frustrated at their conspicuous lack of success in achieving it. Some of the possible reasons for this may be that they are targeting the wrong area or system, or the right target but in the wrong way.

External assistance may then be sought and part of the change agent's skill should be:

(a) to locate the actual area where change is required;

(b) to have knowledge of the kinds of change which will be required; and

(c) to know also what kinds of effort will be needed to bring about the necessary change.

Given that such a level of external organisation of change is available, this gives rise to the next question.

4. Does the target possess, or can it acquire, the basic requirements for effecting the intended change in the designated area?

Change requires effort and, usually, requires commitment, it also requires information and ability; it brings about costs which may contain elements of fear, threat or discomfort about them. Of course individuals and groups have unrealised potential and, given that the need for change is desperate and/or that the consequences hold promise of some kind of acceptable reward, it may be possible to develop and exploit this. Such a calculation of potential is very difficult to make, by either the change agent or the target, and can usually only be made on the basis of precedent or a sanguine faith. The latter may be a warm human experience, but it often proves to be a poor basis for effective change if it is not accompanied by some reliable evidence of potential.

5. Is the target aware of the possible consequences of the intended change?

The risk element in change can also only be calculated on the basis of precedent. In this respect, the external organisation of change stands a greater probability of being based upon a larger and more comprehensive system of precedents which are part of the individual's, group's or organisation's experience. Into this assessment must come an appreciation of the costs, but also of the rewards, based as ever upon what is known or expected to be achievable.

It can be seen from these questions and the suggested answers that there are several stages in a change effort where lack of information, and insufficient knowledge of alternatives, possible outcomes and risks may make the target individual deficient in the wherewithal to make a decision about where, and when and how to proceed. It is at these points of individual deficiency that the change agent becomes the externally co-operating influence.

Other-directed change, I think we can now clearly state, is seldom one in which the pressure to change is directed in a one-way process at the target of that intended change. If the basic definition of effective change must contain large elements of acceptance and integration by the target, purely external pressure can, at the most, expect to produce only a form of conformity which will be dependent for its continuance on the original or similar pressure being maintained.

Thus other-directed change must be at least a co-operative endeavour because, ultimately, it is the target who changes – and either makes the changes stick or rejects them as unintegratable. The power difference between change agents and their targets is one which concerns knowledge of the processes of change, their implementation and of the potential of targets to accept and absorb them. The skills which exist in the exploration and matching of change efforts to need; the ability at all stages to decide what is required and, ultimately, to decide on whether it is possible or not in view of abilities, risks and possible consequences, are all part of the power differential.

The risks for the change agent contain the possibility that he or she will have an overwhelming belief in him or herself, and in the particular methodology and theory of change, that can effectively overcome the negative possibilities in the change situation so that success will eventually be achieved. Indeed, such confidence is almost a prerequisite of becoming a change agent. As we shall discuss later, this particular risk is not only hidden by change agents, but may well be the mainspring of claims of success that cannot be substantiated by evidence at the level at which it is asserted that effective change has been made.

6 Issues and Problems

Since 'tis Nature's Law to change,
Constancy alone is strange.

John Wilmont, Earl of Rochester (1926)

The four previous chapters in Part One have been used to present some basic ideas about the process of change from the general to the particular, and in so doing have exposed some aspects of the change process which need to be discussed and some which seem central to some of the problems which invest and, in some ways bedevil, intended change. These matters will be discussed here.

One of the first issues to examine is the apparent contradiction between the universal nature of change and the stated goal of many change agents, which is to change individual or group performance by generating a more effective level of operation and then to stabilise the new behaviour at that level. If change is a constant of life, then either the concept of equilibrium is false or it has to be of a transient nature. Given the wide use of the terms 'stability' and 'equilibrium', it must be preferable to argue that such phrases are time-limited and to establish the period during which, in reality, such a state can be said to truly exist.

There is also the problem that stems from the fact that most stable situations, if not actually stagnant, comprise a system of containment. By this I mean that unstable or chaotic elements of the situation are held in check and in some form of order. This can then appear to be a stable situation. Intended change must essentially become a challenge to the continuity of this order/containment, and in so doing must stand a fair chance of diminishing the containment function and revealing or releasing some of the turbulent elements which had been held in order.

In a sense this disruption of behavioural patterns is very similar to that of other highly optimised systems where an imposed order contains the elements of chaos. In Catastrophe theory, for instance, which is a multi-dimensional attempt to explain (and predict) sudden discontinuities, the effects of even small perturbations in highly optimised systems can result in large catastrophes.

For example, a motorway is a highly optimised system in which a motorist may make a small driving error – a small perturbation – that causes a large pile-up of traffic – which is a large catastrophe.

Variations in the behaviour of organisms usually arise from perturbations entering the behavioural system. If there is negative feedback, the effects of the perturbation can be controlled; if not, variations arise and remain. Perturbations can be dealt with by being controlled, being absorbed or being minimised in a large excess capacity within the system. But change agents do not often deal with human behavioural systems that have large excess capacity available.

The inadequacies of the human behavioural system that often entail the need for change to be introduced can occur in two main ways – either by the system being too erratic or by its being too stable. In the former, the system changes while the context in which it exists remains the same; in the latter, the system remains the same while the supporting context changes – the system then becomes maladapted and the situation begins to generate tension.

First I would like to address some of the problems of change in general, then deal with the fascinating issue of equilibrium and stability. This leads inevitably to ideas relating to change as being perceived as a threat, and to a weakening of existing control and containment elements, and thus to other perceptions about change.

Some Issues Concerning the General Nature of Change

How do we *know* that change is accelerating? There is after all, no absolute way to measure change. In the awesome complexity of the universe, even within any given society, a virtually infinite number of streams of change occur simultaneously. All things – from the tiniest virus to the greatest galaxy – are, in reality, not things at all, but processes. There is no static point, no Nirvana-like un-change, against which to measure change. Change is, therefore, necessarily relative.

Tofler (1970: 28)

There are two points in Tofler's dramatic assertion which I believe are issues about change that are worthy of consideration here.

For centuries people have stated that change was universal. We now have Chaos theorists telling us that chaos, disorder, is a more normal state than that of order. But the logical conclusion of such arguments must be that changes which are made to the human condition as an exercise of will, take place within changes already occurring to those individuals and to everything about them. Thus Tofler's second point is valid; there are no static points against which to measure such changes; for all available points are themselves moving and changing. Changes are, therefore, relative.

For example, an individual who is a member of a family is of necessity away from that family for a long period of time. During this period of absence this individual's experience causes him to review himself, his attitudes and his position vis-a-vis the other people in his milieu. The assessments he will make in relation to his absent family will be largely based upon the perceptions he has of them which will no doubt be founded on his recollections of them as last seen.

When he returns to his family, his expectations of the effects on them and on himself are based on the changes he has brought about in himself, and he is immediately faced with the fact that the family have also changed. Some changes, such as people age-ing, he may have allowed for, but others which he could hardly have anticipated have also occurred.

The process of change is universal, but the perception of it is definitely time-related. Some changes are so small that over the life span of a human being they appear to be non-existent, whereas over thousands of years they can be cumulatively vast. However, unless we take a dynastic approach to existence, the human life span is the adopted measuring rod of human change.

For the change agent one of the problems of the relativity of large change is whether the changes that he or she intends to make in the lives of others are actually going in the same general direction as the existing change patterns, or across them, or against, them or operating in an entirely different area. When the processes of development are in full swing, changes which are instigated that go with the general direction of the processes of development, either physically or mentally, are inevitably more success-ful than those which run counter to them. For instance, children display a great desire to learn, but not necessarily those things we would wish to teach them; when instruction and the desire to learn, which is a developmental process, coincide, then indeed learning becomes relatively quick and easy. Conversely, when the desire to learn does not coincide with the instruction on offer, or where there is no instruction available, the developmental process, in this case learning, goes astray and, in some crucial areas which are time-related, may never occur at all.

Tofler's first point is much more controversial when he writes that there are no 'things', only 'processes'. This has echoes of the systems theorists' dictum that all systems eventually decay because they use more energy than they can produce, so unless energy can be drawn from elsewhere an entropic action is inevitable.

Human beings interfere with this entropic process in the people systems they create because they can perceive the need for inputs of energy and are thus able to postpone the process of decay in such systems. We also interfere with the individual human system in order to bring about change to processes which, if left unregarded, would diminish the effective functioning of that individual system, both in its own right and as a unit member of several social systems.

Indeed, on many occasions the survival of some individuals is maintained at a very visible energy cost to others. This is something which frequently happens, for instance, when one member of the family takes on the full-time responsibility of caring for another member. The process of growth and decay of human beings is one which no amount of energy input can divert but it is a 'process' and it can be changed at many levels of experience which are peripheral to its central course.

Change agents are themselves subject to the universal process of change, which is sometimes admitted in terms of the learning they derive from those they work with, but which is present in other forms anyway. So, because of the universal nature of change, both changer and changee are more like two planets in constant motion around each other than the static relationship which is most often presented of the intended change process.

> A state of equilibrium may be defined as follows: if a small force is impressed upon a system, a change or adjustment takes place within the system, and once this force is removed, the system returns to approximately its previous state.
>
> Chapple and Coon (1955: 54)

This is a common enough use of the word equilibrium in group work literature. At first sight, Chapple and Coon would seem to be implying that a state of equilibrium can only be achieved by a system which actually resists change, or at least as much of it as is possible and by so doing returns to the state of balance of all its elements which existed prior to the introduction of the change that they describe as 'a small force'. This would be a description of a system in a state of near stagnation; probably not, therefore, a system that is dynamic and adaptable.

But later the authors introduce the element of time – 'the degree to which a state of equilibrium becomes stable depends upon the length of time that the interaction rates, of which the equilibrium is composed, remain constant'.

What is in effect being suggested here is that a system, in this case a group, which is dynamic and not stagnant, has periods in its existence when all its elements achieve a state of balance; an equilibrium. But then forces occur which disturb that equilibrium and allow movement and change to happen. Thus over a long period of time, the life of a group can be seen to be a procession of states of change between periods of stability or plateaux when a new and different balance obtains from that which existed previously.

Obviously the process of movement, of change between plateaux or states of equilibrium, does not necessarily always go in a positive or beneficial direction. The changes can exercise a retrograde influence quite as easily as a progression.

Stability and the negative element, stagnation, occur when a plateau continues to exist, resists all efforts and forces, and the balance of elements becomes fixed and rigid.

There are two important points about this:

1. There is a great insistence in the literature of intervention in human behaviour on the achievement of a new stability – which has an implication of accommodation and of integration of new and different forces.

2. It must be obvious that the time-scale used to measure what is happening to an individual, group or organisational system can make a crucial difference to the perception of whether a state of equilibrium is a final and desirable goal, or merely a stage in a system of many steps.

I propose to examine these two points in some detail because they have considerable relevance to the process of intended change and to some of the claims made by change agents.

The essential characteristic of an equilibrium is that it has no tendency to change.

Wilden (1980: 313)

Wilden's statement is true in the sense that the elements which constitute an equilibrium are in balance with one another. However, if we accept that all states of equilibrium are time-related, admittedly on vastly differing time-scales, and also that a state of equilibrium can at any time be unbalanced by even a small change in any of its constituent elements or by the incursion of external elements, then we have also to accept that an equilibrium state is a dynamic situation wherein constant small adjustments in the constituent elements maintain an overall state.

Thus any state of balance in an individual's or group's behavioural position may contain within itself the possibility of change, or be susceptible to change from without. This must be so otherwise changes would never take place at all.

The concern of change agents with stability therefore acquires a different significance when viewed in a dynamic perspective. Basically, the changes which are sought for an individual, group or organisation are those which move from a stable state, which is in some serious way inefficient or inadequate, to one which is better suited to the prevailing conditions. But it is also necessary to accept that, if these conditions are themselves in a state of flux either slowly or quickly, then further adaptation of any improved stability will be essential if it is not once more to resume a state of maladaptation.

A very obvious example occurs in the growth through various stages of an individual in a community. As that individual grows older, his or her community has different expectations of him or her, and so changes in the patterns of adaptation and stability need to be made in the progress from childhood through adolescence to adulthood and increasing age. A static pattern formed at any one stage of this process is no guarantee that an equally stable pattern will be formed at the next and subsequent stages. In some societies the so-called 'rites of passage' were used not only to mark the need to change from one stable social state to the next, but also to form part of the preparation for these changes.

Of course, when help is needed during the process of change from one stable state to another which has different requirements, it is possible that part of the change process will be the acquisition of greater awareness; both of the need for adaptation, and of those processes by which it is acquired. In which case, future needs for adaptation may well be met by the use of an acquired skill and knowledge and outside help may not, therefore, be necessary.

We must now consider the possible effects of a change agent deliberately setting out to change a stable pattern of human behaviour which is considered ineffectual, damaging or inadequate.

Discussing the work of Chris Longton of the Santa Fe Institute, New Mexico on why life first emerged, Roger Highfield wrote:

Using a measure of complexity called the Lambda parameter, he [Longton] claims to have identified a new regime, dubbed 'the edge of chaos', where systems are highly sensitised to change without becoming completely unstable, where unpredictability co-exists with creative adaptation ... This seems to capture an illusive quality of living things which combine the ability to change and innovate with the stability of feedback systems that ensure a stable shape, metabolism and heart beat for instance.

Highfield (1994: 12)

This may be unproven research, but the idea it proposes of the 'edge of chaos' state in live entities has some obvious relevance, through the processes of change, to the intended intervention made by change agents in the lives and behaviours of their target individuals and systems – not least because it generates a different kind of description of the nature of the state which can be receptive to change without 'becoming completely unstable'; different that is from the concept of equilibrium and plateaux of consolidation pursued earlier.

There are similarities. It is agreed, for instance, that in equilibrium theory when any change that is introduced does take root in a system, that system must be neither so stable that change is resisted, nor so unstable that the force of the change will actually help to destroy the system to which it is introduced.

This has implications for change agents in two ways: (1) in the need to assess the stability of a system in terms of its receptivity to certain forces of change; and (2) to assess what kind of change, at what intensity, power and rate of production, the system can tolerate and absorb or accommodate. Frequently, change efforts are designed on the basis of criteria which exist outside the system to which they are applied, and it is not surprising that they are, as a result, not very successful.

It is axiomatic that stress, crisis, trauma and accident can break what seems on the surface to be a stable state. They all appear to generate what, in Catastrophe theory, is called a 'discontinuity'. The underlying theory here would indicate that the working and accepted performance of every individual could be described as an overlay of thought patterns, habits, behaviours, attitudes, opinions, and so on, which have solidified over time to form a compromise – an interface between the outer and inner worlds of the individual. Such a facade,

if well formed, contains a degree of flexibility but it is always susceptible to partial destruction by unpredictable changes occurring on
either side of it. Its maintenance requires energy, and often changes
in energy demand are the most important triggers of fractures.

The other side of this condition must of course be that, because
the facade is a complex compromise which maintains a satisfactory
balance for the individual, the dynamic elements between which
the facade exists remain in place. Hence, if access can be gained to
them they can become the essentials of change, and of a new
facade being formed between them. This process was succinctly
expressed by Kurt Lewin (1991) as that of 'unfreezing, changing
and re-freezing' at the new and more effective level.

The process of maintaining the operational facade is fuelled not
just by the individual but also by the context in which that individual exists, and the networks of which he or she is a part; all of
which have learned to have particular expectations of individuals
and all of which influence individuals.

It is accepted in crisis theory, for instance, that not only does a
crisis tend to damage the operative facade of an individual, but also
that it seems to release energy which can be used to develop a new
and different level of coping.

The 'edge of chaos' theory, which refers to natural effects,
appears to be stating a similar thesis. In essence it implies that
behind apparent stability lies chaos, and when that stability is
fractured in some way the elements of chaos become primary. If
they become total, or near total, the organism or system disappears
from its usual form; but if the elements of chaos are still sufficiently balanced by those elements which maintained the original
stability, energy is generated and change is possible.

In the case of Mrs Jones, quoted earlier, the family had a tenu-
ous stability – threatened by considerable chaotic elements. That
stability was dependent upon the maintenance of the family unit,
so when one major part of that dependence structure was removed,
the elements of chaos became supreme, resulting in a gradual disintegration of the family.

The essential point of this statement is that, however florid the
language, it describes an important fact regarding intended change
processes: no valuable change can take place in an individual,
group or organisation which does not require some rupture and
replacement of those elements which created and sustained the
original working compromise. In this process there is always the
possibility that it cannot be adequately controlled or that fear of
the possible consequence will generate a substantial resistance.

The factors which occasion change in individuals are many and various but the results they achieve all demonstrate two inalienable points:

1. Change only really occurs when the individuals involved accept the change; whether this is done by personal and conscious decision as something that needs to be achieved, that is possible and that any effort involved will be worth it; or through any number of persuasive to coercive pressures.

2. Unless some form of support for the acquired changes is forthcoming, either from the will of the changed individual or the assistance of others or circumstances (e.g. a sufficient gain from the change itself), that change will tend to fade or be displaced.

There are various forms of acquiescence to external pressure to change that appear as willing acceptance of, and conformity to, change influences. But such apparent changes are often only produced as long as the perception of the presence of the pressure which created the changes in the first place continues to exist. Such changes are thus essentially a survival procedure – which is not to say that no residual change effect remains when the pressure to conform is withdrawn. Indeed, such pressure may only have existed in the perception of the individual in any case, and may well have become integrated as a result.

In essence, the distinction between a conformity which exists in public and an acceptance which is really private is, in practice, neither clear nor complete. Frequently individuals will disclose that they have accepted without reservation some parts of the change process, but are ambivalent, resistive or even hostile to others. But there is always the factor of self-preservation – the need to be accepted by those who seem to possess the power of reward or of punishment – to take into account.

There are countless instances on record of social workers entering a family situation with the express purpose of bringing about change through the process of developing or refining skills (e.g. budgeting, parenting, interviewing for jobs, etc.) where initially, under guidance, a measure of success ensues. But when that guidance and that presence are withdrawn, there is a reversion to a previous low-skill behaviour.

The problem is then to decide why this has happened and to realise that only two factors are different from the original state: whatever lack of skill existed previously, it can no longer be held to be caused by a lack of knowledge of how such a task can be performed; nor can the belief still remain that the ability to perform it does not exist. So the social worker is left with an incentive deficit which was obscured previously by his or her encouraging pressure; or by the counter-influence of circumstances that were either not apparent or not present during the learning period (i.e. depression, or the effect of others in the individual's milieu, or some lack or disturbance of character).

If the case study of Mrs Jones (Chapter 3) had many lessons for the change agents, one which does stand out very clearly must be the effect of the system in which the various agents worked. The doctor, the social workers, the psychiatrist and others involved all worked in circumscribed situations which supported them and defined their roles, but which also constrained quite markedly what they could do. One of the major effects of this sort of situation is that any person who goes to or is brought to any of these professionals, leaves his or her system and context and enters the systems and contexts of the professionals.

Take, for instance, the psychiatrist in this particular case. He had a case history of Mrs Jones compiled by his social worker and he had the GP's notes, but he was faced with what he could quite clearly recognise as a picture of depression. Of course he would know the social conditions in which his patient lived, and no doubt he took them into consideration. But, by virtue of his training and of the National Health Service hospital system in which he operated, there was little he could do about the client's system which constrained and supported her, except to advise her about it and seek to moderate it by asking the social worker to talk to other members of it. What would probably not occur to him was that he had become part of Mrs Jones' system in the same way that she had become part of his, and by so doing each had defined some part of each other's role.

In essence, many change agents create situations which previously did not exist precisely in order that individuals may be able to see and do things differently; use resources they did not know existed; take command and control over areas of their lives they never thought they would, and so on. But such workers cannot claim to be non-directive; their very presence and encouragement, even, in some cases, their refusal to do or say anything, has brought them in as part of the context of the individuals with whom they work. Their influences are many and various and in no way limited to those over which they believe they exercise such complete control.

Indeed, much is often made of these hidden influences under the rubric of creating and maintaining relationships, the generation of trust and of controlling behaviour which would counter the explicit and stated purposes of the care agent. This is not intended to be critical of the nature of these influences, but only of the attempt at deception on the part of those agents who believe that their influence in the lives of others, even by just being there, can be designated as non-directive. All human interactions are directive and influence situations, whatever the conscious intent might be.

Part Two:
The Targets and the Agents of Change

7 The Individual: The Essential Target

... at no time is an individual without a history ...

Jaspers (1963: 694)

If it were possible to know how a person arrived at his or her current state of being; or how all or most of the ways in which the various elements and influences involved in this process had interacted with each other in the development of that state; even then the process of intervention to produce change would be less than soundly based or certain of outcomes, because there would still remain all those elements which, though at present inactive, could be set in motion by chance circumstances that would include even the event of intervention itself. Thus, unlike machines which, however complicated they may eventually become, are constructed and designed by human beings and can thus be serviced or changed by other human beings with a total knowledge of how they were created, the change process initiated by human beings for other human beings cannot be based upon a comparable degree of knowledge, even in a physical sense, and certainly not in a behavioural context.

However, man has never seen fit to do nothing in the face of his lack of sound knowledge of the antecedents of human behaviour and thus it behoves all change agents to assess the quality of the knowledge which is at their disposal and upon which their change efforts will be based. The immense complexity of what there is to know, combined with the essential problems surrounding the methods of investigation, must lead inevitably not just to accepting what little we do know as the basis for change efforts but also to accepting that the quality of that knowledge is adequate. For, like computers, the quality of the data we feed into a process governs with absolute certainty the quality of the product, in the sense that the second can never be qualitatively better than the first. In the case of change efforts, however, it can be worse.

Nevertheless, the concept of intended change as defined earlier implies certain things. For example, that the change effort is directed; it has an end or ends, and efforts are made to achieve them. There also follows that unless any change effort is almost wholly a 'let's-try-this-and-see-what-happens' approach, there should be some understanding, not only of what exists but also of how it is sustained, and finally how the intended change may be brought about.

Change (i.e. a logically conscious effort to alter something from state A to state B) implies, above everything else, that state A should be known; thus it is necessary to make some brief and general survey, not so much of what one knows about the development of behaviour in humans, but about the processes involved and how, being universal, they produce manifestly distinct individuals.

The opening of our concern about how human beings can develop into individuals who may need to be exposed to change processes has to be with the nature/nurture debate. Although these are often regarded as separate processes, and behaviour is commonly ascribed to innate or genetic factors or to the influence of the environment, the two are inextricably linked. So, whereas it is necessary to try to envisage which parts of behaviour may be dominantly innate in origin or environmentally inspired, it is equally valid to say that no living organism can be understood except in relation to its environment. Later I will be arguing that this latter statement is the source of one of the great problems for change agents – the extent to which they can become aware of the environment of an individual or group, usually referred to as the context of that individual or group. Even if they do become aware of the context of their target, there is still the problem of the possibility of significantly different perceptions of the factors involved.

What human beings inherit through their genes as part of the process of being created can be divided roughly into two large categories: features they hold in common with all other human beings, but which vary in terms of magnitude; and those which, like eye colour and finger prints, are essentially unique. The differences of magnitude are differences of height, size, disposition, and so on, and these are the differences which are likely to be affected as they develop by the environmental factors to which they are exposed. For instance, a child may inherit from its parents the capacity to develop a large physical frame, but if in the process of growing that same child is exposed to being constantly deprived of adequate nourishment or to a serious or debilitating illness, then the potential of its genetic endowment will be grossly diminished.

This leads to another and central point about genetic endowment: as in the circumstances quoted above, a child does not inherit a physical frame from its parents, it inherits the capacity or potential to develop one. That is, the genes which transfer to the child have the ability to produce distinct properties. That ability can be fully developed if appropriate environmental situations are available; it can be retarded or diminished if environmental factors are antagonistic or inappropriate.

Changing human beings in terms of their innate characteristics would mean resorting to the process of selective breeding, or to some way of interfering with gene structure in potential parents. Of course such changes of gene structure do occur accidentally, for instance in terms of the exposure of potential parents to high levels of radiation or drugs like thalidomide. These situations, however, produce uncontrollable changes – usually in terms of being destructive or creating deficiencies in growth potential. Breeding in animals and plants has shown that it is entirely possible to influence genetic outcomes from the selection of parent stock possessing, or able to produce, some of the desired genetic characteristics.

Essentially, however, from the change agents' point of view, each individual has been endowed by his or her inheritance with potential which is often of a largely similar kind to his or her neighbours, but sometimes may be vastly different. In either case, it has been subjected to environmental influences and also to some attempts at conscious control. The change agents' problem is how much of the innate properties of an individual can be used in previously untried ways in order to bring about change, and how much the factors of environmental influences on that potential can be used to effect required change.

No individual is self-sufficient: the individual exists only in an environmental field. The individual is inevitably, at every moment, a part of some field, which includes both him and his environment. The nature of the relationship between him and his environment determines the human being's behavior.

Perls (1973: 16)

If the environment can be defined as the 'entire world' in which an individual exists, then it may be necessary to divide this enormous potential influence system into some smaller and more manageable sub-systems. For instance there are parts of an individual's world which can be described as direct stimuli; that is, they influence through direct impact on the individual's sensory organs and awareness. There are other factors of which the individual may not be continually conscious, some of which are those influences which are stored as part of his or her memory, like traditions, the perception of the opinions and expectations of others. In this sense there is a complex network of absorbed influences which tends to hold an individual in a particular relationship to the others of his or her immediate and 'known' community.

There are other elements, however, which, enter the human community and thus into the immediate consciousness of individuals, but have their origins outside it. Thus information flows into, and is interpreted by, the community through all the media and communication channels. How these interpretations are made in the interaction of members of a community in the process of their daily lives, at work or at leisure, has to be conjectural, but made they are and individuals in such communities are aware of how others feel about national and international events, and what it is acceptable to believe and what it is necessary to reject.

We must accept that the explosion of information technology has created, and will continue to create in the future, more of the standards of behaviour and acceptable opinions than we have heretofore allowed to be the case. There is no doubt that for some people, often those whose network support system may be somewhat threadbare, or those looking for support in making a deliberate change; the people appearing several times weekly on TV and radio are more substantial as persons than some of the real people who are within their milieu but infrequently encountered.

In any one individual there meet many different lines of influence; which gives point to the ecological studies of human beings; and the obvious need for change agents, working with individuals to bring about intended change, to be aware that they have entered into the individual's network; to realise how vast or how small it may be; how numerous the strands; and how strongly or otherwise such networks hold the individual in place.

It is common enough for change agents to accept that an individual derives a considerable degree of awareness of his or her own identity from the feedback received in interaction with those whom they select as interactive participants. Such people form the bases of a reinforcement programme for the self-image which is already in place. But even this may be only a part of a much greater system of intertwined influences, some known and acknowledged, some not but none the less effective for that.

The whole process of learning, of acquiring experience, is part of the influence of the environment; not just for the content of that learning, but most importantly for the manner and timing of its acquisition and who and what else was involved in the process. The fact that some part of the individual's existence may at some time cause that learning and experience to become inadequate for him or her to cope adequately with developing situations, thus requiring help in some form or other, reveals that some of the environmental influences have acquired a changed value; but they are still there, and probably still retaining a strong influence on behaviour.

It thus behoves change agents to realise that effective change not only requires a basic commitment on the part of the subject individual to the process, but also some need to discover what originates, maintains and supports the behaviours which need to be changed and, finally, what ability to effect and sustain the intended change is available or can be developed.

Each individual makes sense of the world in which he or she lives through the processes of experience, comparison, adaptation, memory, and so on, all of which, and other factors, have to be acquired using the genetic endowment. Differences exist both in this genetic endowment (the equipment) and in the quality, quantity and timing of exposure to situations which offer the possibility of learning. In each case, therefore, an individual develops relatively unique sets of ideas and patterns, habits, thought systems, attitudes, opinions, and so on. Nevertheless, despite the differences, there are still large areas of similarity in environments; and in the situational exposures of those living in close proximity, large areas of similarity tend to be created. Similarity in turn tends to engender acceptance, and the need to conform can cause differences to be less exposed, except in private.

As most change efforts appear to be directed towards increasing an individual's production of socially acceptable behaviour, these differences and the energy and needs which sustain them become an area of 'need to know'. But because they are usually not only hidden but also largely unknown, this is extremely difficult to achieve and can be very time consuming.

Ordinary consciousness is an exquisitely evolved personal construction, 'designed' for the primary purpose of individual biological survival. Sense organs and the brain serve to select the aspects of the environment which are most relevant for survival. Our ordinary consciousness is object-centred; it involves analysis, a separation of oneself from other objects and organisms. This selective, active analytic construction enables us to achieve a relatively stable personal world in which we can differentiate objects and act upon them. The concepts of causality, linear time and language are the essence of this mode.

Ornstein (1975: 61)

Ornstein's definition of 'ordinary' consciousness was the first in several steps to enumerate other forms of consciousness, but for my purposes the 'ordinary' variety will serve to illustrate an essential part of the intended change processes.

The separateness to which Ornstein refers develops from the point where a baby eventually becomes aware that it is not part of mother, and then that there are other beings in the world as well. Like everything else that human beings develop with growth, this kind of awareness varies between individuals; it also varies in one individual at different times in his or her life; and between different situations at roughly the same time. But awareness of self is the basis for being aware of events and situations that are affecting that self.

This means, in effect, that some of the problems that a change agent may be faced with, in the process of establishing the influences on certain areas of behaviour which have been selected as targets of intended change, relate to the levels of awareness of the individuals involved. That is, both the awareness of the self as a separately existing entity and awareness of how circumstances are affecting that self are involved. The problems are complicated even further in that the individual's awareness in both areas may be at quite a high level, but intrinsically distorted by the interpretation which that individual has placed upon previous perceptions, so that although, as Ornstein describes, a relatively stable set of personal constructs has grown up, its bases may be in some senses false.

I am aware that 'false' is a question-begging use of the term in this context, because it may imply that there is some standard of 'truth' or 'reality' against which such bases may be described as 'false'. It is equally pointless to say that such a standard resides in the 'norms' of constructs for the community in which the individual exists, yet it must be accepted that behaviour assumptions, ideas and constructs *are* all judged against what such 'norms' are commonly accepted to be.

But the argument about the application of intended change to individuals needs to be pushed some way past the individual's state of awareness, both of him or herself and of the impinging circumstances, into the realm of meaning, and thus into the ideas related to intelligence.

Intelligence

Intelligence is an attribute of human beings which is essentially extremely difficult to define. Despite this, what everyone considers to be 'intelligence' is widely discussed, apparently measured, and applied to various kinds of behaviour in all manner of situations. For our purposes it will be sufficient to understand that we are concerned with what might be described as 'intellectual activities' – some being innate and others involving the use of memory and experience. The cardinal point at issue is the difference in the way that individuals are able, or not, to understand events and situations of which they become aware, and how they cope with them.

Given that an individual is aware, in whatever way that might be described – real, unreal, distorted or not – the main issue becomes the kind of meaning that the individual ascribes to his or her sense of being, and of the factors of influence which apparently surround them. If the awareness which we have discussed here has produced a series of constructs by which the individual establishes the meaning of those elements of his or her world which are important, then all new elements of awareness will be judged against these constructs and meaningful connections will be made, which, in simple terms, means that they are interpreted.

One definition of intelligence included the idea that it was a human faculty largely concerned with the degree of ability to deduce correlations; to establish connections between things and events where none previously existed, at least as far as a particular individual was concerned. For example, some people cannot easily see any connection between their behaviour and the way others respond to them. Such people appear to have a construct about the behaviour of individuals which indicates that, except in very gross impact situations, each individual operates very nearly independently of all others.

In essence I am accepting that, whatever intelligence may be, intellectual activity equates in everyday activities with the process of thinking and of reasoning. Certainly it is essential that, in order to think, an individual needs to have some impressions to think about, certainly the process of thinking and of reasoning relies on information already stored and upon memory and experience. But the ultimate point is that differences in intelligence relate to degrees of the ability to make connections and to some extent, also, to the speed with which these connections are made. Essentially intelligence performs the function of making sense of whatever the individual becomes aware of, with different degrees of facility and with different degrees of rationality. This forms the basis upon which an individual can make choices about the appropriate actions to take, bearing in mind that the quality of the choice will be only as good as the degree of accuracy of the perceptions upon which it was based.

Chance

The environment into which an individual is born establishes the patterns of opportunity which will be available to him or her. The genetic endowment with which an individual is born may establish the parameters of possibility of what he or she may be able to achieve, but the environment is the main effective ingredient in determining whether, or how, that potential will be achieved. Thus the factor of chance enters into the equation.

Chance, a term seldom employed in the discussions about nature and nurture, is, in my opinion, a very salient factor, largely because in very fundamental ways what kind of environmental elements are significant in a child's and an adult's functioning are subject to chance – in the way they operate, in the changes that can occur and, in other words, are chance because they are often unpredictable and uncontrollable.

Even in relatively stable communities, events occur which significantly alter the kind of environmental pressure, the people, the opportunities which may be available for the members of that community. Take for instance the situation of the break-up of the former Yugoslavia. The amazing changes of location of populations; of fortune; of stability, created by a cruel war may have been predicted as a possibility by someone aware of the disturbed history of the Balkan states, but hardly by the vast majority of the population going about their daily tasks. Almost without warning, and with dreadful speed, their expectations of life changed dramatically.

Such magnitude of change, while fairly common, is seldom predicted by those whom it affects the most and so, in a very dramatic way, apparently chance occurrences have created unforeseen environmental pressures and, whatever the genetic and innate characteristics which existed in those affected by them, the interaction between the characteristics and the chance situation which has arisen must generate a vastly different outcome from what might have been expected before the changes occurred.

I think that even in a society which is regarded as stable, the occurrence of unforeseen, unexpected changes is quite high and may indeed be a phenomenon of increasing prevalence in recent times. The essential nature of chance occurrences is that they are unpredictable. They have for centuries been ascribed to the interference in human affairs of divine beings, to fate, to the malign influence of other powerful human beings or to plain luck. There is, I suppose, a logic which would suggest that if it were possible to know all the factors involved in any chance event it would be clear that each was the culmination of a series of events and thus eminently predictable. But as we are never in the situation of being omniscient, many events must remain as the apparent outcome of chance elements.

In his book *The Psychology of Consciousness*, Ornstein (1975) quoted a story about Nasruddin Hodja which I think illustrates the problem of knowing a sequence of events well enough for the culmination not to appear as mere chance.

'What is fate?' Nasruddin was asked by a scholar.

'An endless succession of intertwined events, each influencing the other.'

'That is hardly a satisfactory answer. I believe in cause and effect.'

'Very well,' said the Mullah, 'look at that.' He pointed to a procession passing in the street.

'That man is being taken to be hanged. Is that because someone gave him a silver piece and enabled him to buy the knife with which he committed the murder; or because someone saw him do it; or because nobody stopped him?'

Choice

Maslow believed that a truly autonomous person was one who was able to be conscious of the nature of influences in his or her life and able to make rational conscious choices about how they were responded to. It was suggested that most human beings were not able to make rational choices about large and important elements of their lives for the simple reason that they were unaware that choice was available. Indeed, many believe that it is not possible to choose to do this or that because in reality no choice exists. Often choices are made on the basis of what a knowledgeable but unbiased observer would be compelled to say was inadequate information, or else upon inadequate understanding of what information there is.

Part of a change agent's approach to creating intended change has always been to remedy, if possible, these informational deficits by revealing alternatives previously unknown to the target; to demonstrate the nature and quality of the information upon which choices were to be made; and generally to increase the awareness of clients of the pressures and influences involved – so making it possible to avoid the habitual and unregarded patterns of thinking and behaviour which diminished the element of choice by the process of 'tramlining'.

Thus when an individual becomes aware of those factors of influence in his or her life, thinks about them and ascribes meaning to them in relation to his or her life patterns, the basis has been formed for choosing what to do about them, if anything. The quality of the awareness and of the thinking in fact prescribe the response – in which a major factor may be a limited knowledge of what responses are available, or even a marked reluctance to embark on what would appear to be the appropriate path.

Explanation

> The implications of different assumptions about human nature and human behaviour become apparent when we examine their consequences. Crucial social issues, such as destructive human aggression and the learning and development of sexual identity, are dealt with in quite different ways by psychobiologists, cognitive theorists, behaviourists, psychoanalysts and humanists.
>
> Medcof and Roth (1979: 323)

We must start from a very interesting point here: both those who investigate behaviour and those whose behaviour is investigated are human beings. The fact of being human is that one knows what it is like to be a human being, hence the scepticism of the man in the street about the pronouncements of social scientists on the subject of human behaviour. The difference between individuals is obviously acknowledged, but the factors which human beings hold in common are usually extrapolated from individual and local experience. The differences of the specialists, noted above, only enhance the ordinary person's estimate of the worth of his or her own experience and the extent of the contempt felt for the utterances of psychologists and sociologists.

The material that such people find so unacceptable is in large part the basic information that the change agent has to use. His or her target is the individual, particularly the individual who needs to achieve some form of change. The change agent's knowledge of that target must derive from the theories of human behaviour, plus whatever personal experience is relevant. The nature and quality of those theories will be looked at later; here we glance at the kind of information they provide for the change agent, on which decisions about how current states of individual behaviour were actually achieved and, from this, how to devise the most effective ways of producing the required changes.

The two most tangible facts about individuals are their physical and material existence and the observable behaviour that those existences produce. It would seem logical, therefore, to look first, very briefly, at explanations of behaviour which have some tangible and probably measurable factors on which to base assumptions, explanations and theories.

As we have seen, what are accepted as the three major creative factors in the development of human beings are genetic or innate material and propensities; the influence of the environment; and the cognitive faculties – of which the latter may be considered to be largely innate. Thus it can be no surprise to discover that the major contributions to explanations of human behaviour accept one or other of these main influences as the basis of theory, or in some cases a combination of two or more.

For some theorists the division into genetic, environmental and cognitive factors has always appeared to be somewhat illogical and they prefer to see such factors as being part of the same process and wholly interdependent. While I agree with this standpoint, I will note briefly the important explanatory assumptions under the three traditional headings.

Biological Determinism

Theorists who subscribe to the overwhelming dominance of the genetic elements in human behaviour believe that individuals are mainly controlled and directed by internal and unconscious forces, primarily the instinctual forces of sex and aggression. Innate factors are always primary and the effect of the environment is to promote the functioning, well or badly, of these innate factors. The motivation for behaviour is regarded to some extent as pleasure oriented, but is essentially for the relief of tension, and thus purposive.

Environmental Determinism

Environmentalists tend to believe that, given that human beings have a genetic endowment, the dominant feature of their development and behaviour is the environment – which provides conditioning, history and opportunities for learning. Motivation is regarded as being a response to stimuli arriving from the environment. Such theorists are extremely aware that the social conditions into which a child is born and in which he or she will grow, will be the major factor in the formation of behaviour patterns and allow little in the way of personal freedom.

Biological and Environmental Determinism

Under this heading fall those theorists, mainly physiologically oriented, who believe that behaviour arises from a continuous interaction between genetic, biochemical and constitutional factors on the one hand, and environmental factors on the other. These interacting factors are essentially pre-set in that the former set the boundaries within which the latter can operate. Aggression is regarded as an essential survival trait and sex as genetically determined.

Non-deterministic Approaches

Theorists in this fourth category, mainly cognitive and humanistic psychologists, believe that human beings are free to determine their own behaviour and that the genetic/environmental discussion is an irrelevant one – indeed they regard it as an abstraction. In the case of the humanisitic approaches, this turns into the assertion that both genetic and environmental factors provide the boundaries in which development and growth is free. Ultimately behaviour stems from the struggle to grow, and each individual is responsible for his or her behaviour, whatever the outcomes they may be seeking.

The words of Medcof and Roth at the head of this section on the implications of the various assumptions about human nature can now be seen to be very true. Each of the approaches assumes one or more of the essential, known and observable facts about growth and development and behaviour and asserts this as the most important factor in understanding, and thus, also, as the essential basis for the process of changing behaviour.

It is because of this partiality that such a diverse number of change processes have developed, yet in any real sense they all stem from the same pool of factual knowledge about human beings. The problems arise, I believe, from the process of attempting to use what knowledge is available to establish the causes of behaviour in some cases and in so doing creating elegant and logical explanations which come to have the force of received wisdom, indeed of faith.

> Since personality has such a strong biological basis, it follows that people in general are much more different from one another than might at first be supposed. We tend to believe that most people are like ourselves, perhaps differing slightly due to events in their past. We also believe that they could quite easily be converted to our way of thinking and change their behaviour to be more like us. But this belief is quite wrong. The long history of our failure to rehabilitate criminals, make vandals behave like ordinary human beings, cure neurotics and so on, is eloquent testimony to the fact that people differ profoundly from each other.
>
> Eysenck and Eysenck (1981: 110)

It is impossible to visualise a biological organism apart from the environment in which it exists, so the interaction between genetic endowment and environment is always there, and whatever potential is built into the first requires the appropriate stimulus and support from the latter to develop as fully as possible. A biological organism has a built-in developmental sequence, but that sequence at any stage, even right from the beginning, can be enhanced, supported or diminished by environmental factors. The truly important discussion about human behaviour has to revolve around the dominance and quality or otherwise of nature or nurture.

But other factors which we have considered here, like consciousness, will and intelligence, are also important because they pose the possibility, not so much of the urges and drives to particular forms of behaviour, but to the control of its execution. This kind of control may be total or partial exclusion of certain areas of action, or may be directed at the nature and quality, and direction and timing of its execution. So, for instance, a fear of certain kinds of situation may be removable, but it may also be suppressed or more effectively dealt with by a process of learning to cope with its manifestations.

The alternative approach would have to arise from a belief that it could be possible to discover where this fear of a particular situation originated, and then to endeavour to remove its power. Given that behaviour arises to meet the perception of situations, and may be retained for no good reason long after the situation which aroused it has disappeared or changed, the essential first ingredient of this approach must be extremely complex and difficult to the point of being impossible. Even if it were achieved, it may also prove unsuccessful.

8 Groups, Organisations and Situations as Indirect Approaches

> It is a structure that emerges from the interactions of individuals, a structure which itself produces changes in individual members.
>
> Bonner (1959: 20)

Groups and organisations are frequently targets of change efforts, indeed groups are increasingly deliberately created with the express intention of using the dynamics which operate within them as the medium of change.

Some of the major factors which promote the use of groups as change targets will be discussed here for the simple reason that these factors lead directly to the techniques of intervention which are employed. The concepts of credibility, conformity, security, resource development and use will be considered alongside cohesion, isolation, confirmation and contagion.

In organisations the process of change may be either organic, which is analogous to the developmental sequence in humans, or related to the functional efficiency of the organisation. In the latter case there are two main strands both of which are structural. The first is change of the organisational structure – which is a planning exercise inspired to some degree by those who believe that they know what kind of structural planning will deliver the end product for which the organisation was set up. Thus individuals become parts of the organisation. The second strand is relational in nature in the interaction of the human elements – their perceptions, images, needs, and so on, are considered important, even essential, to the functional efficiency of the organisation. In other words, people are the organisation – not just parts of its machinery of operation.

Groups and organisations have been designated here as indirect approaches and some explanation of that designation is required.

In Chapter 7 I suggested that the essential 'target' of all change efforts was the individual human being. There is an insistent logic behind that suggestion which would indicate that individuals are irreducible entities, whereas groups and organisations have individuals as their basic elements and, no matter what ties, bonds or influences exist within them for the individual in whatever form or combination, it is the individual's commitment to that combination which actually makes possible its existence as a unit. Equally so, it is the individual's continued presence in the group which allows the possible development of factors of influence.

Thus when groups and organisations become the targets of change efforts which are directed at influencing that group or organisation, the ultimate factors which have to change are the attitudes, opinions, commitments and behaviours of the individual elements of those combinations. Which is why one of the processes of organisation/large group change often centres on efforts to change key people who then influence the rest of the group in the desired way.

The distinction, therefore, between direct and indirect attempts to change individuals has two basic factors.

1. In one-to-one situations, the individual is wholly aware that he or she is the only target of the change agent's efforts. It matters not whether the target individual is a voluntary target, the evidence of physical confrontation leaves no room for the target to believe that he or she is not the focus of what is going on.

2. In groups and organisations, the attempt to change individuals is just as important but, unless a confrontation with key individuals is produced, the change efforts are directed indiscriminately at the individual membership in terms of loyalties, fears, influences, etc. That this can be seen as a direct influence I am well aware, but the more important aspects of all group change efforts are linked to the fact of the individual being in the presence of others not usually seen as the direct focus of change. Such factors as contagion, imitation, fear of isolation and of not being acceptable are very powerful forces. Indeed, most of these conformity pressures operate without any clear awareness on the part of members of the group or organisation that such an operation is actually occurring. In this respect many change efforts take place in an indirect, non-confrontational and, to a large extent, non-aware manner.

The unawareness of group members of the pressures and influences to which they may be subjected just by virtue of their membership has given rise to the effective use of such pressures in propaganda, and consequently to a great discussion of the ethical nature of such influencing situations. As the quotation at the head of this chapter indicates quite clearly, a group is a structure which contains a number of interactive individuals and will usually bring about changes in those individuals.

When groups first began to be studied it was quite common to see the offer of the development of a 'group mind' as an explanation of the difference between a group and the individuals who were its component elements. The rush to emphasise the 'difference' of a group's performance inevitably resulted in the excessive exclusion of the fact that the group, however different in the performance of tasks to the performance of individuals, was still composed of individuals, who, if not to be regarded as wholly independent, were also members of many other groups and capable of some degree of independent and critical appraisal of the situation.

What group theorists have noted about the relationship between group members and the units in which they congregate, is that their abilities as previously assessed as individuals do not provide a good basis to predict the performance of the group. The process of transformation of individual ability into group performance appears to be a complex process affected by many diverse and little-understood factors. What is reasonably certain is that they appear to set an upper limit to the performance potential of the group and that they are markedly affected by the nature of the interpersonal relationships which obtain within the group. Thus there is much concern, not so much with the ability of the individual member, but with their status within the group – though ability and status may be related – the major point is that status tends to reside in the perception of members about an individual member, which could be entirely a matter of presentation.

It is customary to discuss groups under two very wide categories: those groups which pre-existed the change process, were originally created for some other purpose and have since been adapted as change targets; and those groups which are specifically created from selected and available individuals. In the latter case they then have to go through a process of 'becoming' a group before the process of being used as a focus of change efforts can be truly said to be possible. In this chapter we will concentrate largely on the latter version – groups created as specific targets.

In the created category of groups the act of creation is the most important factor – for the simple reason that the process of creation is not guaranteed to be effective. It may not generate a group, or, even if one is created, it may not function effectively with regard to the targets of change for which it was created. Indeed, all the influences which exist within groups can only be effective if the group not only has an existence over a period of time, but also can receive various influence inputs from change agents or group members.

It is common knowledge that some groups can affect their members in an extremely short period of membership; it is equally well known that such profound and immediate changes are rare occurrences. It is much more usual that group members go through a period of adjustment, which is partly a presentation of themselves and partly learning about the group they have entered. There is a relationship which is constantly being adjusted between the element of personal safety, usually characterised by caution and withholding, and the element of immersion within the group and its ways and thus eventual commitment to it.

There is nothing uncommon in this process; variations in the time individuals take to integrate with a group or to reject it are conditioned by individual personality, past experience and the cultural traditions of the individual's social background. But the process of integration, if it takes place at all, appears to follow reasonably well-defined stages. These stages of group development have a good deal in common with the development of relationships in society in general and are considerably influenced by the expectations of change agents.

When a 'created' group has been formed, and even during the process of its formation, it becomes an instrument of change, the aims of which are to alter some aspect of the lives of the group members, which could be a change of an added factor, like support, rather than a change of existing elements. There are many areas in which a group can exert influence on its members and, as it is these factors which change agents (who may be group members themselves) seek to use to attain their ends, I propose to look briefly at the most commonly listed of these areas of influence and to discuss how change agents attempt to use them.

The presence of others has, from birth, exerted influence of some sort on the individual. Indeed some authorities would assert that human beings need interaction with others in the same way that a plant needs nourishment – that is, it is essential, not only to their growth but also as a necessary confirmation of their self-identity. It is noteworthy that perhaps the most common punishment apart from death that humans have devised and used is isolation. There is evidence from the studies of sensory deprivation that being cut off from stimulation and, in particular, from one's fellows, soon leads to a disintegration of the individual. Relationships and contact also tend to mask the fear of the recognition of the actual separate and isolated state in which we exist.

Group theorists postulate that in normal life our ability to choose relationships is limited, thus if we want to use groups to affect change in individuals, it is advisable to select group members very carefully, on the basis that they will, when brought into contact, affect one another in particularly desirable ways. Such a condition, however, depends upon an ability to predict how people will behave – which we do not possess to any marked degree.

It is difficult to categorise the influences which have been listed as occurring within a group for the very simple reason that all of them are concerned with perception, and thus relatively idiosyncratic reporting occurs. Consider, for instance, the influence designated as the 'attractiveness' of a group. Is that 'attractiveness' an intrinsic quality of a group so described; a perception of those individuals who are potential members; or a combination of both? Certainly the very same observable characteristics which make a group appear extremely attractive to one potential member may be regarded as unattractive by another. Without doubt, when a group is attractive in some measure to all its members, for whatever reason, then those members stand to gain more from continued membership than any costs that may be incurred, for the factors of member satisfaction and perceived attractiveness of the group are apparently different sides of the same coin.

Given this problem of defining the nature of group influences, it is instructive to look at what is available for change agents to use in their attempts to bring about intended change – bearing in mind that much group literature emphasises the concrete existence of the variables we shall be considering.

'Interaction' is a much overused word and has connotations of activity which are also overstressed. Nevertheless, the prime fact of a created group is that it brings a number of individuals into a circumscribed situation and thus makes such individuals available for contact with each other by the simple process of, for a period of time, eliminating the possibility of contact with others, except in the form of some imaginative exercise. Quite a large proportion of that contact may be, especially initially, a passive one – often mistaken by change agents for resistance and lack of commitment, but just as likely to be caution and a requirement to satisfy some security needs by 'seeing', rather than by being told, how the group deals with certain big issues.

If a selection process has been possible and has been exercised, then these group members will find that they have some interest, problem or need in common. This may not be an obvious one, for they may have been selected or chosen themselves on the basis of difference. But the reason for that difference may have been to illuminate, clarify, solve or learn about something which they all have in common.

Many processes operate between people brought into close physical contact with one another. Among other things, individuals become quite visible to each other, and thus their behaviour is open to scrutiny. As the group progresses, members demonstrate – just by being there – something of their feelings, knowledge, skills, experience and personality, all of which may have direct relevance for the other members of the group and also some degree of credibility. These factors and others are often referred to as constituting the group's resources because they have the possibility of increasing each individual's understanding of his or her situation and of adding previously unknown and untried coping skills to their repertoire.

Often the group leader may be the initial source of new ideas, information and ways of coping and, depending on how much the leader as change agent becomes and remains the main resource element, so the group will be leader dependent. The more the resources of the individual members become the main factor, the more the unit becomes group centred.

Other processes which occur in a group and which serve to influence members are imitation, confirmation, comparison, contagion and acceptance. All of these are indirect and often invisible processes. For instance if a group member finds that in a particular group he or she is accepted by the members; his or her views find favour, understanding and support; and that he or she is surrounded by role models of a very acceptable form, then that individual member's level of satisfaction with his or her membership is high. Consequently, the group has a deposit of goodwill and commitment upon which it can draw in the form of demands upon that member, up to the point where the costs of those demands approach the perceived level at which they negate the individual member's satisfactions. At this point, membership becomes debatable – the group's credit has been eroded. If it is possible, at this stage a member will seek to leave the group, or change it in some way.

The activities of a group are another potent source of influence in that they provide interest, learning and excitement for members. Once again a credit rating can develop, and group members will provide energy and commitment to the group as long as that rating is in a favourable balance.

Equally, groups can support members, provide security, discipline, codes of behaviour and often a great degree of relevance. They can generate and sustain self-esteem and form sub-groups with special interests and ideas. Schutz (1959) suggested that these processes of member support could be contained within three large areas: inclusion, control and affection – each of these areas being seen as two-way; thus, for instance, control included the member's desire to control others, plus the degree to which that member was prepared to allow the group to control him or her.

Groups provide roles for members to play; provide standards of comparison and have access to external resources often far in excess of those available to individual members. All these factors are, of course, monitored through the perceptions of the individual, but one of the major factors as far as change agents are concerned is that many of the pressures are invisible, hence not regarded by the members as pressures, and certainly not as compulsions affecting their behaviour. The preoccupation of the change agents is, therefore, to guide and control the production of those pressures which are regarded as most liable to generate the kind of changes which are intended.

A large problem exists for change agents in that the connection between particular group pressures and the production of intended change is not exactly clear, although it is often expressed in the literature as if it were so. Another problem is that the means of control, in terms of intensity and direction of the required influences, also have little of precision and exactness about them. Despite all forms of assessment, individual group members cannot be exactly known quantities. The degree of difference which can emanate from individuals in the same circumstances is quite large. In addition, for most group members the time they spend in the group is only a small portion of their lives, and thus influences from outside the group manifest themselves within its confines, and vice versa. It is for this reason, amongst others, that some change agents targeting groups prefer to isolate group members from all other forms of contact for some considerable periods of time, to ensure that all influences manifest themselves within the group.

Group as System

The properties of the elements of physical systems are ultimately what decide their actions. The properties of the elements of human systems, however, are not so clearly definable, therefore any consideration of them must include the factor of element awareness and the ability of those elements to effect change by taking decisions and by deliberate action.

As a result, the commonly proposed argument – that a human system, large or small, can be understood in terms of the deterministic laws of physical systems – cannot be countenanced. This, then, would tend to suggest that all the regularities which we believe we observe in human systems are more likely to be determined by the interposition of human intelligence and awareness upon the system by the elements of which it is composed than to arise from the nature of the system itself.

The process of group work; that is, the deliberate intervention by change agents in the group process, is to convert the perception that the members have of the system so that it conforms to and adopts a pre-conceived patterning which, by altering the actual elements of the system, changes the probable outcome in a selected direction.

Organisations

An organisation may be defined as a partially self-controlled system, at least part of which comprises human beings, where responsibility for possible actions is divided between individuals or groups of individuals, and which is comprised of functionally distinct sub-groups that are probably aware of each other. The system has some freedom of choice, of both means and ends.

> Social organisations are simply large social groups in which the leadership hierarchy and role differentiation have become formalised into fixed ranks and offices, norms have become rules, and in which methods of communication and work are prescribed.
>
> Argyle (1972: 272)

The historical development of organisations has shown the rise of a hierarchical form, based upon early military and religious models. There are various names given to this form of organisation, but probably the most frequently used is that of 'bureaucracy' – largely because it usually comprises a series of bureaux, or sections, which have a certain degree of responsibility, but fit into a pyramidal system of governance, with the ultimate decision-making, and thus power, at the top.

As processes in industry became more complex and were increasingly gathered together in one place, it became essential that, to control them and to ensure the most effective and economic production, a well-defined structure of management should be employed. Such structures provided a rational basis for controlling increasing complexity. They were able to provide:

1. impartial rules;

2. rational organisation and management;

3. systematised record keeping;

4. specialisation and division of labour; and

5. a clear role structure for members of the organisation.

But as industrial processes changed towards a much higher level of sophistication of equipment, this form of bureaucratic organisation was found to be wanting. Indeed, modern theorists believe that the bureaucratic model is best suited to a situation where required changes are gradual and where relevant technologies are stable and also relatively non-complex.

Definition by structure now contains the organic model of organisation brought about because the static classical bureaucracy could not adapt to change with sufficient speed to remain competitive. Organic structures are flexible – designed to meet changes which are not only rapid but also of major importance; to cope with a technology which is complex and constantly growing and being updated. Change is constant in such organisations and the great problem is to design a system that has enough stability to be productive while maintaining enough flexibility to be innovative. In such a system, the quality of the work-force is of paramount importance because they are largely highly skilled and their quality of life and job satisfaction are highly valued.

Others, like Amitai Etzioni (1980) for instance, have defined organisations, not in terms of structure, but in terms of the kind of authority which is exercised in them and the motivations of the members. Thus he suggests an organisation may be:

- Coercive   e.g. prisons – the authority being based in the concept of punishment.

- Utilitarian   e.g. industry – authority rests on the ability to apply legal power and the provision of monetary and other rewards in exchange for work.

- Normative or moral   e.g. churches, voluntary and professional organisations – authority rests on the management's ability to harness the motivations of members and to engage their commitment to the aims of the organisation.

Blau and Scott (1980), suggested that organisations could be classified on the basis of who stood to gain most from the activities of the organisation – for example, the members in a mutual benefit society; the owners or managers in commercial or industrial concerns; the particular clients of an organisation providing a service such as a clinic or a school; and the public in general with government departments.

The complexity of definition is matched by the complexity of types of organisation, enhanced by the current rapid spread of advanced technology and the consequent decline of labour-intensive organisations. Change agents operate in this widely varied field as management consultants, trouble-shooters and analysts of all kinds. Once again they are faced with the same problems as those found in small groups, but in these instances the network of groups which makes up an organisation is much more intimately connected with the serious business, as far as the members are concerned, of earning a living.

As we shall see later, the change from hierarchical and rigid systems of organisation – where individuals were almost cogs in a machine – to more flexible systems, has been marked by a much greater emphasis on the level of reward in personal terms, as well as financial, which accrues to the work-force. Starting from the experiments of Elton Mayo in 1933 and 1945, concern about the effects that interpersonal relationships can have on the efficiency of organisations has steadily increased.

Change agents working with organisations still have the individual within the organisation as their essential target but, with certain essential exceptions, the approach is usually indirect –

through the processes of learning and discussion, by exposure, and by the exploitation of pressures both within the organisation and from outside it. Indeed, the approaches of change agents may be classified in three ways:

1. Personnel approach – effected through the processes of selection and training.

2. Human engineering – effected through the processes of job modification to suit those who are available to do the work; also by the design and modification of equipment and the methods of its use.

3. Social psychological approach – including studies of: motivation, incentive systems, interpersonal relationships, group identification, alienation; all affecting production, job satisfaction and morale.

There appears to be much more scope for agents to effect lasting change within organisations, because, with certain exceptions, organisations which survive are already in a process of change and adaptation. The scale of such a change operation also makes feasible a great variety of key points and personnel and, above all, the economic and financial motivation can be remarkably strong.

9 The 'Agents' of Change

... it is no surprise that a new profession has begun evolving to do the job. The role is that of the 'change agent', and it may truly be classified as a modern phenomenon.

Golembiewski and Blumberg (1970: 292–3)

In a paper called 'Change Agents', (1970) Warren Bennis described his subject as 'professionals, men who, for the most part, have been trained and hold doctorates in the behavioral sciences'.

The professionalism of this twentieth-century phenomenon was being sedulously advertised in order to establish a form of credibility with other professionals and also with those who would become the 'targets' of their operations.

Most human beings operate as change agents, however, if a common definition of the term is employed – one which leaves out the appeal to professionalism and doctorates in the behavioural sciences. Many times in the life of an individual he or she sets out to change, to modify, to alter the behaviour, opinions, attitudes of those who impinge most upon his or her everyday life. The process may not be extremely 'professional', but it is one of influence in the same way as that performed by the 'change agents' of Bennis' description. Indeed, we often operate as change agents to ourselves when we make a conscious decision to attempt to alter some aspect of our lives or behaviour.

This generalisation of the idea of being a change agent is not intended to detract from the concept of professionalisation which the founders of the term had in mind. Their concern was that anyone who proposed to interfere in the lives of others without the bond of some existing relationship (e.g. kinship or friendship), should be as well trained to perform that function as the current understanding of what would be required and available would allow.

Nevertheless, I am concerned with the activity of change agents and the processes, methods, concepts and beliefs which support them, whether they are trained professionals, as described above, or the friendly helper.

Who Are the Change Agents?

Professional 'change agents' must, in one sense, comprise all those medical specialisms like psychiatry and psychotherapy, through the ranks of psychologists, social workers and into the ranks of trainers, the standard-setters, the religious teachers, parents, friends associations of various sorts, and so on. But when discussions about change agents are held after some crisis has occurred, when some attempt at changing an individual's behaviour has signally failed, those professionals most likely to be under discussion are psychiatrists, psychologists, social workers and other 'carers' who are seen as having a professional and often legal responsibility to decide that change has been effected.

It constantly strikes me, reading through the literature of intended change, that Bateson's point about words not being adequate to describe what goes on in complex behaviours is fully justified. There is a great sense that writers coin phrases which seem to them to fit admirably some situation in which they have been involved, but which, when subjected to later close scrutiny, are often found to be implying something which cannot actually be true.

'Intended change' (my phrase) which is wide enough to cover all attempts by a person or persons to bring about deliberate change in others, is the subject of a bewildering array of euphemisms which are actually much more likely to describe the ideas, philosophy, theoretical orientations and beliefs of the individual who produces and uses them than they are to have any relevance to the actual process of attempting to exert some form of influence to effect change in another.

Take, for instance, the word 'care' which is so beloved of social workers. Essentially 'care' means 'looking after', in the sense of keeping alive, feeding, protecting, having affection for – indeed being a composite of all the familiar attributes of human beings who have a loving and willing responsibility for the well-being of others. But the 'caring' professions are change agents. Even if what they do is to stem a process of deterioration, they have generated change. By becoming involved in a person's, group's or organisation's existence they have changed the pre-existing position and, as the intrusion is deliberate and motivated by the intent to change (for such is the process of the profession) they have added to any 'caring' which may have existed before the process of change. Support; help – whatever name is given to intrusions of this nature –

only adds to the obfuscation of the process of intended change by masking the basic intent with emotive descriptions.

Of course it matters greatly to both change agent and target how the process of change is effected. It is possible to change human behaviour quite markedly by acts of unspeakable brutality, by the forced administration of neuro-surgery or drugs, all of which have been used within this century and inside so-called civilised societies. Under normal circumstances such methods are forbidden because of their enormous infringement of human rights, but because of the need that change agents have to appear to stay well within the limits of ethical behaviour, a considerable degree of obfuscation concerning those processes of change which are used occurs in the literature.

Having said that, it is necessary to point out that, within acceptable ethical limits, much of that literature asserts an ability to be extremely directive and to affirm an extraordinarily close and precise link between interventive action and intended outcome. This is just as bizarre in its way as the attempt to disguise deliberately intended change efforts as 'loving' or 'caring', and must stem from some need to aver certainties which, in all conscience, can only be probabilities, and these not of a very high order.

Lacking the certainty of the physical sciences, which, occasionally, is itself challenged, the social sciences and their applied forms seem to need the psychological shield of an assertion of reliability of outcome to maintain their status. Our society is prone to play image-creation games and it is quite understandable that some degree of credibility is a necessary prerequisite for the practice of intended change. But it is very noticeable that change agents whose background lies in an already accepted discipline like that of doctor or psychologist, have a better public image than social workers who, in Etzioni's definition, are a 'semi-profession' – created as change agents from a standing start, as it were. Indeed social workers often seem to be the scapegoats of a society that wants changes to be effected in some of its members, but is highly critical of those who attempt to perform this function, particularly if their efforts are publicly exposed as failures.

The essential point here is that, however the processes of intended change are described or justified, whatever ways are found to give the change agents credibility, at bedrock they are simply attempts to change behaviour by the application of some form of influence, direct or indirect. Their success or failure depends not so much upon the creation of an acceptable public image (i.e. credibility), but upon a genuine understanding of how human beings are able to be changed, which, in turn, depends upon an even more important understanding of how individuals arrive at their current state when some form of change becomes necessary or desirable. And I suppose the final understanding must be that change – real change – can perhaps only exist if some factors, which did not exist previously within the individual system, continue to exert pressure to create and maintain change. There are only two directions from which that pressure can come; either internally or externally.

Later in this book the suggestion will be made that a great deal of the theory about the practice of intended change comes not so much from academic theorist or experimentation but from a particular kind of practitioner. These individuals appear to possess two well-defined characteristics: (1) they appear to achieve a greater than average success in their chosen sphere of operation; and (2) they are blessed, or cursed, with an active and creative imagination.

If these two characteristics are examined in some detail, it will be found that the components of the first appear in many forms, but always at the base is an apparent ability to understand the predicaments of others in a relatively inexplicable way. This apparent sensitivity to clues unavailable to others has been variously described as 'intuition' or 'empathy', neither of which entirely satisfactorily covers what actually happens.

Miller (1966) wrote that tacit knowing, which is a stage of a child's development towards explicit knowing, represented a state in which a great deal more was known than could be understood, and it is not unlikely that some element of tacit knowing would be found in this process of 'intuitive understanding'. Because such knowing cannot be understood in logical terms, there is always a danger that some individuals may believe that it is present in their work, whereas what might actually be occurring are the productions of a fertile imagination. The only applicable test for the existence of such an activity must lie with the assessment of the results of its use.

As a basis for change operations, however, it is scarcely adequate since very few people appear to possess it to any marked degree and, of those who do, many have only a partial sensitivity, hence are nearly as dependent on the analysis of ordinary sensory data as others. Indeed I suspect that such people are as rare a phenomenon as those who possess special aptitudes like musical, artistic or mathematical skills.

The second factor appears to be more widespread. Thus, individuals faced with the dilemmas and predicaments of others, tackle the situation not by 'the book' (whatever text that might be) but with genuine creativity, and devise original, different and imaginative ways of working with those in difficulties. If, combined with this creative process, there is also the ability to pass on to others, either by word of mouth or in writing, what started out as an individual creative response, this can form the basis of an addition to the change agent's repertoire.

The problem with both these characteristics is that they appear on the fringes of logical validation and are thus not only 'unscientific' but also 'unprofessional' in that they can neither be theoretically substantiated nor, as a result, taught to others. What is astonishing is that we appear to be able to accept with envy, but with no hesitation, musical genius like that of Mozart, or even the fact that a small girl of 11 years can solve mathematical problems with greater facility than established and mature mathematics specialists, but we cannot quite accept as valid that an individual, by the light of nature as it were, can understand the dilemmas, feelings, and difficulties of another person.

Perhaps this may have some basis in the fact that, while skills in mathematics, music, art or even physical ability seem to have been covered under the heading of special aptitudes, no such heading exists for an aptitude in understanding human behaviour.

For this reason, most change agents are taught and learn their skills in a manner which stresses logic and rationality and uses supervised practice and the analysis of perceived data on the basis of available assumptions or theories of the sources of behaviour. Of course there is still some room for the use and development of different forms of 'knowing', and often such factors are acceptable provided that, in the course of practice, they demonstrate a particular tight relationship to predictive accuracy as shown by successful outcomes.

The Enforcers

Some change agents bring about change in those with whom they work by the application of force – they enforce change. As one of the main contentions presented in this book is that lasting change – durable change – can only take place with the willing co-operation of the persons subject to the change process, the fact that a category of enforced change is considered, which by implication frequently requires no co-operation on the part of the subject, has to be explained.

In effect, legitimate enforced changes are almost always of a physical nature. At one end of this scale there are, for example, operations which reduce the capacity of the stomach by sealing off part of it in order to bring about quite drastic changes in eating behaviour. This is an 'enforced change' in that, although the patient may agree, indeed may demand, the operation, when it has been performed, unless it can be reversed, the individual is compelled to change his or her eating patterns – there is no choice. More dramatically, a thief who has had his hands removed may still possess whatever drive he had previously to steal things, but now no longer has the ability to fulfil the dictates of that drive – at least as far as stealing articles from other people is concerned.

The essential fact of the 'enforcers' branches of the change agents' ranks is that they all tend to make it impossible for their subjects to pursue a particular kind of behaviour; thus change has to occur because the original behaviour is no longer possible. Into this category must also come doctors who prescribe medication which, while not making selected behaviours impossible, makes them much less available. For instance, violence, aggression, anxiety, depressive behaviours and sexual drives can all be modified by the use of drugs, and all have an element of enforcement about them, as have some training processes.

But such matters as enforced change are of great moral interest when the behaviours which are being eliminated are based not so much on the best interests of the subject, as in, say, dealing with eating disorders or anxiety, but on the basis of controlling socially disapproved behaviours. The line between the two can on occasions be woefully thin, and when the social disapproval is largely politically motivated the factors of duress and control become ethically dubious. One of the reasons for the use of such enforced change processes is that they usually have a fairly high success rate in eliminating the target behaviours. What kinds of behaviour, if any, arise in the place of those so controlled is another matter, and it must never be forgotten that the ultimate form of enforced change which eliminates all behaviours is execution.

The Persuaders

Quite obviously most change agents are not enforcers in the sense just described, but they do employ differing degrees of more subtle forms of pressure and influence to bring about intended changes, some of which, it is more than likely, they themselves have little awareness of using.

The essential belief is that human beings can and do change. The evidence for this exists all around us in the same way that the evidence also exists for the long-term stability of some major behavioural patterns in the face of all kinds of situational change. So, what change agents know is that human beings can actually change their behaviour – if the circumstances in which they find themselves are appropriate, one might almost say propitious. The real problems arise when change agents come to consider what those propitious circumstances may be, and how they may be set up, created as it were, at the right time, at the right intensity and in the right way to produce selected change in particular individuals.

Change agents learn that people can be persuaded to change by rational approaches, by pressures both direct and indirect and by approaches which involve their emotions. But they are also aware that behavioural patterns are maintained not just by habit and desire, but by many influences both past and present, some real, some not; by responses to the way situations and relationships are perceived; and by a host of other factors, so for any form of change process to be successful, it has at least to counter some of these contextual sustaining influences. For information about these factors, the change agent has to use his or her sensitivity to social situations, knowledge of the major theories of behaviour and a variety of skills, both verbal and action-oriented, to exert pressure to change.

All human interactions can be read as influence situations, so the idea of influencing the behaviour of another is common to all human beings – what is different in the performance of change agents is that it is planned and executed with clear intent, focused as to outcome and backed by knowledge and skill in the available methods of achieving that change.

Personal Characteristics

Most change agents are part of what are loosely called the 'helping' or 'caring' professions. By implication they are people who have some urge to help those who find themselves in situations with which they cannot adequately cope; or who have been recognised by others to have behavioural problems, either of a deviant nature or otherwise. But this basic caring factor has also to be balanced by the fact that, as we have just noticed, change situations involve the use of influence which, in other terminology, means the exercise of power. Many change agents will aver that their main purpose in being involved centres round 'empowering' their clients. To attempt to generate power for others is essentially an exercise in power itself. Other change agents accept quite readily that, in order to be effective, they need to be expert – a form of power – and able to control and direct the change process.

Need Fulfilment

There has been a remarkable proliferation in this century of those who, by the definitions presented here, are practising as change agents. There are two possible explanations for this: (1) the work of the change agent has become increasingly necessary in the kinds of society which currently exist; and (2) such professionals have become remarkably successful at advertising and selling their services. The two are of course inextricably linked. Modern societies are full of people who are no longer constrained by tradition, religion and other social forces to accept their lot. Change agents offer the possibility of becoming different; of being better liked; more powerful; less bothered by stress, anxiety, guilt and depression; more able to utilise those forces which the Human Potential movement has consistently stated are available; of being able to counter the influence of genetic deficits or lacks in skill and social competence; of the deficiencies of parenting, and so on – the list is endless. Many of the problems which change agents offer to tackle are real and handicapping deficits in individual lives; many may be fantasy, but the need in this particular sphere is great.

Since human beings have been freed from the inevitability of their state, any who offer an apparently scientific, professional and accredited method of effecting desired change are in business.

The other area of need for the skills of change agents lies in dealing with those forms of social behaviour which society regards as unacceptable, and for which it requires some form of effective change; so that such deviants can be returned to society, adapted to its norms and no longer desirous of pursuing a life of crime or of other anti-social behaviour.

The division between these two represents a great gulf for the change agent. Those who seek change have the essential ingredient of success already in place, a great willingness to become involved and a readiness to bear some costs, of all kinds, in order to achieve their desired ends. Those for whom change is sought by others, by law, by the society in some manifestation of its power, are much less likely to be willing co-operators and very much less inclined to bear the costs involved.

The process of intended change has been supplied with its informational base by the various disciplines and semi-professions which practice some part of it. Thus that base largely consists of theories of human behaviour, both psychological and sociological; a form of practice which owes a great deal of its structure to the medical profession; some concepts of social policy; and some ethical concepts based on ideas of the value of human beings which probably started with religion. To this have been added some ideas from philosophy, linguistics, systems theory and, latterly, ideas from cybernetics. But the whole, when considered as such, can be seen to have eschewed ideas which, though probably very relevant to the practices of intended change, have appeared to practitioners and theorists alike to be untenable because they deal with ideas rather than action.

Thus the need to be validated as professional practitioners and theorists has created a dilemma for change agents between that need and the essential 'hands-on' activity-based process which is their practice. Perhaps the main results of this have been: (1) individual theories (e.g. psychoanalytic ideas) have been accepted as possessing a degree of certainty similar to, say, the theories of physics – which is patently not true; and (2) what has become acceptable theory is firmly fixed at a level of thinking about human behaviour which is considerably below that of the most potent of philosophical ideas.

For instance, when ideas based originally in a simple mechanistic form such as systems theory are taken over into that variant of intended change known as social work, the outcome is such a dilution and distortion of the original concepts that it is virtually unrecognisable. Admittedly the process of adaptation of theoretical material from one discipline to another is often a very fruitful process, in that it produces a different viewpoint and possible explanation of circumstances to that which currently existed. In the process, however, huge areas of the original thesis are often not just adapted but omitted, then not only is the process of adaptation enfeebled but also probably invalidated because the essential concepts, which were the basis of the original thesis and formed its logical structure, have been ignored.

All the sciences that are based on the study of human beings have something to offer the change agent – not torn, bleeding and emasculated, from their context; but accepted for the extra light they can throw on the complexities of behaviour and the probability of effecting beneficial change. Even ideas from the physical sciences, dealing as they do with matter, can often serve to demonstrate meaningful connections which, seen as relationships between individual objects and forces in a situation, can be extremely revealing of situations of which human beings are a part.

For instance, in 1926 Werner Heisenberg produced his Principle of Uncertainty. This principle stated that, in order to determine the current position and velocity of a particle, it was necessary to shine light on the particle. However, as the accuracy of the revealed position of the particle cannot be more precise than the distance between the wave crests of the light used, the shorter the wavelength of the light the more accurate the measurement. But it is not possible to use an arbitrarily small amount of light because light comes in 'quanta', thus using a quantum of light will disturb the particle illuminated and change its velocity unpredictably. What this means, in effect, is that striving for greater accuracy of measurement of position produces less accurate measurements of speed.

Heisenberg's uncertainty principle is a fundamental, inescapable property of the world.

Hawkins (1995: 61)

In terms of the interaction between change agent and target, and very simply stated, the principle of uncertainty would imply that the closer the former attempts to assess the latter the more the former will actually cause what he or she is trying to understand to move away from what was the original form in which it became the focus of interest. In essence this is another way of saying that the change agent becomes a part of the client's context, but adds some indication that the change so effected will be one which moves the client away from his or her original state.

But what really matters is the idea. The fact that the elements involved in the original form of the idea were matter and light matters little. Essentially, the core of the idea is that the very structure of an intrusive process, primarily the awareness of that presence, tends to move all the 'observed' away from what we would like to assess. Indeed, as the cyberneticists continually point out, the intrusive presence becomes an interactive part of the system being observed and must be calculated as a part in any attempt to understand that situation.

This is in itself a reversal of earlier teaching, where change agents were instructed not to become involved with the client systems they worked with, in order that their judgement should be as objective as possible. Such apparent separateness was essentially illogical, and also unlikely to be understood by clients except as an artificial form of relationship, with authority and superiority its main manifestations.

The Relationship

In that large category of change agents which I have called 'persuaders', the concept of the 'relationship' is crucial. It is instructive to consider why this is so.

In the first place, whether the change agent has been invited by the person or group into their context or is intervening on behalf of some person or institution with the authority to request such a process, the arrival of a change agent creates a new situation in the milieu of the subject(s). The whole process by which change agents operate is to influence, to persuade, to convince and to convert, by methods which rely heavily on appeals to reason, to response to emotional pressure and to example, by the practice of selected activities; thus it is very much one of interaction between agent and target.

The criteria by which individuals judge the quality and value of the influences and pressures that they are aware of in their lives are largely based in past experience. Thus the advent of a change agent may be a wholly new kind of event, and the criterion of judgement will then be based upon perceiving some similarity, however vague, with past experience and with any knowledge, however accurate or inaccurate, of the work and nature of the change agent and of intended change processes. Past experience and knowledge has known value and has gained an appropriate level of trust; the advent of the new and unfamiliar can only be regarded as an untested quantity. If an influence process is to be established, a degree of credibility has to be established which may be founded on rational levels of information, on the establishment over time of the worth of the individual agent and, ultimately, on a proven level of experience and trust.

The element of difficulty here is time. If a lot of it is available, the two parties to the intervention process can pursue the establishment of a suitable level of trust at a rate which is compatible to both. In many instances, however, this compatible rate is not available, due to the lack of time. Thus change agents learn to apply those factors of the relationship-building process that they know have been demonstrated to be the essentials – deliberately and with intent. For instance, they know that a trusting relationship tends to be founded on the ability of the involved individuals to predict the major response patterns of each other with a reasonable degree of accuracy. Such predictive ability is usually developed by the personal observation individuals make of each other's behaviour, which allows each to see how the other responds; then that experiential knowledge, which directly relates to their sense of security in that situation, becomes the basis for the level of offered trust.

Change agents know that one factor which delays the development of such security is inconstant behaviour. This renders prediction difficult, if not impossible, and so they practise a high degree of consonance between the various aspects of their own behaviour – for example, between verbal assertions of behavioural intent and the actual visible manifestations of that behaviour.

The relationship, then, is the channel through which acceptable communications between subject and agent can pass in either direction; some of the main barriers to communication will have been removed when this is established, and thus the value of the communication it carries is increased.

But there is another side to this process. Whereas individuals may accept a deliberate attempt by others to establish a relationship with them under 'normal' social conditions, they are rightly suspicious of attempts made to establish contact when the motive for so doing is outside their immediate understanding and experience. The degree of apparent artificiality equates with the degree of suspicion. Change agents stand to rouse suspicion and accusations of insincerity and artificiality because the mechanics of the establishment of a relationship may well be observable. The process of establishing a relationship as an intended part of the change process, especially by a stranger who may well be perceived to possess power unknown to the subject, will very probably be largely unfamiliar.

Without doubt, one of the greater defining characteristics of change agents is what they believe. By this I do not mean that their religious affiliations fulfil this role, although they may well affect some of their attitudes, but I mean their beliefs about the way in which human beings develop; their beliefs about the sources and causes of behaviour; about what are the most effective ways of bringing about change; and about the problems of resistance and lack of success.

There are two considerations to make briefly here, as the effects brought about by change agents and their activities will be more closely scrutinised later. Firstly there are those effects of belief of which the change agent is wholly aware, and then there are those effects which occur stemming from the beliefs but of which the change agent has little or no cognisance.

It is all too obvious that beliefs, as defined above, will not only set boundaries to what a change agent thinks possible to achieve and equally define those areas of human behaviour which he or she will choose to approach, but also the methods of that approach. Thus a Behaviourist who believes that the causal past is unexplorable, or at least an unreliable source of evidence for current behaviour, will approach his or her target almost wholly in terms of that current behaviour and isolate that part of it which can reasonably be defined in terms of antecedents (immediate) and consequences (also immediate). Such an agent will then attempt to isolate the reinforcing patterns and change them so that the essential target behaviour can be diminished or eliminated.

The outcome may well be successful, but what has been achieved is a method of controlling emitted behaviour which in itself may be rewarding. The pressures of whatever kind that originally generated the behaviour are often still in place, otherwise control would not be necessary. More essentially, the fact that the specific form of behaviour that has been controlled may have been linked to a whole series of other behaviours and situational factors is not dealt with – particularly so if these elements appear to the change agent to have features outside the scope of immediate or current behavioural emissions.

This selective effect is by no means confined to the relationships between change agent and subject; it occurs frequently enough in medical practice, where concentration on one manifest area of illness can result in ignoring others which may be equally or more important. But, besides conveying a scale of priority to his or her subject, which is a conscious part of their belief system, change agents are also conveying attitudes and impressions over which they apparently have no control. One of the results of this may be a noted dissonance between verbal protestations, say, of intent and observed behaviour. Many change agents who use and deliberately foster relationship-creating behaviours to carry out their purpose are horrified to realise that, whereas being clearly visible suits one aspect of their intentions, it may equally clearly highlight other facets which convey much less suitable or appropriate signals. This is particularly so when the individuals involved see themselves as vulnerable, and indeed threatened, by behaviour which is outside their normal experience. Sensitivity to discrepant signals often becomes very acute as personal security is at risk, and responses can then become very defensive and defeating of the change agent's immediate objectives.

But apart from the actual interpretative effect this particular form of belief has on the change process, there are other aspects of belief which may be political or social. Currently some of these ideas, such as those which concern oppressive behaviour, discrimination, race and gender factors, create considerable effects, and they replace other ideas – no longer current – that at one time were equally capable of creating effects which would have been regarded as beneficial, or at least based on consideration for the subjects and targets of intervention.

10 Issues and Problems

For the human infant is born – biologically considered – some ten or twelve years too soon. It acquires its human character, upright stature, ability to speak, and the vocabulary of its thinking under the influence of a specific culture, the features of which are engraved, as it were, upon its nerves; so that the constitutional patternings which in the animal world are biologically inherited are in the human species matched largely by socially transmitted forms, imprinted during what have been long known as the 'impressionable years', and rituals have been everywhere the recognised means of such imprinting.

Campbell (1973: 45)

Probably the fundamental problem for those who need to be able to change human behaviour is to find adequate explanations of its genesis. If that should prove to be impossible, the next problem such individuals face is how far and by what means can the behaviour that is generated and, for whatever reason, needs to be changed, be modified when those generating factors are wholly or mainly inaccessible?

These problems, and the solutions that are offered to them, tend to divide agents of change into two main groups: those who believe that they have some rational and logical explanation of the genesis of behaviour; and those who admit that such explanations, while they may be logical, are incapable of proof, and that all that is actually accessible is the observable behaviour of individuals and such methods of controlling it as can be applied at or near to the point of manifestation. This fact must form the basis for any realistic assessment of the claims of change agents to be effective in what they do, or at least to establish what degree of effectiveness it would be reasonable to expect, given the problems just noted.

As I hope to show later, however elegant and apparently complete the explanations of the genesis of human behaviour may appear, they are essentially assumptions, in the sense that the only forms of proof which have ever been available lie in, firstly, some evidence that work done with clients on the basis of these assumptions produces results which are probably significant, though not strongly so, and, secondly, that an accumulation of similar incidents and events does produce a reasonable belief in some form of meaningful connections, dubious though such a belief may be in the eyes of a genuine statistician.

In the second approach, which concentrates on current behaviour, its immediate antecedents and its consequences, the limitations are immediately obvious. Whatever the genesis of the behaviour, genetic or environmental, the fact that it may become possible to control and thus change the current manifestation, does not allow one logically to assume that a different manifestation stemming from the same unaltered causative elements may not arise at any time. Nor is it reliable to suppose that large and very strongly maintained behaviours which cover many areas of an individual's existence can be changed.

Such arguments inevitably bring to the forefront, not the change operators, but those with whom they work, the so-called targets. Behaviour is produced by individuals responding to situations and to innumerable forms of pressure, training, experience, and so on; changes to any aspect of that behaviour have ultimately to be sustained, maintained and accepted by the individual concerned. Hence the assumption is made here that the ultimate target has to be the individual, whether the method of approach is direct, that is, to the individual; or indirect, that is, through the group or organisation.

The fact that change, immense and dramatic change, is possible in human behaviour is beyond question. But the essential question is, when it does take place, what are the most frequent and thus powerful causes? As far as I am aware, no one has as yet prepared any statistical evidence which would offer a definitive answer to this question. So, relying wholly upon my own experience, I would offer what can at best be only an educated guess that in the greater number of such behavioural changes, however they may have been initiated, the individual concerned has been the prime factor. Which is a roundabout way of admitting that effective change has to be a matter of individual choice or will-power. In other words, people cannot be changed effectively by outside pressure alone.

Obviously this is not wholly true, for we have enough evidence in this century alone of people being changed drastically by outside pressure, often to the point of destruction. But if, as I have assumed, we are discussing changes which have as their intent benefit to the individual or society, then the sole use of external pressure, unless maintained for extremely long periods and of an unremitting nature, does not appear to work very well.

To return to the basic point, it is necessary to show the reasons which give it such a pole position. If a mechanism performs in an erratic way, or indeed ceases to perform some essential parts of its designed function adequately, it can, if not totally defunct, usually be restored to functional efficiency by virtue of operations to replace or repair the deficient parts or operations of its system. Likewise, if change to some element of its total function is required it can often be obtained by partial or total restructuring. By analogy, any mechanism which needs to be changed can be altered by those who know how it was built and how it functions.

Living organisms can be changed in terms of some of their physical functions by virtue of the existence of the same kind of knowledge of structure and function. But when that organism possesses not just built in response patterns, but a brain, and has to a large extent the possibility of being self-directing, the problem of change based upon logical and provable knowledge becomes a matter of some uncertainty. The physical aspects of human behaviour may be reasonably well understood, and the connections between causes and effects seen to be meaningful, but the conditioning processes which programme the self-directing potential of human beings are largely unique, unpredictable to a great extent and often influenced by factors, both currently extant and from the past, which are not only unknown but probably unknowable.

The individual is a nexus of all the influences, experiences and learning which have cumulatively impinged upon and effected the genetically determined biological organism which each person is. From this basic fact it is logical to state that such a process of influence is always dynamic in origin, but produces effects which may be either static or relatively unchanging, and also others which maintain their dynamic nature. Significantly for change agents, what is available without question are the behavioural outcomes which these processes produce. These are observable outcomes, but the reason why such patterns emerge in such ways in such conditions is seldom a matter susceptible to logical proof.

It would appear that explanations of behaviour have always been sought, and range from the provable – in terms of physical conditions – to the unprovable – for instance the interference of spirits. But the need for explanation is relentless because it is essentially the basis of understanding behaviour and, equally, that of changing it. Thus elegant theses of causation exist, built around unprovable assumptions, but which appear to explain what happens in behavioural patterns. Most of such theses have more in common with religious faiths and beliefs than with scientific understanding and, in similar manner, can become remarkably complex once the basic belief is accepted as true. I accept that there are more forms of truth than can be established by scientific research or theory, but the fundamental problem here is not that such ideas exist but that change agents seem bent on trying to establish their sort of theory as equivalent to scientific theories, and this an inappropriate comparison. The capacity of such theorists to continue to postulate ever increasing degrees of complexity on such an unsound logical base is only indicative of the enormously powerful need that they appear to have to acquire expert scientific status.

This must lead to a consideration of what is realistically available to enable change to be effected, which is without doubt the influences and pressures, the networks which originate and maintain patterns of behaviour. In essence, the search for these factors could then lead to an approach using elements of the context and milieu of the individual. What stands to emerge from such a search may well be that the context of an individual is the mainspring of the behaviour patterns which it is deemed most necessary to change; and thus we come to the indirect process of change, which involves the adaptation of existing group systems and the creation of new ones, specifically designed to establish a different context, which can probably generate the required change.

When practitioners discuss the influence potential of groups, the usual starting point is the effect that the perception of the presence of others can have on the patterns of an individual's behaviour. This is logical in that most people are born into groups and spend by far the greater part of their life span in the company of others. Given that other people thus form a large part of the environmental influence to which an individual is exposed during times when he or she is most vulnerable to external effect, as well as when the individual is resistant to influence, the possibility of using the presence of selected others to form an influence system is extremely promising.

Thus, created groups appear to be a pragmatic use of the known processes of influence which arise spontaneously within so-called 'natural' groups. But even with this much of an enhanced reality factor established in the process of intended change, the control processes that are necessary to ensure that the intended change is the principal outcome of employing the group process are extremely difficult to isolate. Group theory tends to be the product of cumulative experience, and suffers in consequence in its predictive quality, because no true theory can be based upon what is basically a process of counting. The fact that some event has occurred a thousand times in certain recorded circumstances does not and cannot alter the statistical probability of its recurrence at a higher than chance expectation.

Groups, of the kind which I have often referred to as 'contextual', are usually designed with the influence of the leader as the main factor of influence and the presence of others a minor, but nevertheless important, accompaniment. The interpretation of behaviour within the group has all the connotations of individual intended change efforts, while still being one which takes place in the context of not one other but several, all with some vested interest in the process. The main shortcomings are the same in both cases – that the interpretations will inevitably be based in theoretical concepts which are fundamentally unprovable assumptions about the drives and patterns of behaviour.

Without doubt, the creation of a specific milieu for the process of producing intended change can be very effective but, like all change processes, it is dependent ultimately on the individual group member. Other problem factors relate to the intensity of the experience; the time during which an individual is exposed to the group's influence compared with the time during which he or she is exposed to 'normal' social influences; the eventual value of the experience to the individual; and, as stated earlier, the ability of group leaders to ensure that those influences which are desirable have a greater effect than all the others which are equally available within the group situation.

For instance, groups which are designed to change behaviour and which are held within what Goffman called 'total institutions', have to compete with the much more prolonged and intrusive influence of the institution itself, and frequently are seen to lose. But it is not feasible to promote a learning process by exposure to the behaviour, ideas and experience of others which does not also contain the possibility of promoting the learning of material which may be detrimental to the intended objectives. After all, the essential change experience is ultimately one which the individual should have the chance to accept or reject, and the process of learning to learn, once acquired, can be directed to many different ends.

In using designed groups to effect intended change, what change agents have actually accomplished is the 'professionalisation' of very ordinary human influence situations and also they have taken on the mantle of those who are 'expected to know'.

This means that they tend to have created the perception in their clients of possessing what French and Raven (1959) referred to as 'expert' power.

The expectation that society appears to have of change agents is very ambivalent. On the positive side, there are many human situations where someone possessing the expert ability to bring about change in human behaviour is eminently desirable and devoutly wished for. In these circumstances society is prepared to accept the change agent's evaluation of his or her expertise at face value.

It is interesting at this point to realise how the ideas of change agents have become an integral part of everyday communication about human behaviour, despite the scepticism with which some of the activities of change agents are greeted. For instance, writing in the *Daily Telegraph* on 3 October 1995 about the O.J. Simpson trial, Anne Applebaum said:

> Most of the time, in fact, the talk about the Simpson trial was evidence that Americans have become so used to applying the language of psychotherapy to everything that they no longer know when to stop. In the language of psychotherapy there is never anyone who is guilty or innocent: we are all victims. No one can be 'bad', only 'damaged'; no one can be evil, only in need of healing. Psychotherapy also treats people, objects and events as symbols to be interpreted, not real things in and of themselves. (1995: 24)

Given that this degree of assimilation of the language and beliefs of change agents is common in the general public, it is somewhat surprising that scepticism still exists in such magnitude. The reason may well lie in the fact that in so many ways and instances the public acceptance of that expertise has been palpably demonstrated to be wrong. The acceptance attitude produces a situation at present in which no single disaster or problem of any kind can be overcome without the intervention of 'counsellors'. The sceptical attitude produces the scathing public and media criticism of the events like the discharge of mentally disturbed individuals into society without adequate supervision, who then proceed to kill innocent victims.

The pressures on change agents are thus immense. They have to be seen to be successful, hence the assured certainty of their pronouncements, and the obfuscation of essential issues in language which is beyond the comprehension of most of their clients. There has to be more expression of a need for certainty in a profession which is essentially based on uncertainty than in one which has a more assured base.

It is essential that a change agent has a basic belief in him or herself; otherwise what they enter into in terms of working to change people and their behaviour is remarkably daunting. However, it is interesting that the failures of change agents are seldom recorded as being based in their lack of understanding or in the form or methods of their practice and its suitability for the particular situations in which it is applied. Much more frequently the resistance of the target or client is cited as the cause of failure; their inadequacy and their inability to take advantage of what was on offer. It has always been my personal experience and also that of others with whom I have worked, that any professional who is confident of his or her skills is generally able to accept that they can be wrong; that they can make mistakes, and, indeed, often be completely out of their depth.

I have every sympathy for change agents who can never have real confidence, by virtue of the very nature of their area of 'expertise', i.e. human behaviour. They can never have certain knowledge that what they do is based upon logically substantive fact. Yet they are all that we have, and our society's expectations are immensely high despite the scepticism. It might perhaps be better to meet society's need for change agents and what they expect they can do with a more realistic assessment of what is possible and why, rather than to accept the unreasonable expectations that currently exist. Society, any society, needs methods of dealing with those of its members whose behaviour patterns cause social and individual distress, but it also has a right to expect that those methods will be based in reality and that the cost of their use will not exceed the benefits they produce.

Part Three:
The Processes of Intervention

11 'Necessary' Intervention

For centuries formal religion has stressed the primacy of man's relation to God, to the neglect of the interpersonal dimension of human experience and existence. As a result, ever larger numbers of people have 'sickened' in a peculiar way; and, in despair and desperation, they have turned to (and thus, in considerable measure, created) the modern professions of psychiatry, clinical psychology and social work. But here again the emphasis has, it seems, been a mistaken one: not, to be sure, upon man's relation to God, but upon man's relation to himself.

Mowrer (1964: iii)

This section looks at some of the main facts about the process of intervention in the lives of selected targets, by change agents with intent to bring about change. It covers some of the general situations and ideas which are seen as the bases for making changes in behaviour considered 'necessary' by society. It attempts to show that, in the process of effecting 'necessary' intended change, the actions of intervention are based upon collected and assessed data which, when interpreted in the light of theoretical concepts of behaviour, form the foundation of active intervention of many different kinds. Such interventions into the lives of individuals, groups and organisations are briefly scanned. Finally, the problems and difficulties and the successes of intervention in these areas are critically discussed.

These are my politics; to change what we can; to better what we can; but still to bear in mind that man is but a devil weakly fettered by some generous beliefs and impositions, and for no word however sounding, and no cause however just and pious, to relax the stricture of these bonds.

Stevenson (1882)

Bearing in mind what Stevenson wrote about our attempts to change and to 'better' others, and in particular those attempts which appear to be considered necessary by society, we will be faced with considerable moral and ethical dilemmas. These occur for the simple reason that, although our basic concern is with the ways in which the behaviour of human beings can be changed, when the essential prime agent of that change is society through its institutions, the decisions about why such changes are considered necessary should entail very careful scrutiny, in order to preserve the rights of the individual.

Thus when we come to discuss, very briefly, the social reasons for the need to change certain kinds of behaviour, the preservation of rights, the preservation of society and the freedom of the individual become relevant issues.

Such large issues cannot be fully discussed here, but their relevance to a considerable amount of the work of, for example, a social worker as a change agent may well be concerned not just with elements of control but with attempting to produce behaviour in clients which is consonant with accepted social norms (i.e. an imposition of standards which, in themselves, may or may not be questioned).

In doing this we also have to look at the processes of intervention, that is the actions which change agents take in order to bring about changes which are required by society, and ultimately we should look at the nature of those changes.

Intervention is Action Taken to Achieve Change

We must start from what reasons exist for requiring individuals to change; what mandate exists for the active interference of some in the lives of others. Ethically and morally involved in this process, and in legal terms also, is the fact that some laws give specified individuals the right to interfere in the lives of others in prescribed circumstances. There are some questions which emerge here:

- What are the social control factors involved in intervention?

- What are the significant differences between overt directive interventions and the processes of enabling intervention?

- What are the practical approaches to intervention, and upon what theoretical bases do they stand?

- One of the major ethical problems relates to understanding, e.g. if an individual has no real understanding of the change processes to which he or she has agreed or accepted, is this morally indefensible behaviour on the part of the change agents involved?

If

If, as happened recently, a man stabs a young woman to death in the presence of her two-year-old child and in a public park, there can be little doubt that his behaviour is abnormal. If such a man is to be able to exist within society as a free agent ever again, some change has to be brought about in the ways in which he thinks, feels and behaves.

If we discover that this man has had fantasies for most of his adult life which revolve around the brutal and unprovoked slaying of a young woman, and that a slippage of the boundary between reality and fantasy may have been the occasion of this particular young woman's murder, how can the necessary changes be brought about? Can they indeed ever be brought about? Must the realistic answer to the question of how to deal with such a person be that, for the protection of others, there is no provable and effective way which is also morally and ethically defensible of ensuring that he will not produce another slippage at some time in the future?

Even if drugs could diminish his response to the fantasy stimulation, there still remains the problem that at some stage in his life the administration of such drugs will become the responsibility of the man himself, and there can be no guarantee that he will continue to take them – especially if he should feel that there is no need.

Even more recently a man in secure hospital accommodation to which he had been committed after an attempted murder, was released having been declared by his psychiatrist to be fit to live in the community. This clinical decision was backed by a tribunal and based upon many months of clinical observation. Within a matter of days this man had killed and cut up into pieces his own father and strangled an elderly couple in their home. He was recorded as saying that he had always wanted to kill his father, and the elderly couple were a 'practice run' for his intention to kill and eat some young person later.

In the environment of the hospital this man was regarded as 'safe'; in society at large he was a wholly unrepentant and merciless killer.

Of course these two cases are extremes, but they serve to high-light two very important points:

1. Society, any society, has a great need to be able to protect its members from those who pursue deviant and often destructive agendas.

2. Apart from elimination, the only options available for use in this protection appear to be total exclusion from society or some form of behavioural change.

The latter brings into question the whole matter of the efficacy of such change processes as are available to us and, in particular, the processes by which they are chosen and applied.

In any association of human beings, no matter how small or large, if it is to continue in existence and fulfil the purposes for which it was established, there has to be a certain minimum number of rules of acceptable conduct. The different natures, appetites, conditions, needs, ambitions, and so on, of the individuals in such an association have to be governed in such a way that the maximum freedom of the individual to pursue his or her own way is obtained that is compatible with the least hurt to the others and with the maximum benefit to the whole. Given the dissimilarities of individuals, some will find even such democratic constraints upon their behaviour irksome and untenable, and will behave in ways which threaten the association's stability and the safety of its members. Indeed, quite often such rebellion will seek to overthrow the association as a whole and re-establish it in terms that are more favourable, or apparently so to the rebels.

The larger the association, the greater the disparity of individuals within it – in terms of both their ideas, rights and needs, and their access to what the community has to offer. Ambition, the search for power, wealth and status, may all be available through the legitimate channels of a community, but are seldom equally available to everyone. As a result, there are members who will attempt to gain their ends by wholly or partially unacceptable means. By and large society, as I have already mentioned, has three methods of coping with such breakers of its rules: it can eliminate them; it can take them out of society and keep them where they cannot operate; or it can attempt to re-fashion their behavioural patterns to be more in accord with the accepted norms of society.

The third of these processes is one of intended change.

A great problem for society exists in the actual effectiveness of the changes that are made in the name of that society to those individuals and groups who are considered to be deviant in some way. By 'deviant' in this instance, I mean being outside the area of tolerance of difference which a given society maintains. As we saw in Chapter 3, Eysenck and Eysenck (1981) believed that, as far as change in terms of rehabilitation of criminals was concerned, 'the traditional methods are almost completely ineffective'.

The problem then, from a society's point of view, is quite simply that it has to maintain law and order; it has to guarantee standards of protection for its citizens; and in order to do just that, it has to remove or change those who cannot, for whatever reason, operate within the limits of society's tolerance. Removal by extermination is still debated, but is not currently accepted on moral and ethical grounds, though it is apparently increasing in favour as a permanent answer in some parts of America, and has always been available as an option in other countries. Removal by incarceration is expensive and questionable on other grounds, which leaves the probability of change. But if change efforts do not work very well, this also becomes an expensive process, which at the very least needs constant repetition in order to maintain short periods of compliance.

Essentially, we are faced here with a problem that runs throughout the whole of the intended change of human beings: without some clear and unequivocal understanding of the causes of behaviour which any society needs to be able to control, change efforts are confined to dealing with manifestations. That is, they are attempts not so much to remove or change the mainsprings of behaviour, but to instigate some form of control over behavioural manifestations. This process usually implies some form of learning being imposed between impulse and action, and its principal weakness lies in the fact that the use of control factors is concentrated eventually in the hands of the individual who, as far as is known, will continue to be subject to those impulses to behaviour which still exist and which brought him or her into conflict with society in the first place.

This leads me to ask two questions:

• Have we wrongly estimated the potential of human beings to change?

• What are the current beliefs about how well changes, however brought about, can be maintained?

In answer to the first question, it is essential to make clear that estimates of the potential for change have varied from nil to vastly more than most people using ordinary experience would be prepared to accept. The whole process, is of course, complicated by individual differences – so some people may be capable of vast changes of behaviour, given the right commitment and stimulation, and others hardly any at all, whatever the approaches currently available that may be tried. The factor of genetic endowment once again sets boundaries to what may be achieved.

The nature of the 'psychopathic personality' is discussed elsewhere in this book and provides a prime example of individuals who appear to be deficient in their ability to learn from experience in that they constantly repeat the same, often self-destructive, behaviour patterns (see the illustration at the end of this chapter). It must be true that the ability to change, to possess the potential to change, is related to the ability to learn from experience. For, essentially, the prerequisite of all change must lie in the recognition that change of some sort is necessary. Admittedly, recognition of a need to change and having the potential to effect it may not always be a straightforward link, but lack of the ability to recognise the need to change certainly obfuscates the possibility of discovering if any potential exists. However, the psychopathic personality has been shown to be able to understand rationally the need to change, and may even be willing to attempt to bring it about, but seems almost always to be wholly incapable of success. It cannot escape us that there is therefore no potential, and that of all the psychopath's behavioural abnormalities it is apparent that it is the inability to change by learning from previous experience which seems most unusual to ordinary mortals.

Further, the fact that many individuals may possess an almost unlimited capacity to change and grow is indisputable; but the fact of possessing that ability is not invariably accompanied by the ability to use it, or even of the knowledge of how such an ability can be fostered. Nature is notorious for over-providing, but many organisms still function infinitely within the capacities they have been given. Equally, the capacity to change may exist but the actual willingness to employ it may be completely missing.

The second question was essentially about our beliefs concerning the durability of such change efforts as we can make. Indubitably people make staggering changes to their behaviour patterns every day; through religious and ideological conversions; through the development of insight, persuasion, accident and circumstance. But wherever such events take place, and whatever the instigating factors may be, one essential appears central – not just to the change itself, but also to how long and how well it is maintained. Stated in bald, unequivocal terms that essential seems to be that the individual or group accepted and embraced the change even though its initial impact may have been hurtful or even dangerous.

Changes

'Necessary' changes to patterns of behaviour, like all other changes, are either analogue or digital changes – as discussed earlier. In essence, analogue changes are those which make some alteration in behaviours already in existence, whereas digital changes are those which are brought about by the development of new and different patterns. Thus the former are changes concerned to supply deficiencies in existing patterns of behaviour by developing and expanding what already exists; by changing the quality and application.

'Deficiency' in this sense may best be interpreted as inadequacy or inappropriateness for the situation in which the group or individual exists, and as such may originate in genetic endowment, the environment, learning, experience or opportunity. There is also the possibility that behavioural skills may exist at a very high performance level, but be misdirected in terms of social norms. In this case the analogue change is one of redirection, a technique frequently used by those whose job it is to rehabilitate offenders.

The reasoning behind the use of analogue change efforts for social offenders clearly divides into two main streams based upon two principal ideas. First, offending behaviour is believed to arise from the fact that 'normal' social conditioning has not 'taken' in certain areas. This may have been due to intent (i.e. having been brought up in a socially deviant sub-community so that the result is produced with some degree of intent); or it may have been due to absence or lack of so-called 'normal' conditioning; or it may have been due to a lack of the essential potential to benefit from whatever conditioning was available. In all these instances, the change approach is to attempt to supply what is missing up to the limits imposed by genetic endowment; the hold which previous conditioning may have; and the time and resources which are available. The whole process is one of adaptation, development and redirection of what already existed.

The second idea stresses the fact that it was not the case that conditioning and potential were there, but defective in some

way or inappropriately developed; rather that, in effect, the necessary social learning and conditioning were actually missing in
large amounts. What apparently needs to be done here is to
attempt to build what is missing, whether it be in terms of new
learning or new opportunity.

As we have seen, genetic potential may be either missing or
undeveloped due to lack of appropriate stimulation; in either case
the behavioural effects often appear very similar. When either of
these approaches is involved, however, certain factors immediately
become apparent – taking the form of resistance and lack of success in bringing about change. We will look at these factors in
some detail later, so it will suffice to state them briefly here.

All human behaviour is held in place by a network of support
from the milieu, tradition, experience, the reactions of important
others, so changes aimed at the individual cannot succeed unless
this factor is at least taken into account and, if possible, also
changed to become a positive influence in the intended change
process, or at least so that its negative qualities and its sustaining
of past behaviours are minimised.

The change processes may also meet resistance because, even
though they can be seen as extensions or developments of existing
patterns, they are being offered from despised sources, or the outcomes are not seen as being consonant with previous conditioning.
In short, the effort required is a cost which is not, to the individual's way of thinking, met by an appropriate reward. Indeed, new
skills and new behavioural patterns may be learned avidly, but the
problem then is how to sustain them and it is one of great magnitude, particularly if the new patterns do not fit contextually in the
social milieu of the person who has acquired them. There is also
the probability that these new patterns may be adapted and used in
ways appropriate to that milieu, and not in the ways in which the
change agents and the larger society would have wished.

Of course the dichotomy of causes and approaches is not as
clean cut as it is presented here. The bases of anti-social behaviour
(criminality) may rest on potential directed at variance with the
social norms, but whatever its source, change cannot conceivably
be effected and sustained unless it is wholly accepted by the participant in the process. And even that acceptance, when made, can
be rescinded at any stage later in the process. There has to be
some viable reward, not only at the point of change but from then
on – viable in the sense that it means 'reward' to the participant
and not just to the change agent. One of the greatest costs in this
business is that change requires effort, and the intensity and dura-

tion of that effort is often something which eventually destroys the continuation of the new or enhanced behaviour patterns.

Our concepts of deviance emphasise patterns of behaviour that tend to endure over time, be sustained by social and personal forces, and persist unless these forces are changed. The helping practitioner must, therefore, energetically intervene to modify clients' behaviors and situations, Only by direct, active involvement in the relevant processes can practitioners accomplish desired change.

Vinter (1974: 6)

Intervention

Intervention is a process of interfering in the lives of others to bring about intended change, or alternatively the deliberate alteration by an individual of some of the processes of his or her own life for the same kind of end. It usually follows a logical sequence:

1. Recognition – that change is necessary, desirable or essential.

2. Search –
    (a) an approach which will bring about the required consequence;
    (b) to decide whether appropriate resources are available to achieve this, or can be obtained.

3. Actions – taken in the belief that these will produce the required change.

4. Monitoring – some simple or elaborate process of comparison to discover if, and how effectively, the action of intervention has elicited the required consequences. If it has not, to abandon the process, redirect or try something different.

There is some evidence that the process of helping others (i.e. intervening in their lives) may be powered by a biological need. But even if this is not so, the major urges to intervene can be seen in the belief systems of a society which produce the concepts concerned with the value of helping others through developmental change. The idea of making better, and also the ideas which relate to the protection of society from the behaviour of those who do not conform to its rules, form a strong basis for intervention. The security of existence within a community is dependent to a large degree on members of that community abiding by the major rules. Threat of the different has to be mitigated by a process of obtaining an acceptable degree of conformity.

This is a huge area of concern and can only be touched on here in order to assert that change, particularly of the imposed kind, is a basic drive to maintain the structure of communities and to improve the quality of life.

Any society, however large or small, can only continue to exist as long as a majority of its members are prepared to abide by the larger or more important rules that such a society's structure imposes. Indeed it would not be too strong to say that a society is a structure of rules, so that the maintenance of that society is dependent upon ways of dealing with those within its confines who do not or are not capable of keeping within the bounds of tolerance. Part of the conflict of a racial nature is brought about by incomers to a society whose rules differ in some major way from those of their society of origin. To abide by the laws and customs of that society of origin, which in essence defines their cultural identity, may well bring them into conflict, not just with the legal system of the host country but also with the more informal but equally powerful controlling elements of tradition.

But apart from this situation brought about by an influx of people from different cultures, every society has also to deal with those of its own people who do not conform. This then becomes a very complex issue because societies which are not wholly static and stagnant change and develop. Most of the impetus for these changes comes from those members who are not satisfied with the way their society performs; they agitate for change and, in the process, they may well come into conflict with the establishment and offend those who are primarily satisfied with the way things are.

The complexity arises because of the difficulty any social group has in deciding whether disagreement and conflict about the current state of governance is legitimate; that is, proceeding through the accepted channels of complaint, controversy and conflict which most societies provide where change, within certain levels of tolerance, is seen as something which may well be beneficial; or whether it is destructive, appearing to be an attempt to destroy some part or all of the existing system, whether an alternative is offered or not. The ultimate problem of any community can be complicated even further by the factor of selfish gain.

In all societies, the concept of achievement, of ambition and of selfish gain is accepted, though in most some limitations are placed upon them, conditioned usually by some idea that gain should not be to the detriment of and wholly at the expense of other sections of the society. Inequality in the access to and the use of resources is a fact of life and all societies contain those sections whose quality of life is infinitely worse than that of other sections. The whole basis of criminal and social laws is founded upon some attempt to regulate exploitation, most often with some success, but also often with some large areas of palpable injustice.

Given that such regulation exists, it becomes the basis for judgements about the acceptable, or otherwise, nature of the behaviour of members of the society; and this, in turn, brings into question the process of necessary change. If a society believes, as most appear to do, that existence depends upon its insistence on a level of conformity within the bounds of a given tolerance, it is faced with the problem of discarding or changing those who do not conform. Fear of punishment is a deterrent, and the creation of punitive acts has the effect of raising the costs to those whose behaviour, in society's opinion, merits punishment. But large communities have the problem of locating and bringing to justice those who offend, which means that the raised costs produced by a punishment system can be reduced by the miscreants by a simple calculation of the odds on being caught.

So-called 'humane' societies use in conjunction with punishment the concept of rehabilitation, which implies that change, if it can be effected, may be a better method of dealing with deviant social behaviour. There are several issues in this point of view which are relevant to the thesis of this book.

As I have said before, human beings are capable of some of the most astonishing changes of behaviour, but the major question is how do such changes occur? Almost inevitably they appear to be brought about by a set of circumstances which have an impact upon the individual or group which, either in the long term or the short, are accepted; not only accepted, in fact, but integrated, and the different behavioural patterns implied are adopted almost without reservation. It would seem that, in the terms of a cost/reward analysis, the individuals and groups concerned have accepted that the change has either greatly increased their current and/or potential rewards or greatly diminished their current or potential costs. Also it would seem that the process of change in these instances, although it may have been an 'out of the blue' situation, is one which was accepted.

- The problems for change agents working with those whose behaviour has been deemed to be socially deviant are:

- How can the changes they wish to promote be offered in such a way that this level of acceptance will occur?

- How can they have any reasonable certainty that those required to change will not do so only on a temporary basis, having reasoned that by this method they will free themselves from the incubus of the change agents and be able to resume their previous activities?

- Above all, how many of these people are actually capable of making such a change, not because they are essentially or necessarily deficient in the ability to do so (though some may well be), but because their training, environment and social behaviour patterns – the influences in their lives – may run strongly counter to such behavioural change? Indeed there are those who, when faced with the pressure to change will embrace it with open arms and minds because the circumstances are propitious at that time, but later, when circumstances are different, the pressures change and reversion becomes all too easy.

Addiction units have long known that when individuals are in a desperate state, at the very bottom of the pit, change becomes not just acceptable but even desirable, no matter how harsh and severe the regime may be. But as change is effected there comes a point in the process when the change regime starts to become less tolerable, because the individual is no longer desperate and is no longer at the bottom. At this cross-over point, many individuals will opt out of the programme – long before its completion. Logically, it might be thought that the costs have become greater than the rewards.

Most socially deviant behaviour carries costs, not just for the individual deviant, but for others as well – the families, the victims and society at large. The difference between those whose social behaviour is brought about by circumstances over which they have no control and those who appear to choose consciously to act in deviant ways is again a very complex area, but it certainly makes some considerable difference to the potential for change – if only by implication that one form of social act is one with a large element of choice and control in it.

A second implication may well be that choice indicates responsibility. But the development of responsibility for one's behaviour, particularly in regard to the rights of others, is socially conditioned and programmes of reconditioning have to accept that, although they can substitute intensity for experience over time, the long slow process of acquiring whatever sense of responsibility an individual possesses is extremely hard to counter by these methods, especially if a willingness to change is not apparent. In any case, the natural process of conditioning or learning took place at a time in the individual's life which is usually much more appropriate for its acceptance, because it is unchallenged and is absorbed at a far deeper and more central level of the individual's being.

It would seem that society's need to effect change for the sake of the safety of its own structure and the protection of its members brings into sharp focus the efficacy of the intended change efforts which may be employed. Indeed, the essential co-operation of the individual concerned would seem to be an important element – and not just co-operation, but willing co-operation. It would also seem that our calculations of the ability of people to change may not be effective enough to give a sound basis for change efforts to be successful, nor is our ability to discriminate between public conformity responses and those of private acceptance, of a high enough order.

A final point in this particular issue, and probably the most important in society's attempts to change 'deviant' individuals and groups, is directly referred to in the quotation from Vinter (1974) earlier, that all behaviour, deviant or not, endures over time and is sustained by social and personal forces. The fact that behaviour manifests in an individual or group should not leave us to concentrate change efforts wholly at the point of manifestation, i.e. the individual or the group. The sustaining forces referred to by Vinter and many other commentators, are probably by far the most important factors, not only in sustaining behaviour but also, as we shall see in greater detail later, in resisting change and in bringing about a deterioration in achieved-change states and in minimising the effects of change.

The stabilisation effects on behavioural patterns are potent and extremely beneficial when the patterns which are stabilised are acceptable and within the society's area of tolerance, the so-called 'anchors' that Carolyn Sherif (1976) comments upon. Their potency does not change when the patterns they sustain are socially deviant, or different. Indeed, because of the pressure which may be employed by the larger social unit, they may be even stronger because of an increased need to be defensively protective.

Illustration – Ian Kay

On 20 July 1995, Ian Kay was sentenced at the Old Bailey to serve a minimum of 22 years for the murder of John Penfold, a Woolworth's shop manager, while being illegally absent from prison after a period of home leave.

Ian Kay was born in France but came to England while very young. His parents having separated he lived with his grandfather in various places. He left school with minimal qualifications and was described (by an Educational Psychologist) as a disturbed and maladjusted boy who had no real permanent home.

In court he was described as being unemployed, a thief, robber and drug dealer. He was 28 years old. Psychiatrists offered opinions that he suffered from an abnormal personality disorder, but they could not decide whether this impaired his ability to accept responsibility for his actions. Kay claimed that he was presented with violent impulses which he found impossible to resist. He also went on record as saying that 'have-a-go-heroes' (i.e. people who attempted to stop him committing his crimes) got what they deserved. He was depicted as being plagued by violent fantasies, obsessed with the occult and very prone to be violent to both human beings and animals.

In September 1990 during a raid on a newsagent's in Kew he stabbed Richard Boston, who was then 17, in the armpit – severing an artery. Seven years later Boston was still partly paralysed in one arm. During this period Kay staged a series of robberies with a sawn-off shot gun.

In December 1991 Kay was jailed for an attack on a shopworker which was almost identical to the attack on Penfold three years later. He was also known to have committed 16 shop raids in West London, netting a haul of some £25,000. While on leave from Maidstone prison he robbed a Post Office and then calmly returned to jail.

In August 1993 he was given leave of absence from prison and absconded, going on what was described as a crime spree during which he was believed to have been dealing in drugs and getting deep into debt. He was known to have threatened a Woolworth's assistant with a knife, in this instance the female assistant was able to snatch back the £200 he had taken from the till and Kay ran off.

The robbery at Woolworth's in which he murdered John Penfold who was attempting to stop him escaping with the £165 he had taken from a till, took place on 3 November 1994. At no time did Kay express any remorse for this murder, as witness his statement about 'have-a-go-heroes'. During the course of his trial Kay also admitted seven robberies, theft and attempted theft all involving threat with a knife and all but one taking place in Woolworth's stores.

In July 1995 Kay was sent to Broadmoor.

Issues

1. Kay's diagnosis of personality disorder does not enable an accurate prediction of behaviour to be made.

2. There was an incompatibility between the response of the diagnostic system and the legal system – i.e. between abnormal personality and criminal activity.

3. There was a problem of behavioural inconsistency. Under scrutiny Kay's behaviour was possibly reasonably adaptable. Away from scrutiny, his behaviour became self-seeking, ruthless and unconcerned for others.

4. In Kay's case it was clearly established that he knew what he was doing. What change is possible in a person who deliberately and with forethought makes such choices as demonstrated in this brief history?

12 The Data Bases of Intervention

We are often data rich and information poor.

Cochrane (1996: 12)

In the training programmes of change agents of all kinds, an assumption is made that effective change must be based upon some degree of understanding, not just of the processes of change which can be employed, but also of the 'target' of the change operation and, in particular, of those areas of behaviour which have been highlighted as the possible focus of change.

Change efforts are thus based upon information about targets and their problem areas and what sustains them.

Whereas this would appear to be an acceptably logical approach and one not subject to question, the problems of what kind of information is required; how it is obtained; the constructions that are placed upon it; and, ultimately, the processes of intervention which arise out of it, are indeed enormous.

Since the sum total of the traits of any empirical phenomenon is infinite, anybody attempting to describe it must decide (consciously or unconsciously) what to note and what to leave unrecorded, and how much attention and space to give to each mentioned item or aspect.

Andreski (1974: 309–10)

In the process of collecting information about other human beings, there is little that can be regarded as factual or, more precisely, as objectively verifiable data. For the change agent, choice – influenced by many factors such as training, education, beliefs, personal preference – cannot be avoided. What a change agent will see or hear or feel will be largely determined by his or her interpretative process, which will have been selectively programmed. For instance, the cancer specialist who concentrates on what he suspects may be a malignant growth in the throat, which is after all his special area of interest, and then sees his patient die of a heart attack – the symptoms of the approach of which were never noticed – is a case in point.

In this chapter I hope to present a brief survey of the kinds of information to which a change agent may have access; to discuss how such information arises; how it is usually collected; the processes of attempting to make sense of it and, ultimately, how it may be used. In Chapter 19, the problems relating to this complex process of data collection and use will be discussed, together with the probable effects that these problems of the quality and quantity of data and use may have on the intended change process.

Kinds of Data

To categorise the available data into that which is observed, recorded, heard and assumed is a somewhat arbitrary process and bears little resemblance to the actual processes of the assimilation of data in practice. For instance, the separation gives the false impression that the sources of data can be dealt with one at a time, whereas in practice they may all be in use at once. Logically, most intervention procedures used in change processes start from some sort of referral or request, and often the first information available will be that which accompanies the request and is therefore written or spoken.

But a large element of mistrust of recorded and spoken information emanating from sources other than the individuals who are to be the subject of change processes has traditionally existed among the more highly qualified professional change agents, and the preference for direct contact, 'to see for oneself' has been strong. There are reasonable grounds for this behaviour, as we shall see later, which relate not only to the idiosyncratic nature of reports and the different approaches and practices but also to the different needs and circumstances. After all, there is usually a lapse of time between a report being made and its being presented to another person in the form of the accompaniment to a request for intervention.

So we must start from the kind of data which a change agent can derive from direct observation of intended targets, which will include their behavioural patterns and appearance as well as the kind of milieu in which they live. The latter poses some problems when individuals are brought to be interviewed from an environment with which they are wholly familiar to one which may well be considered strange, if not also alien and frightening. But even when interviewed in a familiar environment, there is always the problem that the interviewer is a stranger and his or her appearance on the scene has altered the context and the perception of appropriate behaviours on both sides of the interview.

Recorded data is any information which has a substantial existence in whatever form that may take (e.g. writing, film, video, photograph, etc.); unlike verbal data and observational material which, unless translated into recorded data, are ethereal and subject to the operations of memory storage and subsequent recall, with all the possibilities this entails of slippage and selectivity.

The next category I have called 'assumptive', because it is the kind of information which one is aware that one appears to possess about situations and people, yet there exists no clear recollection of having collected it. It includes understanding which appears to be based in the recognition of 'similarities' with past ideas and experiences, and also imagination and intuition.

One final point to be made here is that the whole process of collecting data about individuals and sources often seems to omit the perceptions of those about whom the facts are being sought. Their perceptions of the situation, of its apparent nature and of those involved, of what it means to them, are equally to be considered as an influence on the information which emerges.

Observation

> ... perception is the extraction of information from the stimulus energy impinging on human sensory receptors.
>
> Erikson and Erikson (1972: 2)

Observation is used here to cover information about an individual or group acquired by the change agent by directly watching and listening to those involved and also noting the environment in which they exist. As person perception is widely covered in the literature, I propose only to mention here the various categories of the sources of data with brief comments.

Observation of individuals in a familiar environment gives the observer the opportunity of seeing them in their least constrained form, apart from the fact that the presence of the observer is bound to have some effect. Such observations would include the nature and quality of the environment, its condition and the individual relationships to it and to the others which it contains.

Included here would be the perception of smells and sounds which appear to be an integral part of the environment.

Observation would also include the behaviour of the individual, both verbal and non-verbal, in relation to others within the environment. It will be obvious that all perceptions of the behaviour of others have to be interpreted by the observer, and the fact of seeing things from a different standpoint (e.g. the well-documented difference in the perception of a single event as seen from the viewpoint of observer and actor taken into account).

Recorded Information

This kind of data includes all forms in which information can be stored, either permanently or temporarily, and later recalled or referred to. In this category would thus be found interpretive forms of recording, that is, the making of notes, either at the time of observation or by later recall, and their redrafting, in writing or taping; and also direct forms of recording by tape or video which occur at the time of observation.

Different forms of recording contain greater or lesser degrees of dependence upon memory and interpretation.

Verbal Data

Talking and listening to the individual produces what can be called 'verbal data', again very much dependent upon the process of interpretation. Weldon (1953) suggested that words have no meanings only uses, and 'use' in this context means that which is commonly accepted.

Verbal information is rendered complex by two factors, the first being a basic assumption that we can understand what is being said when it is obvious that there are large communication gaps between speaker and listener – especially when what is being communicated is emotional or indeed anything which goes beyond the realm of simple provable fact. We will look at the barriers to communication later.

Included in these problems of communication are the facts of cultural difference; of status difference; of education and experience; perceptions of what is required in an intervention situation; assumptions, etc.

Assumptive Information

The significance of the phenomenological approach lies in its attitude to facts and does not arise from the feature that, at most of the places where its application is most relevant, the facts are of a social nature.

Leighton (1973: 515)

The idea of 'tacit knowing' derives from Piaget's work on the development of logical thinking. It occurs in the period of the development of formal operational thought at 14–15 years in ordinary children or at 11–12 in the outstanding, and is defined as the ability to know a great deal more about things than is actually understood. What this amounts to is that there is a kind of knowledge which cannot actually be codified or even readily communicated. It is apparent that some of the understanding of human behaviour is of this nature, where logical explanations or factual evidence cannot be produced to support it.

The pursuit of discovery is conducted from the start in these terms; all the time we are guided by sensing the presence of a hidden reality towards which our clues are pointing; and the discovery which terminates and satisfies this pursuit is still sustained by the same vision, it claims to have made contact with reality: a reality which, being real, may yet reveal itself to future eyes in an indefinite range of unexpected manifestations.

Polyani (1967: 24)

In essence, this is a phenomenological approach which is based in the idea of 'understanding'.

Of course, understanding the social and psychological situation of any person or group about to be the subject of change process is fundamental, but understanding itself is a complex factor and can also be founded in so many different kinds and orders of 'facts'. What phenomenologists imply is that understanding a person must be the kind of understanding which an individual would have of him or herself; thus implying that any understanding a change agent may develop which does not have as its basis the client's interpretation of his or her perception of his or her situation is suspect.

Forms of the Production of Data

The actual source of information may have a great deal of bearing upon how it is considered in the process of evaluation by the change agent. Some sources will be trusted absolutely, and may indeed be over-valued because they appear to come from a source held in great esteem. Others will be discounted because their source is deemed to be of little value. But above all some sources of information about individuals and groups protect that information and, indeed, the situation can range from a total refusal to produce information at all because of a professional belief that some fellow workers should not have access to it; to being swamped with what may well turn out to be irrelevant data.

Collection of Data

Sundel, Radin and Churchill (1974) writing about understanding problems, state that the assessment procedure, which they refer to as 'diagnostic', comprises activities 'aimed at collecting and synthesising information which will enable them to set specifiable intervention goals'. The medical terminology of diagnosis and treatment was not uncommon when this paper was written and, while it might be criticised for borrowing terminology from a profession which has developed a much greater precision in the analysis of information, it correctly delineates a similar process which is performed with a different set of data.

That process is simply one that involves the collection of evidence which can then be used as a basis for making a decision. It is interesting also to note that the authors refer to the situations about which they wish to make a 'diagnosis' by the term 'problem'. Much has been written and said about defining human situations as problems but the one outcome which always inevitably occurs is that the method of coping with a situation so defined resolves into attempts to find a solution.

If the situation in question happens to be a problem, as for instance is the case when an individual does not have adequate information to deal with a situation, the problem is one of lack of information which can then be supplied as an answer allowing the individual to cope. But even though in this case the 'problem' has been solved, it may not serve to resolve the situation. For instance, the fact that the individual apparently could not solve the problem because of lack of adequate information may have masked the much more serious deficiency that, even had the information been present in adequate form, the individual concerned would not have been able to handle it.

This leads us directly to a consideration of the nature of the data upon which intervention may be based – where it may be found; its quality and value; the processes of collection and analysis, which are all subject to the fallibility of the individuals involved and the idiosyncratic nature of their perceptions – all of which is compounded by the hidden and inaccessible nature of much data which would be relevant. But the trigger for this process of the collection of data; of analysis and decision-making is the simple recognition that a situation exists which displays some compelling need for changes to be made.

Recognition

An example of the collection of data upon which to first make a diagnosis, and then prepare an intervention to effect change – which was made in some of the most advantageous of circumstances – is illustrated in the following description of the process in a university Department of Psychiatry, both as a genuine diagnostic tool and as a vehicle for student learning.

The recognition of the need for change had, in this instance, been made by a combination of the patient's relatives and the GP, so when the patient arrived in the department for investigation a considerable amount of preliminary work in collecting information had already been done.

With the patient came the clinical notes from the GP which contained some information about the patient, his visits to the doctor, his treatment and the tests and previous admissions, etc. The department taught its students the simple facts that: an accurate diagnosis could only be made on the basis of adequate information; the life of any individual was remarkably complex, both in terms of inner and outer life and that merely collecting masses of information was useless and indeed often counter-productive – information had to be assessed and structured.

The collection of information was the simple part. The patient was interviewed when this was possible and assessed by observation. Members of his family were also interviewed with the dual purpose of completing a history of the patient through the major events of his life and of the family going back several generations.

Social workers, nurses, psychologists, doctors and students in the department were all allocated areas of this possibly vast network to explore and record, so that a detailed history of the patient from birth to the current time could be compiled, together with a simpler but still explicit history of those in most contact with him over that period. School records, comments by friends, relatives, employers, by anyone who could be contacted, were collated so that differences and similarities could be exposed, divergences noted, areas uncovered by comment recorded and major events logged.

From this mass of material there would then emerge evidence of genetic endowment and the processes of environmental influences and learning, but only when some structure had been imposed upon it. Such a structure was designed to highlight two very important facts, one being the need to be able to pinpoint *changes* in the behaviour patterns of the patient and the other the *coincidences* and *consequences* of major events, across not just the patient's history but the whole network of connections over time.

This structure was produced by the use of something resembling a matrix on which the vertical columns represented the event history of each of the major members of the network starting as far back into the family history as was practicable and ending at the bottom with the present. The horizontal time levels would then show the significant events in the network across all the involved members. This matrix was time oriented and thus offered sequences such as, when the patient was two and a half years old his sister was born; his mother was 28 and had just had a serious illness which had required hospitalisation; his father had been absent for three months and was later found to have deserted the family; grandmother had come to live with family two months before, and so on. There was nothing unusual about this data except that it presented masses of possibly related information in ways that meant its relation in time could not easily be missed or ignored. This assessment is based on the theoretical assumption that the past produces the present state.

Finally all those who had been working in collecting the data, patient, students, family and others, plus tutorial staff met together to discuss the data, to add to or comment on it and to offer personal opinions, and to notice patterns and developments. This final process would reveal whether the information yielded evidence of some known pattern, required more data or needed a different form of structuring. If some known pattern was clearly visible or the majority of its elements were clear, then a diagnosis was proposed and a treatment plan, if applicable, set up.

Few change agents have this kind of resource available to them, but that is not the point. The process of data collection and its comparison with known patterns is clear in this instance because the discrete elements were made independent operations by virtue of the numbers of those employed in the process. But the same process is, or should be, followed when pursued by one individual, The problems start with the factors of time and contamination. Time particularly, in that the pressure to do everything must dilute the quality and quantity of what can be undertaken, except in phenomenally unusual circumstances. Contamination occurs because there can be no comparisons of perceptions of the nature of the data with others equally involved, other than the target. These problems will be considered in more detail later.

No change agent starts as a clean slate upon which the information regarding a situation can be recorded uncontaminated. Each individual already possesses experience, knowledge and a collection of tentative ideas about any 'new' situation that is encountered. It is wholly possible that acceptance of these previously existing factors, and their clarification by conscious thought about them and their consequences, may reduce the individual's degree of possible bias and prejudice. But against this must be set the fact that tentative ideas are actually essential in providing lines of possible enquiry.

There has been for some time a difficulty in deciding whether to use serial processing of information, that is, one item at a time; or parallel processing, that is, several items at once. There may also be other ways of handling information but it is feasible to discuss the possibility of

(a) collecting individual facts;

(b) the way we enquire into possible connections between them; and

(c) how complex units may be formed from connected facts.

Facts have the property of being describable in such a way that they are capable of being recognised and identified every time they occur, wherever or whenever that may be. However, the nature of facts can be very different – as, for example, a material inanimate presence, or an information byte established through contact with another human being. Thus some facts can be proved by reference to or against other sources and can be considered for all practical purposes as indisputable; but others are subject to the fallible nature of human perceptions, which can produce great distortions as well as absolute truth.

Next in the hierarchy of facts are those that are of the order of statements which contain some degree of bias and which are opinions. Then there are intentional distortions of observed reality which are produced with some considerable degree of intent to evade, mislead or deceive. Inferred facts are those informational bytes which can be deduced or inferred from other facts – these latter being usually of a higher order of proof than those inferred from them. But on occasion, which happens very seldom, the inferred fact is one of a much superior order of reality, something which may have to be regarded as a special case of inference.

As data is collected, all the evidence would seem to indicate that in reality it can only be presented in isolated pieces about human situations, behaviours and events. Any attempt at understanding has, therefore, to store, recollect and correlate those pieces, a process of integrating which is based upon the perception of existing relationships or connections between them. The connections can of course be falsified, but to be effective they have to be, to use Jaspers' (1963) term, 'meaningful'. Occasionally such connections almost establish themselves, because it is easy to see how one fact arose from another and was dependent upon it (e.g. frustration leading to the displacement of anger). But the problem of a temporal sequence creating the appearance of a causal connection is very real. Causal explanations are one of the two main forms of understanding and are static, in the sense that the relation between cause and effect remains constant; they are, however, only available when the data covering both events is wholly exposed and available. This causes considerable difficulties, for many of the theoretical concepts used by change agents offer probable explanation as defining the nature of cause. Human understanding is limited, but the capacity to explain is not.

Genetic understanding derives from the perception of meaningful connections. The implication here is that what it is possible to collect in terms of data about human situations constitutes only a small part of what actually exists. But we can probably perceive connections between what we have collected and what we do not know. Facts about individuals, for instance, do not and cannot have an existence separate from that individual's life, however simple or complex that may be. Of course objective data, however obtained, are never complete and this is where the problem of interpretation arises. Whereas static, that is causal, understanding leads to the formation of theories, genetic understanding does not. It becomes the yardstick for a particular kind of event.

Finally, understanding of data may be based upon logic or empathy which is often described as an understanding which is felt; or upon what has become known as the 'as if' process, which requires the agent to make a basic assumption of the existence of some central fact (although there is no available evidence that it exists) and to build an understanding of data as if that central assumption was true. This approach is often used when the search for alternative core data has not been completed – probably due to lack of time, but it does tend to preclude any further search for more, real and better explanations.

The process of understanding human situations has to be seen as one limited by the very nature of human beings, and modified by cultural factors and the fact that there must be many things which are completely unknowable.

Giving Meaning to Data

Giving meaning to data about individuals and their behaviour has consistently been presented as an apparently logical process. But this must be a fallacious assumption for at least two principal reasons:

1. The information that a change agent can collect falls into the category of 'facts-as-perceived'; that is, they are perceptions rather than the kind of facts which would be accepted as data by a pure scientist.

2. The ordering of these facts-as-perceived subjects them to a selection process which is bound to contain a large element of subjective bias on the part of the change agent.

As Leighton (1973: 513) also points out, most of such information about individuals and groups occurs as part of a continuum; this puts their appearance at any particular moment in a context; and only in that context can they have any real or valid meaning. Inevitably it must be noted that where facts are not fixed but are defined by the perceptions of others, those perceptions can change and thus the nature of the so-called 'social fact' acquires a different value. Of course this is of value to the change agent because change can be effected in the life of an individual by developing a different perception of salient facts in his or her context.

Much has been said and written about the ways of giving meaning to facts obtained from observational, verbal and other sources, from the point of view of comparison with pre-existing models, theories and constructs of behaviour, and we shall look at some of these now. But it is as well to bear in mind that the actual allocation of meaning is a subjective process with little or no possible back-up in terms of fixed and provable facts. The parameters of meaning allocation have the possibility of shifting continuously and any stability or structure tends to reside solely in the belief of the change agent in the validity of his or her experience and theoretical constructs.

Information Integration

> Memory seems to rely upon the sets of networks of analog patterns retained by the 'grooving' of the pathways in and between the organism or the system, and recall could be described as a sort of plucking at these patterns.
>
> Wilden (1980: 398)

Talking about 'transindividual' concepts that are used to identify whole-group processes, Long (1992: 2) wrote:

> These concepts rely on a careful and intensive description of individual behaviours and interactions within the group because it is the *patterning* of these that provides the data upon which 'group' concepts are predicated. That is, group data are constituted from specific individual behaviour evoked by other specific behaviours in particular patterns.

As we saw in the description of the diagnostic process earlier in this chapter, ultimately the collected and structured data on a target, individual or group, has to be compared for the patterns it reveals with 'known' patterns which have been previously soundly ascribed to certain behavioural entities.

There are two points to consider here. The first has already been made in discussion of the sources of data and is quite simply that, with few exceptions, all such material is susceptible to selection and interpretation. The second is the repeat of processes of selection and interpretation which occur when comparisons are made. The whole attempt at objectivity can only ever be even partially fulfilled by the employment of defences against the intrusion of known bias, which in the case of the illustration earlier, occurred when a process of exposure and integration of several different viewpoints was used.

The process of the recognition of similarities, while having been much explored, does not, I fear yield much of great value to the change agent seeking clarification of the process of comparison of complex data. Of course, as computer experts know, information has to be presented in a form compatible with the process of analysis to which it is being submitted, and it is more likely than not that after the process of collection and ordering there is also a process of re-jigging so that the material is then in a form capable of being compared for 'fit' to known patterns.

Pattern Recognition

The formation of 'known' patterns is typified by Long (1992) in the quotation given earlier, where repeated productions of particular forms of behaviour are gathered together and published as the expected form. These collective entities can then be christened with a particular title in hindsight, when there is proof that over time they have turned out to be what it was suggested they might be. Repetition and effective use produces a 'known' pattern which then becomes the touchstone by which similar patterns are recognised.

All the way down the line from the original recognition of the need for change to the eventual recognition of what needs to be changed, the process is one of constant idiosyncratic interpretations forced into some kind of comparative rigour by the use of known patterns which may or may not become habitual.

Of course, many situations where change is required do not or are not susceptible to such a rigorous process of discovery and recognition as the psychiatric example given earlier. However, the process may be the same and to highlight that process the most rigorous example is preferable to one that is less difficult. But the argument which may be based upon this process is that, even with the most rigorous of processes of analysis of quite simple change-needs, there is little acceptable evidence that it produces an equally high order of success. This alone may well be part of the reason for the obscurity which attends and clouds analyses of effectiveness. If the processes were clear with an adequate record of success, such obscurity and obfuscation would not be needed.

However, the process discussed here eventually produces an initial assessment of what needs to be done. If the need is great and complex no doubt the assessment will change in the light of new data and understanding as the intervention proceeds. It may change completely.

When the hypothesis has been stated, the original data are seen as *entailed* by it, in conjunction with the general laws and the rules of inference. But someone has to state the hypothesis in the first place. It is in the initial *formulation* of the hypothesis that there occurs a genuine creative act with which the logician, as such, has no concern. There is a stage at which someone must have thought up a hypothesis which, in the context of discovery, was, to be sure, suggested by the facts, but is not a formal consequence of them.

Mechl (1954: 57)

13 The Theoretical Assumptions About the Sources of Behaviour

In the name of science we have been wrongly satisfied with mere *conceptualisation*; mere *logical method* mere *clarity of thinking* – these lack objectivity.

Jaspers (1963: 768)

In the last chapter I attempted to show the sources of information which were available to the change agent and, in particular, to note the different qualities which each source possessed. Of course all sources are not equally available, nor is there always time to collect what may be on offer before a decision has to be made about the process of intervention. In any case, all sources of information are subject to the individual perception of the change agent and also to a process of prioritisation in the light of the apparent pressures of the situation.

The theoretical ideas to be discussed in this chapter are the frameworks – the constructs which the change agent uses to order and make sense of the individualistic data which he or she has collected. To call such theory a framework is logical, for a framework imposes an order of relationships on apparently disparate and unconnected facts and, indeed, it is the structure of the relationship of component parts to each other and to the totality which makes a logical and coherent theory.

If theory can then induce order into the collation of facts it also has the virtue of generating some level of understanding of them and, just as importantly as ordering what is known, indicating the gaps in the collected knowledge. This very positive use of theory is limited by one crucial fact which is the relationship which any theory has to actual reality. For instance scientific theories are subjected to experimental verification, produce predictions which must be true and accurate; indeed no scientific theory is of much value if it cannot be proven with evidence, prediction and repetitive testing. When a new idea, new information is tested against existing theory, its value is related to the degree of fit which is produced unless the new information is of such a nature that it invalidates the logical basis of the old as relativity did to determinism.

So the relationship of theory to reality and of theory to practice are crucial in determining the expected level of efficiency of those processes based on them. If it is feasible to establish that the basic theoretical concepts are what Jaspers calls 'illuminating ideas', then the level of effectiveness of change agents can be established as relatively unpredictable. But of course it is not that simple because other factors than the theoretical concepts such as experience, and different kinds of understanding, e.g. tacit knowing, are involved. We will consider these factors elsewhere, here we will only look at those concepts which are available to inform change efforts.

The Sequence of Theory and Practice

Bateson believed that therapy was an art form and that the theories and practice were inextricably linked. But, unlike many who study the available theories in order to found the bases of practice, Bateson believed that the practitioner – the change agent – faced with the actual pressing need to work in face-to-face situations was the source of the development of theoretical ideas based upon careful reflection on the actions already taken.

There are two processes to consider from this association:

• The first is that practitioners, in order to meet the exigencies of practice not covered by theory already promulgated, need to possess creative imagination to a large degree and also the ability to reflect upon their practice and eventually to structure and broadcast it.

• The second arises from the first and is that the process of creating theory from individual imaginative practice generates a very strong likelihood of the resulting theory being idiosyncratic, and probably highly correlated with particular situations and personalities. A good example of this process is the rise to guru status of R. D. Laing.

In a sense, the sequence of practice–theory–practice is fraught with other difficulties as well. For instance, because some theory is originally formulated from the practice of highly creative practitioners, there is always the possibility that much less creative practitioners will follow the same path, believing that they have what is necessary in terms of discipline as well as creativity to work outside and separate from any current established guidelines. Practice without theory can be an extremely dangerous activity – both for the practitioner and those with whom he or she works.

Thus it would seem that the development of theories relating to the practice of effecting change is often dependent upon the emergence in practice of highly imaginative, creative and disciplined individuals. But this is true of all areas of human endeavour; what is significant here is the nature of the theory which arises, and its use by change agents of all qualities who do not always possess the sensitivity of the theory's originators.

The other side of the theoretical coin is the material which comes from non-practitioners who are experimenters and speculators. This material, like for instance Milgram's work on obedience, attempts to produce generally acceptable data about human behaviour. The problems here which worry change agents are that, by producing general ideas about human behaviour, the theorists have made the adaptation of their ideas to practice in particular situations incapable of producing an appropriate degree of specificity.

Pseudo-science

As theory serves a fundamental purpose in the change process by providing the standards of patterns of relationships of the sources, productions and consequences of behaviour against which can be compared the data obtained about a particular human situation, it is necessary to examine theory quite closely – not so much in the detail of individual compilations, but in the quality of the aid they represent for the practitioner.

By virtue of the ways in which change practices are formulated, at one end of the scale they are untestable hypotheses and at the other they belong to what Karl Popper (1959) described as the realm of 'pseudo-science'.

If a change agent wishes to effect change in an individual, this can be produced through the process of training (i.e. by developing a new set of behaviours, enhancing existing ones, or generating insight into those factors which promote and sustain the behaviour that is to be changed, thus offering a choice which did not previously exist about what, if anything, can be done about it); or change can be effected by coercion, by rewarding selected behaviour, by influence (e.g. by using love or fear to bring about effort to control or modify the behaviour in question), by example; or by generating the desire to change, and so on.

In such a momentous and important operation as effecting change in others, are there any theories or guidelines which could, for instance, be used as a basis for teaching individuals how they might learn to do this effectively? Indubitably the answer is yes, because this process of learning and teaching has been going on for a long time. But, it is pertinent to ask, is there a body of logical and replicable evidence which would indicate that by applying these particular approaches (or, more likely, just one of them) to the problems of changing a selected part of the behaviour of an individual, the outcome can be predicted with a degree of certainty which is higher than chance? In simple terms the question is – Can it be stated that by doing this or that a particular outcome will most often be achieved?

Without doubt this level of certainty cannot be claimed for any of the theoretical material which is currently in use to underpin change efforts, with the possible exception of some changes which are effected in extremely confined areas of behaviour. The nature of this theoretical material in nearly every case is inductive and based upon an accumulation of conforming examples. This compilation has then been refined into a more or less elegant hypothesis. What tends to be omitted from this thesis is the fact that much unexplored and unaccepted material, which would not confirm the original idea, or at least which might be seen to dilute its force or call some major part of it into question, has been conveniently ignored.

The inductive process of theory formulation never has and never can consider the whole of the material available, but is of necessity biased and selective.

Another problem deriving from the nature of this kind of theoretical material is that it has to be concerned with the generalities of genetic endowments and their development and can be confounded by other factors such as culture or even location. Consider, for instance, something so radical and so ordinary as the perception of three-dimensional space. How this develops can depend more upon the area of the world where an individual is born and raised than upon any general thesis of spatial perception.

Inductive theorising about human behaviour produces generalities which are dependent in their practical use on the similarities of the individuals to whom they are applied being far greater than their dissimilarities.

This problem is of course not a problem when inductive theory is applied to material entities rather than to aspects of human behaviour.

The human individual however, stands in a reciprocal relationship to the groups which s/he helps constitute. The lessons of social psychology stress social determination, humans presumably being largely derived from social process. However, humans at the same time are creating their social environments.

Long (1992: 1)

This reciprocal relationship between human beings as genetically created biological machines and the environments in which they exist, and which they also create, generates a complex influence and interactive system which not only complicates the production of effective theorising but makes a 'theory of everything' relating to human behaviour impossible.

What follows is not an attempt to cover the complexity of the main theoretical assumptions about the sources of human behaviour, but merely one to show that because of the inaccessibility of the actual processes, the theoretical assumptions are in essence elegant, unverifiable explanations, with the possible exception of those theorists who concentrate on the biological approach. It is only in this latter approach that actual physical and biochemical interactions can be indubitably shown to occur, and the consequences noted and tested many times.

The reason for using the term 'assumption' must become very clear when considering the available explanations of behaviour. Indeed many theorists have abandoned the search for sources as wholly inappropriate and have concentrated on what is actually available – which is the manifest behaviour of individuals and groups in the context in which it occurs. They believe that what is more important than discovering the source of the behaviour is to isolate the factors which sustain it; the circumstances in which it occurs; and who and/or what actually stands to gain from its emission.

When we move from considering the behaviour of the individual and, in particular, from a consideration of his or her internal motivations and drives to the social factors involved in being part of groups and organisations, the attempt to understand internal motivation begins to yield even fewer dividends. But, as we shall see, the alternative of the statistical analysis of group behaviour also provides only wide guidelines of what might be expected to be the variables of group existence; and the similarities of such behaviour often strike an uncomfortable balance, with the effect that predicting consequences and understanding the sources of social behaviour is not and cannot be a precision operation.

The catalogue of assumptions about the sources of behaviour is quite a large one. The simple distinction usually drawn between nature and nurture is a good enough starting point but, on the basis that to change behaviour implies some measure of understanding of its sources, we need to be somewhat more explicit. Indeed the very complexity of possible sources of behaviour is one of the main reasons why intervention has such a large element of the unknown and the unknowable about it.

At birth, all human beings have already been equipped by heredity with physical endowment, and with what can be called certain predispositions. Straight away there are questions to ask, such as: What kind of genetic equipment is involved, of what quality? How well does it function – how efficiently? Is it already deficient, damaged, diseased, omitted or modified in some way?

It is impossible to visualise a biological organism apart from the environment in which it exists, so the interaction between genetic endowment and environment forms the next great source of behaviour. Whatever potential is available in the former requires the appropriate stimuli and support from the latter to be realised. The biological organism has a built-in developmental sequence programmed as a part of the genetic endowment, but that sequence can, at any stage of the organism's growth, be enhanced, supported or diminished by environmental factors. So a large element of chance enters into the developmental process in terms of where, when and under what circumstances individuals are born and grow.

Of the systems of the body which actually play a large part in behaviour, the neural and glandular systems are perhaps two of the most significant, but the basic needs for nourishment, warmth and affection (as Maslow pointed out) have to be satisfied, not only for the organism to grow but also for attention to be diverted from survival to other, less basic, functions.

The peripheral nervous system is responsible for carrying messages from receptors to the brain and for the transfer of messages to the muscular system from the brain. Thus the effectiveness of this system can affect the way an individual perceives his or her environment; and also conditions the ways of responding to it. Equally the glandular system controls factors like digestion, growth, emotional behaviour and stress response, social behaviours and the development of secondary sexual characteristics.

Even at this simple level, complexity abounds. Behaviour may be affected by the physical and biochemical constituents of the individual, and also developmental programming of the use of the genetic endowment can be affected. For instance, the relationship between programming and learning may be one which not only affects how learning takes place, but also what is learned. The problems can arise from defect, damage, the quality and quantity, frequency and appropriateness of stimuli and, finally, from opportunity. All these factors can contribute to the maximisation of the potential that is genetically formed, or they can do so partially, selectively, sporadically or not at all, or they may actively diminish it.

Ultimately this process, with varying degrees of success, produces an individual with a pattern of adaptation to life which tends to become set and adopted as the basis for all future learning. Of course, by deliberate intent, some of these patterns may force a re-evaluation and some effort may be made to control outcomes – usually when the adaptive patterns have become demonstrably unsuccessful.

The genetic and biological bases of behaviour promote the idea that changes in behaviour can be brought about by physical means, and so drugs and surgery can be used to inhibit, maintain or increase the functions of some parts of the physical system.

If the 'givens' of biological genetic endowment yield a very close connection between sources of behaviour and the possibilities of changing it, the same cannot be said for the assumptions about those sources of behaviour which are deemed to be social in origin. By 'social' is meant all the factors of that environment which impinges upon the organism from its earliest days, and about whose presence we have already seen there is a notable element of chance. Broadly speaking, the assumptions in this group divide into four main categories:

- those which are mainly concerned with the relationships between the genetic factors and the environment;

- those which are mainly concerned with the manifest current behaviour, however produced;

- those which accept that the processes of behaviour development are almost immutable; and

- those which are prone to believe that a large element of change can be effected by a conscious effort of will.

As must also be obvious from this simplistic fourfold division, no single part of it when used as a basis for the explanation of the sources of human behaviour is wholly adequate. As a result, though such single-base explanations exist, most in practice contain combinations of assumptions.

Thus psychodynamic theory is biologically oriented, and also holds strongly to the idea of the immutable nature of the early established patterns. But, while believing in the historical determination of current behaviour, it also holds that by bringing these antecedents into conscious awareness some element of control can be exercised over the behaviour so produced.

Cognitive theorists believe that the element of environmental influence is large and that most behaviour is learned, and thus can be unlearned, and other behaviours substituted. They may well believe that the process of developing behavioural patterns consists of the interaction of genetic endowment and environmental factors but, unlike the psychoanalysts, they are wholly unprepared to say exactly how the process operates – preferring to state that what they see as important are the interactions, and the interpretations of those interactions that individuals make based upon the constructs they have developed.

Thus we have theoretical assumptions about the sources and maintenance of behaviour which constitute a straightforward biological determinism; those which stress the pre-eminent determining effect of the environment; those which combine both determining factors, and those which use neither, preferring to see humans as free to determine behaviour according to their own choice.

It must be obvious that if the ideas about the sources of human behaviour are so different – ranging from accepting that individuals are controlled by internal unconscious forces which are largely hidden; to accepting that human beings are largely controlled by their biochemistry; to believing that humans are free to control their own destinies within the framework of their physical and social environment – then there are some questions to be asked about these assumptions. For instance the most complete of all these theories, in the sense that it covers most aspects of human existence is that promulgated by the various schools of psychoanalytic thought. But does this necessarily preclude the ideas of the others? Indeed that apparent complexity of the urges and drives underlying human behaviour could serve to show that if all the assumptions were added together there would still be large gaps in our understanding. However, such an exercise is not possible because some of the explanations are at best alternative, and at worst mutually exclusive.

What seems to be fundamentally clear is that attempts to understand an organism devoid of or separated from the environment in which it normally exists is a nonsense. But this might lead to an eclectic viewpoint of the kind that avers that if there are a number of possible sources of behaviour, it is a matter of attempting to establish which and in what proportion each is active in an individual case. Inevitably such an idea can founder on the fact of diametrically opposed views of causation, and may lead to other forms of assumptions being made which use forms of symbolism to explain behaviour, rather than attempting to discover what are factual reasons for behaviour in areas which are scarcely accessible to investigation.

Humans have existed for a very long time and they have recorded human behaviour at all kinds of levels – as history, as myths, as stories, etc. – and it is possible that in this mass of material may lie the basis of some understanding of behaviour. But by advancing from this direction no claim can be made for scientific accuracy, which in any case would be largely spurious, but only that the recorded behaviour patterns of human beings cannot only show the nature of behaviour, but also its outcomes, consequences and how it might be dealt with.

Ideas From the Studies of Social Behaviour

One factor in the study of the sources of behaviour which has always been readily available has been the behaviour itself. A plethora of investigations into major common aspects of behaviour has yielded considerable material, which has sometimes been designated as constituting a particular theory. Examples of such constructions are the cost/reward thesis; attribution theory; social exchange theory; cognitive dissonance; personal construct theory; games theory; self-presentation theory; the frustration/aggression thesis, and so on.

What all these theories have in common is their starting point in the observation of human behaviour, the experimental testing of some major aspect of the causal sequences revealed in observation and the postulation of a 'generally applicable' thesis with some degree of predictability. The whole process appears to work on the assumption that social systems function according to certain rules, both formal and informal. The formal rules are explicit, but the informal rules can only be detected from watching behaviour over large numbers of situations and inferring that the behaviour so examined appears to operate according to a set of rules.

Take for instance the cost/reward analysis. It is a commonly accepted idea that all human beings seek either to maximise what they believe to be the personal gains they can obtain from a situation or, alternatively or as well, they seek to minimise loss. This sounds, and is, remarkably logical, but at the level at which it remains a logical explanation, it has little or no value in determining what an individual will consider to be a cost or a reward in any particular situation, other than in a very general way.

The same is true of all the other studies of social behaviour, whether individually or group focused. For instance, the idea that holding opposing ideas at the same time develops a tension which has to be relieved by action, is again essentially a logical concept but apart from the usual approach of asking individuals why they behaved in a particular way, there is no way to prove that such tension actually existed. All that can truthfully be said is that the individual behaved as if such was the case. Experimental situations set up to demonstrate the validity of theoretical claims are essentially artificial situations and are responded to as such by the participants. Investigations of real situations can only be an intrusive exercise and, as a result, succeed in influencing and thus changing the event under observation.

Apart from these forms of statistical theory there are also the studies of the effects on behaviour of culture, belief systems, moral and legal systems, educational and political systems – all showing the effects such systems have on the behaviour of those who are subjected to them. The list of possible areas of exploration of effects on behaviour is endless, for the simple reason that human beings have always found their own species the most fascinating subject of investigation and, whereas rational choice has always figured largely in the major attempts at explanation, the unconscious motivations, the drives and the social factors have also been added and complicate the picture enormously.

Studies of the attributes of human beings, for example, intelligence, memory, perception, language and construct formation also abound; as do papers on habits, emotional responses, kinds and levels of interaction, methods and effectiveness of communication, attitudes, opinions, likes and dislikes, social competence, conflict – the list once more is endless. We have studied the kinds of constructs which help individuals make sense of the world in which they live; what tends to be present in the behaviour of socially competent individuals; the development and consequences of prejudice and conflict. So it would appear that there is no important aspect of manifest behaviour which has not been studied in absorbing detail.

What such studies show with startling clarity if their individual attractions for the change agent are overlooked in favour of the overall picture they present in combination, is the embedded nature of the individual. Each person – rational, decision-making, choice-operating as he or she may be – is yet obviously formed in terms of his or her social behaviour by a complex network of interactive systems, and is held in them. Such is clearly demonstrated when that complex network is removed artificially, as in the studies of sensory deprivation or as naturally occurs in many cases during the enforced isolation of old age.

The most important word about behaviour is 'manifest'. What we have is what we can observe and even that is complicated by the idiosyncratic nature of our processes of observation.

Among the more interesting theoretical applications to the processes of intended change are those ideas which have cybernetic and ecological systems at their base. Ecological ideas are concerned with the relationships between living organisms and their environment, which form a considerable counter to the idea that human behavioural problems stem almost entirely from the biological entity and its genetic determination. One spin-off from this has been a realisation that the information available about a particular human situation relates specifically to the context in which it occurs. Similarities with other situations can thus be made at a wide and general level. As a result, the context of information actually gives it most of its meaning, and intervention strategies have to be formulated in the light of the ecology of the origins of the data. Not to do so suggests that, far from beneficially changing the situation, intervention will produce a new and higher order of difficulty. In other words, ecological theorists believe that intervention has to be made in the context of a specific situation and not founded on the application of unrelated ideas. They refer to this process as the 'contextualisation' of intervention.

From the systems theorists and cyberneticists comes the idea of 'feedback' which is essentially a method of controlling a system by feeding back into it the results of its past and current performance. When such feedback takes the form of criticism, the result may be a structural change to the system; but if the feedback becomes part of a learning pattern, the general method and pattern of performance may be changed. Certainly without some form of feedback into a system no developmental change is possible.

The major thrust of these ideas is to show that:

(a) individuals, groups and organisations are not isolated units where change can be effected internally, but they are embedded in other larger systems and contain within themselves smaller systems, all of which are affected by any incident involving the apparently defined unit; and

(b) change agents, by intervening in a system, become part of that system and that involvement must be considered as part of the pattern they are trying to change.

They also emphasise that the patterns of human behaviour are important in that there needs to be a clear relationship between the particular pattern which is selected as a focus of intervention and the nature of the intervention. These ideas also point to the limitations of intervention and prioritise the current social and behavioural systems, the need for a reality orientation and some need to understand the theory of logical types.

Informal Material

Whereas the theoretical ideas presented so far have been of the order of general theories of behaviour and development, there is a wholly different area of concepts which is often given the title of 'practice theory' or 'practice principles'. One essential difference from the theories of behaviour is that practice theory is not really theory in the true sense, for it has no consistent or logical design, but is essentially a collection, an accumulation or a compilation of practice experiences which, having been found to be useful by one or more practitioners, are recorded for the benefit of others.

In this sense they are guides to practice. But once they become common knowledge to practitioners and writers on change efforts, they begin to assume an almost coherent form. The recorded facts do not in themselves change but the regard of those who read, work and teach from them eventually accords them a status which their writers might perhaps not have intended. It is common, for instance, to find lists of such practice principles which have been around for a few years to be accorded the status of being an essential part of that 'body of knowledge' which writers present as the basis for interventive action, along with, and apparently possessing equal status to, the more formal theories of human behaviour – or at least to those parts of such theories as are deemed to be capable of being of practical use.

The basis of practice theory is essentially one of counting. Thus if a particular aspect of interventive action is recorded by various writers over a period of time, then it is almost inevitable that a synthesis of these recorded incidents will be presented as a paper affirming the probability of an occurrence which is substantially higher than chance. It is the fact of occurrence which is important, so little attempt is made in such papers to predict what the essential causes of these recurring behaviour patterns might be; it is enough that they appear to occur with sufficient frequency.

There are several important facts about practice theories as a basis of interventive action which should be noted. The basic idea is sound, and is one that has been around and in use for centuries in the form of apprenticeship systems in which an individual of great experience passes on to a learner the elements of that wisdom. Essentially what are transmitted in such a situation are recurring patterns which have emerged from his practice and which have come to be expected as essentially direct cause and effect sequences by the experienced operative.

The advantage of the apprenticeship system was the direct face-to-face teaching between actual individuals. The disadvantages of the system when it is transferred to a written record of experience comprise the loss of the immediacy, directness and credibility of the contact system and the possibility that it will become regarded as more certain theory than the nature of the material and its uniqueness would warrant. However, it also avoids the narrowness of the individual apprenticeship situation and the probable propagation of idiosyncracies and prejudices.

The second important factor is the nature of interventive action and the high level of impossibility of the occurrence of patterns of behaviour which repeat with any great degree of fidelity in different situations. One of the major effects of creating 'theory' or 'principles' by a process of accumulation and counting, or by establishing the probability of occurrence is a movement towards a greater degree of stability and certainty that events will actually occur as predicted. Indeed one of the great attractions of such constructs for all those engaged in working with others in change efforts is the apparent increment in the predictability or certainty.

But against this has to be placed the fact that, although theories may be and no doubt are in most cases large generalities about the patterns of human behaviour, nevertheless human beings are individuals and, at the very least, they put an individualistic gloss on those general patterns. Thus no two people with apparently the same problem will handle it in identical ways. Indeed this very fact is made much of in group work where the individual and idiosyncratic approaches of separate individuals to a similar problem are used to identify different possible methods and to develop alternative ways of coping for those members who may well have become tramlined in their own relatively ineffective approach.

Thus the generalities which comprise the practice theories and principles are liable to form a very loose fit to any particular set of circumstances, or situation of interventive action. Or alternatively, like much of the work of behaviourists, change agents concentrate on relatively minute areas of problem behaviour with a high degree of precision.

The third point applies to both extremes, but more importantly to the loose fit situation and is that the expectations of what will happen, generated by the apparent certainty of the practice theory, actually occur. Their production, however, would seem to be precipitated more from the pressure on the change agent to discover them than from any suggestion that they had an independent existence.

An interesting comment on this factor of influence was made by Eysenck (1953) when he noted that the patients of various psychotherapists consistently produced the kind of material which the theoretical concepts espoused by the therapists would have led them to expect. Of course this self-same evidence was used as an argument that the theory was thus correct in predicting what was there to be found. But evidence has consistently mounted about the indirect and probably unconscious, or at least unwitting, influence by change agents on the production of usable and indeed expected material in all forms of change efforts. The effects of this situation will be dealt with in more detail later.

A final point about practice theories concerns the production of complete theories by individuals. They are not so much compilations but consistent explanations of a particular phenomenon which appears, or is thought to appear, in change efforts with individuals but more consistently in groups. Two good examples of this kind of thing are Bales' production of the Interaction Process Analysis and the theories of Group Development, most notably those produced by Schutz (1959) and W. Fawcett Hill (1974).

Bales' theory was in fact an attempt to classify the major forms of interaction which occurred between the members of a group. A pro-forma was supplied on which the interactions of any particular group, as defined by Bales, could be recorded and the actual processes of the group and of individual members scaled from it.

The limitations of such a procedure are immediately obvious – by providing a defined scale of interactions Bales compels all users of his chart to force everything that they see in a group into those categories. But the complexity of human behaviour defies a simple classification and, by either omitting those behaviours which are not described on the chart or squeezing them into the categories provided, the whole process of interaction is falsified. In addition, as this was also an observational technique, what could not be seen was not included and, of course, much of what goes on in a group is of the order of the invisible (to the observer).

It is interesting to note the lack of an inclusive theory of group behaviour, or even of the behaviour of organisations. Much material from the assumptions of the sources of behaviour has been taken over to use in multi-person situations, which is one of the reasons why I have put forward the thesis that the individual is the essential target in all contexts.

With the exception of the ideas deriving from systems theory and those which are extensions of assumptions about individuals, most group and organisational concepts stem from observational data. But the whole issue of 'group theory' is bedevilled by the never wholly acknowledged idea that, in some indefinable way, a group of individuals metamorphoses into a distinct entity which acts differently because it is a group. Of course individuals who become members of specific groups do perform differently from the way they behave as isolates and in other groups, because the essence of being a member of a group is to conform to its rules, which somewhat constrains the expression of individuality; and to commit time, skill, energy and belief to the group. It is, after all, an energy system and the source of its energy is the members.

'Group dynamics' is the term applied to a collection of information about how people have been seen to behave in groups, which produces ideas like those on group development. It is logical to expect that, when a group of strangers meet for the first time having been convened to perform a particular function:

(a) they will behave towards each other in ways that they have learned in the past, when faced with similar situations, as being at least reasonably successful; and

(b) as the group continues to meet and the members see one another's behaviour in the context of the group, these initial behavioural patterns will change. What was essentially different and strange has become relatively familiar and predictable.

The theories of group development, as propounded by people like Schutz for instance, offer little more than this obvious social familiarisation progression; but they do attempt to give a precision which is eminently spurious. For instance, for many years group development was presented as a linear progression of defined stages. Eventually it was realised that development towards a functional state was seldom linear, indeed not even spiral, but frequently erratic and often retrograde – depending on circumstances which were not altogether within the ambit of the group. Group development could only suggest what might be expected, apart from one factor which is seldom mentioned. If group leaders have a concept of how a group 'should' develop, there is a strong possibility that it may well appear to develop in this way. We will discuss the problem of unaware influence on the part of change agents later.

The ultimate point to be considered here is not the quantity of theory or assumptions about human behaviour, because it is indeed vast and being added to at an exponential rate annually, but rather its quality. And that poses us with a double problem:

1. The actual theories of the sources of behaviour are inductive – which precludes any possibility of their being verified.

2. All the material on manifest behaviour has to be statistical in the sense that it is based upon the frequency and intensity of production of selected behaviours, and this can, at best, provide only a very loose fit to any particular individual, group or organisation.

But this is what is available. The question is, what use is made of this material, and is it the best use possible? If the answer were to be in the affirmative, we would expect to see that the claims of success in the process of creating intended change would agree very closely with the quality of the theoretical material upon which those change processes were based. There is some evidence that this is not so, and that the claims are considerably higher than the actual quality of the assumptions would reasonably allow us to expect.

There may be two reasons for this. Firstly, there are factors involved in the change process – other than the quality of the theoretical material – which increase the possibility of success.

Secondly, the claims are exaggerated for reasons which are not unrelated to personal and professional prestige, and to anxiety about being seen to fail.

A theory is a good theory if it satisfies two requirements: it must accurately describe a large class of observations on the basis of a model that contains only a few arbitrary elements, and it must make definite predictions about the results of future observations.

Hawking (1995: 11)

14 Methods of Intervention
(1) Individual Focus

After delineation of conditions influencing the client's target and the formation of specific behavioral goals ... the worker plans an intervention strategy ... [which] usually includes steps to modify the client's behavior as well as to control conditions surrounding the client's situation. Modification of the client's behavior utilizes interventions directed toward acquiring, strengthening, weakening or eliminating specific behaviors ... may also make plans to increase intermediate behaviors and/or instrumental behaviors.

Sundel, Radin and Churchill (1974: 120-1)

The language of texts on intervention in human behaviour, as the above relatively typical example shows, is designed to look authoritative, professional and competent. But, given that intervention in human behaviour is an activity (that is, the intervenor actually has to do something), most of what is written is so vague that, as a basis of practical guidance, it is almost useless.

There are several possible reasons for this:

- It may result from an assumption on the part of writers that, as intervention to initiate intended change can only use those processes of ordinary human interaction that are in common use every day – but with probably more conscious effort and deliberate focusing – the translation of phrases like 'modify the client's behaviour' requires no explanation whatever.

- Equally it may result from the fact that statements like the one quoted above usually follow statements of philosophy and principles of practice. It could be assumed that the combination of philosophy, or a set of principles, with statements of intent will unhesitatingly pinpoint the exact nature of the interaction required to produce the intended outcome that has been clearly defined in the 'planned intervention strategy'.

- Or again it may be assumed that to write that a reasonable approach to achieving part of the planned intervention strategy would be to persuade the 'client' by means of a process of outlining in unthreatening terms the consequences of his or her continuing in the present line of behaviour, would demean the intelligence of the reader by appearing to reduce the process of intervention to one of the selection of an appropriate approach from an array of clearly defined interactive processes.

Of course there are texts which do exactly this, which is in essence trying to put into writing a verbal process of instruction. But because of the limitations of such a practice it is little regarded.

This highlights a fundamental problem for change agents – which tends to be resolved through personal preference, or through the processes of trial and error and whatever supervision is available from experienced practitioners. But, despite all the complicated theories and ideas about how the behaviour of individuals and groups can be changed, we ultimately have to face the inescapable fact that they are going to be put into effect by individuals, in a face-to-face situation, using what abilities they possess, and in the available forms of human interaction.

It has been said that all human interaction is a process of influence. It is my purpose in this chapter to try to put into hard realistic fact what methods change agents have at their disposal to bring about intended change. Of course, some methods of bringing about change which may be very effective are also morally, ethically or legally unacceptable. Nevertheless we will consider them in their place. Because, as we have seen earlier, some change efforts are made by individuals and groups without outside help and entirely self-directed, the different slant this internal process puts upon the use of the available interactive processes will also need to be looked at.

If we take as our starting point the fact that human interaction is a situation containing attempts to influence, and from there attempt to define influence, we can then proceed to see intervention as a controlled influence situation which not only has a prepared or planned outcome, but also a preferred selection of means for achieving those ends.

The use of force is a relevant starting point. Force implies the imposition of one person's will upon others. To be successful, in that the imposer succeeds in influencing the behaviour of the others in the intended manner and to a required extent, means that the imposer exercises what is universally described as 'power'. This is a concept which is notoriously hard to define – largely because it is concerned with the perceptions. Indeed French and Raven (1959) made out a strong case for the source of power generally residing in the perceptions of the person or persons who were subjected to it. This claim was based upon some of the factors we will consider later, but is essentially dependent upon the state of mind of those subjected to influence processes.

If I believe that a person who is requesting that I change my behaviour has the ability to punish me for refusal to do so, or to reward me for complying; or that he or she has a legitimate right, which I accept, to make this demand; or that he or she is a charismatic person for whom I would do most things, or one who I believe possesses an expertise in the matter in hand which I unequivocally accept; then that person's power, which in essence I by my belief have given, will succeed in its objective.

But power given in this way, based on perception, can only cover some part of those situations when a person or persons feels compelled to act at the demand of another. Indeed, fear of consequence, which is implicit in the punish/reward situation is a very strong factor. Although this may also be a perception-based acquiescence in part, there are situations, largely physical in nature, which are real. Thus the Muslim thief who has his hand cut off is forcibly prevented from stealing. His behaviour patterns have been modified by an act of physical force. Though such a compelling form of forceful change is neither legitimate nor considered ethical in Western societies, other forms of physical change are, as for instance leucotomy and the application of behaviour changing drugs such as tranquillisers.

But how do most of the verbal forms of compulsion to change operate?

Take coercion – in this use of force an individual is led by explanation to see quite clearly that a distinct connection exists between the behaviour under question and the consequences it will entail. The essential point in coercion is that although those consequences may in some cases be a direct result of the behaviour, even if they are not the implication is that the coercer will ensure that they, or something similar or worse, will arrive. Indeed coercion implies threat, even when the consequences anticipated in a successful change are in the nature of a reward.

Whenever a reward is implied for a successful change, punishment is implicit in failure.

For instance, many parents have found themselves in situations where the management of their children has been brought into question by social workers. They find that the standards of care do not match, in some essential areas, the legal and acceptable standards which society appears to demand. The parents perceive the social workers as having the power to remove their children and to take them into care. It would be only human nature for these parents to feel that any request for changes in the children's behavioural processes made by the social workers is backed by such legitimate power. In other words, they are coerced into conformity by fear of the consequences of refusal.

However, other force-based interventions may rely, not so much on the direct perception of consequence, as on the sense of obligation or duty. Frequently this takes the form of a compulsion to consider the individual's obligation to others, what their legitimate expectations may be, and what shortfalls have been noted. In a sense this is one of several pressure gambits that may be applied, in which a change agent will point to the effect that the individual's current behaviour is having, and will continue to have, on others. Given that these 'others' are of sufficient concern, there will be some pressure on the individual to change his or her behaviour in order to reduce whatever the harmful effect may have been.

In this brief discussion of intervention based on force, an essential point to recognise is that – although force may range from overwhelming physical violence, or the threat of it; to legitimate authority; to the power to exercise influence through the indirect forms of pressure and obligation – the element of choice still logically exists. In reality, however, the costs of making a resistive choice may be such that few would care to select this option. But of course circumstances and the value of options can change. What was a powerful incentive to change, and to accept even great pain and to expend great effort to do so, may, as the benefit accrues, become much less powerful in its effect and other options become more attractive. Historically, where sheer force has been applied to effect change it would appear that it needs not only to be constantly maintained but even increased over time, and its area of application changed, to have continuous effect.

As part of the process of learning in the early days of development and also in what may be referred to as 'training', individuals are not only presented with goals which others think desirable for them to achieve, but they are also subjected to some degree of pressure and compulsion to attempt to achieve them. This process has an element of guidance about it, but the prime element is coercive because the change agents, in this case parents, teachers and trainers, have a basic assumption that they know what kind of goals are required for specific purposes and what kind of efforts are required to achieve them. Their clients, whether young or not, are assumed neither to possess that knowledge nor, often, to be able to see clearly what they are being encouraged to achieve.

Thus an element of force is involved which is directive and compelling and which also has the effect of supplying energy and any deficits of understanding, initiative and involvement. Of course there is always the possibility that those placed under such directive pressure will turn from reluctance to rebellion; will refuse on the grounds that the output of energy required is too great for what they understand to be the goals; and, indeed, may still have the outlook that present gain is far more rewarding than increased potential future gain achieved by deferring present gratification.

If such a process of direction, however, proves to be successful in its early stages, the external force may well gain a very potent ally in the fact that it begins to coincide with a redefinition on the part of the individual of what is possible and at what cost. When this happens, the commitment level of the individual replaces his or her initial reluctance. In economic terms, the enforced saving to produce an investment has begun to show dividends.

Such an application of force and the maintenance of a pattern of behaviour with a long-term outcome highlights the main dichotomy of the change agent's approach. Basically it is only possible to change the situation in which the individual exists, or his or her perception of it. In this case the perception of the individual is changed by a forceful and directed change in his or her situation. Fundamentally, belief that things can be changed is far better demonstrated by actually changing them than by describing how it may be done. But such a process is by no means always either effective or even possible as, generally, the individual subject has the ability to refuse to participate – though for a variety of reasons he or she may not be able to exercise this ability.

Now we must look at the ideas of human behavioural change which lie behind the idea of compulsion. There must be an assumption that human beings can be compelled to change, and that such change can be effected even against the wishes of individuals if the force applied is strong enough, all encompassing and durable.

What the individual becomes is conditioned by his Anlage and his environment. The factors due to the environment can be influenced by therapy, those due to the Anlage only by eugenics. As almost everything that is due to Anlage (disposition) needs the environment for its realisation, therapy extends to the Anlage in so far as this depends on the environment.

Jaspers (1963: 852)

It is an essential part of this exploration of change that the focus of change in all circumstances, must eventually be the individual – no matter how indirect the influence process may be. Concomitantly therefore, it must also be true that the individual has to be the final arbiter of whether change actually occurs and endures. This last statement, while fundamentally sound, has to be qualified in certain ways. Firstly, the individual concerned must become aware that he or she is the focus of change efforts, for if there is no perception that a change process is in operation, the individual focus has no opportunity to choose his or her response to it. This is also true when understanding of the nature of the change process is either partial or false. This can occur both from lack of understanding on the part of the individual, which in truth may be due to an actual inability to understand what is involved, or an inadequate or deceitful presentation by the change agent of what is in hand. This latter may occur when the change agent believes that resistance and reluctance to participate in the change process can be bypassed in the individual concerned if he or she is not wholly or truly aware of what is involved in the change process. Besides being unethical, such a process tends eventually to produce undesirable results, if and when the deception is disclosed, which are of the nature of a considerable dissipation of any element of trust that may have arisen between the participants and a devaluation of whatever changes may have already occurred.

Essentially the second major approach to intended change accepts that genuine change only occurs when the individual accepts the change process to such a degree that he or she becomes the programme operator and, however it was initiated, requires only support from any external source.

The actions which are available in this kind of intervention are based upon a particular kind of deficit analysis. Such an analysis tends to show that an individual's behaviour is initiated and maintained by a series of support systems. If the nature and content of these systems could be changed, the behaviour of the individual would change also. The systems involved are many and various ranging from traditional and habitual patterns of behaviour of the individual, through the quality and quantity of information the individual possesses about salient aspects of his or her existence, to the social systems of which he or she is a part.

Thus if access to any individual is given, it is possible to increase information, demonstrate different and presumably more effective ways of doing things, fill in the gaps of knowledge and of training, generate more and better understanding, train to develop skills, rehearse behaviours in essential areas, and so on. Bound into this kind of deficit analysis is the belief that many people do not realise their apparent potential, not so much because that potential is drastically deficient, but because their progress through life has either not offered the right and appropriate stimulation for its development or it has produced situations which have stimulated alternative or ineffective development in essential areas.

One of the most essential features of this approach is to realise that many individuals are limited by their incapacity to think outside the constraints of their 'tramlining' developmental patterns. They are constrained not so much by lack of ability, but by not knowing how differently fairly simple and common situations may be handled. Consonant with the belief of those who practise this approach is the idea that showing that other ways, other patterns and other possibilities exist, leaves the choice to the individual to make. But, beneath this, lies also the fundamental idea that a true choice can only be made between alternatives when each is realistically understood in terms not just of the alternatives themselves but also of the possible consequences of adopting one rather than another. So a great emphasis is placed upon a presentation in terms and ideas which lie well within the grasp of those to whom they are presented.

Of course, when and if such a presentation is accepted, a more active and interventive assistance may be acceptable, but this is not necessarily so.

Often this approach requires something more than the need to present new ideas, new ways, different outlooks. Such things may be so alien to the individuals concerned that they may need some degree of preparation to be able to start to see their possible value. This is dangerous ground because such preparations can have a marked similarity to proselytisation or propaganda, with all the connotations of unethical behaviour and taking advantage that this implies.

The processes of this approach contain the application of logic to situations, thus detaching them from their personal emotional entanglements; the processing of relevant and available information; guidance; instruction; training; the development of insight and understanding; behavioural practice, demonstration and example. There is much evidence that individuals respond better in learning and growth situations to those for whom they have respect and/or affection, rather than to those for whom their main feeling is one of fear. In that respect this particular approach to changing human behaviour is one in which the performance of the change agent is liable to attract intense scrutiny. If such a performance is not essentially consonant with the expressed intent of the change agent, in the opinion of the target, then that performance is immediately devalued in the eyes of the target and any others who may be participating. After all, as I have just noted, one of the major approaches is that the change agent becomes a model for the kind of behaviour he or she is attempting to promote.

Another prime factor in this approach is that the change agent, acting as a person of some authority, licenses the participating individual to behave, to think, to feel in ways from which he or she may have been excluded or constrained by past training and experience, and to show what development is therefore possible. This is also accompanied by an expanding awareness of the need to be responsible for this and all other behavioural patterns which the individual will accept as his or hers. The process is also involved in making known to individuals the many and varied pressures (of which they may well have been in total ignorance) to which they are subjected and respond, and which produce behaviour that individuals have considered 'theirs' – personally and individually arrived at.

Indeed this process is one which brings home to individuals the nature of the choices available to them. This may be a very frightening procedure and one from which many will shrink. But the ability to influence the behaviour of others in selected ways and directions which goes commonly by the name of the exercise of power, is exercised by those who understand some of the pressures and choices which exist, over those who more than likely do not.

The approach usually called 'skill training' brought into prominence the idea of deficit analysis. It amounts to the making of comparisons with an ideal or norm of behaviour. Thus, if an ideal human being existed, he or she would be perfectly capable of coping with anything that happened and their deficit analysis would be nil – the whole of the genetic and social developmental sequences would be flawless. That such a person could exist is never actually considered, but if human problems are believed to arise from deficits of genetic endowment, of development, of socialisation, then, because deficits are the lack of something, there has to be an ideal from which these lacks can be assessed, even if the process is partly a fantasy.

The skill training approach defines those deficits it can deal with, such as social competence, believing that social competence is largely comprised of learned behaviour patterns. It was maintained that if such patterns had been badly, inadequately or maladaptively established, they could be dealt with by learning or re-learning more adequate skills, given that the basic capacity to learn such things was available. Like all such training and learning or re-learning approaches, its success is limited by the capability of individuals to perform the tasks which are required. In this there is as always a deficit, which may well be unalterable.

But the concept of deficit can be useful in a much wider aspect than social competence. Indeed most of the major theories of human behaviour are deficit theories. For instance, psychoanalytic concepts of behaviour indicate that current behavioural deficits stem from deficits in genetic endowment and/or deficits in the developmental programme, all of which are more or less permanent. Such biological determinism holds out the hope of change in the individual not in being able to repair these historical deficits, but in being aware of them and the consequences which they entail. Thus, given that other deficits in understanding and ability are not also present, those consequences can be ameliorated by conscious effort.

The Humanistic approach can be seen as defining a deficit of choice, circumscribed by circumstances, i.e in not understanding the choices which are available.

In like manner, those approaches which bear the title of 'treatment' can be seen as embodying deficit ideas – in this case that something has gone wrong and requires to be 'cured'. The idea of making better something which was ill, or at least attempting to bring about some relief from suffering, presumes an attitude of mind which regards some form of human behaviour as 'sickness' – which is as valid an approach as any other, but does have connotations of casting the change agent into the role of healer and the target into that of patient. On the edge of the treatment approaches to behavioural problems are those which are described as 'remedial', based on the clear idea of putting right something which has gone wrong.

The interesting point about this is that most of the approaches are defined by the perception of the change agents, and the techniques they use in all cases are of decidedly similar nature. For, as they would probably be very reluctant to admit, there are only an extremely limited number of ways in which human beings can be approached in terms of changing their behaviour.

In any situation where one person intervenes in the lives of others, that person, by the action of intervention and subsequent interaction, creates costs and rewards for both parties. If those costs and rewards are consciously used to achieve certain ends, the process becomes one of reward and punishment. Intervention to achieve intended change, because of its conscious and deliberate nature, must therefore employ punishment and reward.

This may appear to be a huge generalisation until the nature of punishment and reward is examined in more detail than is usual in the common usage of the words. To increase an individual's costs in an interaction as a means of bringing pressure to bear is a form of coercion. The punishment element is related to a form of implied or direct threat that behaviour must change in the way which has been indicated or this punishing effect, whatever it may be, will occur, remain and may increase.

Such a situation may be brought about by the change agent expressing displeasure. If the person concerned has reason to believe that such displeasure is deleterious to his or her well being then he or she will seek to remove it. Parents often imply to their children that they will withdraw their love from them unless their behaviour is modified in defined ways. Much human behaviour is, and always has been, modelled and shaped by the threat of the loss of some factor which the individual values, whether it be affection, esteem, material things, freedom and so on.

One of the reasons why change agents are often very concerned about the nature of the relationships they make with their clients is precisely because they have learned and indeed have been taught, that at both the affectionate and the power ends of the relationship, the perceived ability to reward and punish is extremely likely. But however 'natural' a professional change relationship may be, the very fact that it exists – the presence of the change agent in the lives and context of his or her clients – possesses all the possibilities of reward and punishment. There are irritant qualities of intrusion which clients may well wish to rid themselves of and thus discover that the means of doing so is to conform to the requirements of the change process with which they are being presented. There are also factors of liking, of fear of consequence, the use of time, of energy, all of which can be either penalising or rewarding according to situation and use. Even where change agents have a personal mandate from their target person, these factors will still operate.

Many contracts between change agents and targets indeed do carry not only an element of compulsion and discipline but also strong implications of punishment if commitment to the process and performance within them does not meet the desired standards.

Intervention aims, in part, to generate feelings and states of mind which change agents deem appropriate to the achievement of intended change.

15 Methods of Intervention
(2) Group Focus

First it is clear that demonstrable changes, both in how people feel about themselves and in how others see them, do occur as a result of attending a group. These changes are sometimes on the small side, and they tend to fade over a few months.

Oakley (1980: 88)

Human groups appear to be aperiodic systems and the process of leadership, from whatever source it arises, is a process of the imposition of some form of order.

No human system can be regarded in the same way as a physical system for the simple reason that the component elements of human systems are conscious and possess the capacity to become aware of any system of which they are a part, and thus able to make deliberate efforts to influence it. Thus when order is found in a group it can be assumed that it comes from two principal sources: (a) the ideology and intentions of any leader; and (b) the experiences, expectations and social conditioning of the group members.

The developmental sequences which have been recorded in groups and promulgated as one of the very few apparently cohesive theories about group behaviour, are deterministic and predicate essentially identical starting points or initial conditions. This cannot, of course, be true. So developmental sequences are not universal patterns, and perhaps would not be seen as patterns at all if it were not for the similarity in any community of the two influences noted above.

Tiny differences in input could quickly become overwhelming differences in output.

Gleick (1988: 8)

The process of using specifically created groups, or of adapting groups already in existence, to pursue the goal of individual change has many forms and many theoretical orientations, but, equally, all such groups have many and very basic similarities. There is also a great deal of supposed differentiation in approaches and a considerable amount of this is based, not so much upon discrete and discernible elements of difference, but upon a process of coining a different terminology which then becomes the hallmark of a school or particular approach.

If we examine closely what actually constitutes the process of creating change in individuals by working with them in groups, there are only three areas of logical interest: the individuals who comprise the groups; the individuals who create the groups; and the actual effects which being in a group can have.

I have called working with groups an individual change effort for the simple reason that all that exists are individual human beings and putting them into groups or using groups of which they are already members as a unit of change, cannot affect that basic point. Being a member of a group may, and does, affect the way an individual will behave because he or she will have perceptions of what is to be gained from being a member and, equally, perceptions of what will need to be given to the group in order to obtain these gains. The pressures and influences which a group can exert are only effective in achieving ends in so far as the individual members of the group perceive these pressures and influences as valid, either in the short or the long term, and are prepared to bear the required costs. Thus descriptions of groups as separately existing entities have a large element of truth in them because that is how it appears. But the ultimate factors which determine how a group functions are the human individual elements of which it is, often transiently, composed.

In this sense there are two things to consider: that the influence of the group on the individual is indirect, and that the group itself changes and develops in particular ways, probably as its members become clearer about what commitment to the group they actually want to provide.

If we look at the factor of indirect influence first, we will note that it has several complicated factors. All human beings are born into and grow up in groups, sometimes large, sometimes small. They enter into many groups as life progresses, and most people accept that they are the natural manifestations of the social nature of human beings and of the existence of societies – whatever their fundamental difference of culture. Thus a basic familiarity with operating in groups is formed, which is not necessarily a knowledge of groups per se, but an experience – from which some learn well and others do not. Without doubt, the fact of being in groups is a major factor in influencing the way the individual develops, but to a large extent most human beings remain ignorant of the extent of that influence – except in special circumstances, and often with hindsight – for their perception tends to be skewed by the concept of individuality which, at least in the West, reigns supreme.

The arguments of change agents for the use of groups as instruments of change has often been founded on the idea that if 'natural' groups are so fundamental in the formation of the individual in ways which are accepted as natural and seldom thought about or questioned, then the same processes generated in specific group situations should be efficacious in changing selected aspects of the individual's behaviour. Thus some groups are formed on the basis that individuals who are to be changed will become members and, with minimal guidance, will be subjected to similar pressures and influences in a similar situation to those group processes that formed them in the first place, and will thus be changed.

One of the major pressures is often stated to be the need to be accepted by significant others, and indeed there is considerable evidence that human beings need a constant flow of interaction with others to support them in the maintenance of their identity – it often does not seem to matter a great deal what the nature of this interaction may be, but it must exist. The fear of isolation is perhaps the most potent human dread, although largely unacknowledged.

Obviously people cannot just be placed in groups and left for those groups to work the magic of change. There are far too many possible outcomes. The role of the change agent in this respect is to create or adapt a group and to set up a series of procedures and goals which will tend to ensure that those aspects of a group which are known to affect certain areas of behaviour are the ones which will actually occur, and to actively inhibit others which will not. The problem, as with all change efforts, is that the targets are intelligent individuals and able to make decisions based on past experience and an idiosyncratic understanding of what is happening around them. Which is one of the reasons why group workers may often make the mistake of assuming that, because all human beings have considerable experience of 'natural' groups, they also have a clear perception of the ways in which groups operate.

The range of group use, which seems to be so wide and various, can actually be contained within two fairly simple areas that are widely recognised but have several different names. One contains those groups which are used directly to influence the individual, and the other is concerned to influence individuals indirectly by generating the group as an operative instrument. As the first of these seems to contradict the idea that the group is an indirect form of influence, we must deal with that issue first.

In essence it is a simple situation. If a group is composed of individuals with similar problems, difficulties or needs, and the change agent, in this case the group leader or director, works with each individual member in turn in the context of the group, not only will the direct one-to-one work between member and leader be effective (at least, as much as it would if they were not in the group), but the spin-off of the group presence means that those members not directly involved at any moment can learn and gain insight from the process. Also those group pressures which are involved in a group where the members have a similar relationship to one another, defined by their relationship to the directive leader, can become active.

An example of such a process is what is recorded as constituting psychoanalytic group therapy, which involves the treatment of individuals within the group context. The leader is referred to as a 'conductor' and the emotional transferences of members to the conductor are used to highlight latent motivation and reveal hidden psychopathology. The processes dealt with include defence mechanisms, resistance and the unconscious. Such groups are usually open, members can leave when they are 'cured'; and group processes may be seen as irrelevant.

There are degrees in this process ranging from where the actual group processes are minimal and the contextual effect is largely the perception of similarity and the probable development of insight, through to the active involvement of both the group and its interactive processes. The resource factor of prime importance for such groups is inevitably the leader, but the resources of the group can be used with different degrees of involvement. Thus at the opposite end of the spectrum is group psychoanalytic therapy, in which the individual is still the object of treatment but the group is also used as a therapeutic agency. Communication and sharing experience are stressed; the group has a social structure and a problem orientation. Attempts are made to improve perception, to stimulate interaction, to bring about the creation of multiple transference and the relinquishing of defences.

The second large area alters the focus from the individual to the resources of the group, and equally changes the focus of the group leader to that of a creator of a group where those member resources can be used with maximum benefit. This approach does not deny the group leader as a resource in a contributive sense as well, but shifts the locus of power to the group members. The ultimate form of such an instrumental group is one which can be defined as a self-help unit, where members are the resources that the group as a whole uses to achieve its ends.

Examples of such groups are to be found as sensitivity training groups, basic encounter groups and others which fall into the class of 'experiential' groups. These groups attempt to facilitate emotional expressiveness and generate feelings of belonging, have a norm of self-disclosure and a process of sampling personal behaviour, the sanctioning of interpersonal comparisons and, finally, of sharing responsibility for leadership and direction with any appointed leader.

Most of the group approaches discussed so far have 'change' defined as some form of treatment. But for many other kinds of groups the change may well be focused on support or on learning. Essentially the dichotomy of 'group-centred' or 'leader-centred' still obtains, but more as representing the opposite ends of a spectrum of possible forms than as antithetical forms. Most groups are of no pure form but vary in terms of both ends of the spectrum, so are partly directive and partly non-directive in the same group at different times.

But, as already stated, it is possible to define a number of factors which arise within all groups and which are enhanced or diminished by any particular group practice. It is these factors which change agents use in their attempts to produce selected and intended change within the context of a group. These universal factors can be defined as occupying five large areas:

1. The ways in which members respond to their membership in particular groups.

2. The relationship which exists and/or develops between the individual and the group.

3. The characteristics of the group.

4. The nature of the group purpose.

5. The nature and influence of leadership.

Because whatever changes take place within groups are dependent upon the operation of these five factors, we must examine their component parts in some detail. The effectiveness of group change efforts depends to an enormous extent not so much on the actual existence of these factors, which is an indisputable fact, but on the degree to which change agents can select and use them to obtain their intended goals of deliberate change.

Conditions of Responding
(Commitment, Public and Private Acceptance)

Two components are of major interest here:

(i) member commitment; and

(ii) the quality of member acceptance.

Member commitment

Essentially, a group is a system of which the elements are individuals. Systems require energy in order to operate, in the case of human groups that energy has only one possible source, and that can be described as the commitment of those involved in the group – the members, the leaders and to some limited extent those interested in the group who, while not a direct part of the group, are part of the larger system in which the group is embedded.

The element of commitment may not be rational or logical and may be based upon some wholly unsupported belief, but in most cases it is dependent on the individual believing that, by committing time and energy and presence to a particular group, something which he or she considers to be a reward or satisfaction will either in the short or long term (or both) be forthcoming. The nature of this perception does not have to be based in reality, though it is more effective in producing long-term commitment if it is.

The problem for change agents is how the necessary level of commitment can be developed – in some cases the argument is almost circular. It is not possible to discover the benefits of group membership without commitment to a group; commitment is not entirely feasible without knowing whether the cost and rewards the group will offer will prove largely beneficial.

Quality of member acceptance

The quality of member acceptance of the group, which is also positively related to the degree of commitment, is usually presented as a dichotomy. Simply stated this implies either public conformity or private acceptance. The distinction is crucial.

- Public conformity arises when individuals find themselves in groups in an involuntary capacity; or, having joined voluntarily, find that the group is not to their liking but they are constrained, either physically, morally or psychologically, from leaving. As a security measure they perform what actions are required of them, but if and when they are released from the pressure of that particular group system, they immediately slough off any appearance of conformity to the group's norms.

- Private acceptance implies that members accept the group's norms and requirements because they want to and because they believe them to be beneficial. If the group's influence were to be removed from such members they would have integrated the group norms and would continue to follow them as far as they were able.

Again these are two ends of a spectrum of behaviour on which the individual group member may register at significantly different points at different times during his or her membership. The change agent may well have some difficulty in discovering which aspect each member is presenting, but it must be clearly stated that without some degree of private acceptance the element of change could be diminishingly small.

The Relationship Which Exists and/or Develops Between the Individual and the Group

There are many factors involved in this area. Among the most important are:

(a) The level of attraction the group has for its members.

(b) The status of individual members within the group.

(c) The level of interdependence of members.

(d) The characteristics, abilities, experience and attitudes of members.

(e) The nature and quality of interpersonal relationships.

(f) The 'cohesive' nature of the group – the factor of inclusiveness.

The relationship of an individual to a group changes throughout the life of the contact, from a state of not existing on joining, to whatever degree of involvement and commitment is developed later.

There is no sure or certain way of deciding what constitutes satisfaction for individuals, indeed the only real clue available is the individual's behaviour. But given that access to a group is possible, and departure likewise, those members who stay can usually be regarded as deriving more from attending the group than they would from other available uses of their time and energy, whatever the idiosyncratic nature of the individual assessment may be.

Nevertheless, even for those who stay the relationship may not be essentially positive or productive and, as we have seen, the dynamic energy which is the group's power source comes from the commitment of the members.

The fascinating fact about these relationships as far as change agents are concerned is that they are dependent on the perceptions of individual members. It is one thing for change agents to create a situation in which various individuals will meet and interact and to give them guidance about how they may use and benefit from that interaction, and entirely another, because of individual differences, to be certain that it will proceed in intended directions.

The Characteristics of the Group

If, temporarily, we regard a group as an existing entity in its own right, it is possible to describe its characteristics – i.e. those qualities, processes and appearances which distinguish it from other groups. Again there are many such characteristics recorded, amongst which may be found:

(a) The composition of the group.

(b) The numerical size of the group.

(c) The norms, standards and values which the group has established, particularly those most different from the general values of the society in which the group is founded.

(d) The environment in which the group operates.

(e) The resources of all kinds which the group possesses.

(f) The time; particularly that time which the group is allocated to function, both in individual sessions and over its existence.

(g) The quality and degree of group processes, especially the interactive processes.

(h) The structure of the group.

(i) The developmental sequences and processes through which the group appears to be passing.

It must be obvious that change agents operating in groups attempt to select and/or create a unit possessing those characteristics which they consider to be most effective in pursuing their goals of intended change. Where choice is not possible, the consequences have to be fed into the intended change plan and modifications made, either in the process, or in the nature of the goals which are deemed to be achievable.

The perceived characteristics of a group are directly related to how attractive it appears to its members and thus to the degree of commitment they may give to it. Indeed it is relevant at this point to put forward what most people who work with groups eventually discover empirically, even if they know of it rationally, which is that all the parts of group process that we can define (and some we cannot) are not independent entities, but wholly and almost totally interdependent, so that changes in one inevitably produce changes in others.

Most of the components listed here are well documented in terms of the effects produced by variations in their intensity, quality and presence – which is not surprising for they are all monitored through the medium of human experience.

The Nature of the Group's Purpose

I have used this form of expression rather than that of 'group task' for the simple reason that, while all groups have a purpose, some groups are much more specifically task-oriented than others. The components of interest may be listed as follows:

(a) The competence of members to achieve the group purpose.

(b) The confidence of members in the performance of their roles.

(c) The perceived difficulties involved.

(d) The goals of the group, specifically the clarity of their expression.

(e) The efficacy of the group's decision-making process.

(f) The nature and quality of the information available to the group and the competence of the group in processing it.

(g) The ability of the group to translate information into action.

There is inevitably some degree of overlap in these components and, indeed, most of the factors which are discussed here have some bearing on how, or even whether, a group achieves its purpose. For instance, groups which are successful become more attractive both to their members and to others. Ambiguity affects confidence; difficulty affects judgement. It is usual to discover that group members are more susceptible to group pressure if they find the group task difficult than if it is easy. It is only common sense that, if a member discovers that the objective towards which the group is struggling is one of great importance to him or her as an individual, such a member will have more incentive to make a greater commitment and to conform more exactingly in order to achieve that worthwhile goal.

The Nature and Influence of Leadership

The purpose of leadership is to achieve the ends for which the group was established or adapted. There are two principal areas of leader influence, which may be crudely defined as intended and unintended. In the case of the former, the leader's task is to generate a unit of individuals in such a way that they work together to achieve as many of the group's goals as are possible. To this end the leader, as the person possessing information and experience about how groups function, selects and consciously seeks to influence the production by the group under his or her influence and/or direction, of behaviour which will best meet the group's collective and individual needs.

In the second area of influence, the term 'unintended' is used to mean influence which is not consciously applied but which, frequently, is amazingly effective in generating results. It is a truism of group workers that if any conflict is perceived by the group members between the statements of intent of the group leader and his or her actual behaviour in those intended areas, the latter will be taken as a much truer indication of intentions than the verbal statements. Indeed, some authorities would aver that the major influence factors of leadership are those which are of this unconscious nature.

The change agent operating through groups uses his or her knowledge of the factors which influence group behaviour and, by a process of selection, guidance, direction, encouragement, coercion, and so on, attempts to influence that group's development. Whatever the group may have been assembled or adapted to work on, the process of group work is essentially one of causing the development of the necessary skills, information and resources within the individual members of the group in order that they can use the particular events and processes which occur within a collection of individuals in close interactive proximity over a period of time, to achieve their intended ends.

As I hope to show later, some intended ends are much easier to achieve in group situations than others and also, however clearly described and tabulated group processes may be, the increment of predictability in excess of that available about individual behaviour is not necessarily very great. This should occasion no vast surprise because a group, in the sense of being an instrument generated or adapted to bring about intended change, is only a tighter and more visible and restricted version of the group pressures to which we are all subject in society all the time and which, if we are truthful, make our concepts of highly individual behaviour somewhat inaccurate.

16 Methods of Intervention
(3) Special Groups and Organisations

But in between the context of ideas and the context of atoms and molecules (or even that of the genetic code) there is a single, but enormous, level of organisation which is missing: the socio-economic context of human reality. And this level of organisation contains a parameter which cannot be found in physics, in biology, in information science, in language, in ideas, or in myths viewed as synchronic systems of oppositions: the punctuation of the system by the power of some of its parts to exploit the other parts (including 'nature' itself).

Wilden (1980: 9–10)

The difference between 'special' groups, usually referred to as 'natural', and created groups lies mainly in two factors: the purpose for which groups are created; and the length of time such groups have been an accepted part of society. Thus intervention in special groups has the implication of working with a unit which had a purposeful and accepted existence prior to being 'adapted' as a unit of intended change.

Here we will look at the intervention processes most commonly used in these groups, which involve such factors as inter-member exposure; conversion of the manner of regarding the group from a natural to a working group; insight generation; learning, and so on.

I intend to have only a brief look at intended change in organisations through the processes of management, for the principal remit of this book, as outlined earlier, is to explore a particular kind of change – that is, intended change used by members of such professions as can be classified as 'change agents'.

In this respect, managers and the processes of management can only be accommodated somewhat uncomfortably under the remit, and borrowing Amitai Etzioni's term which he applied to social work, they can be regarded as 'semi change agents'. For although managers may employ some of the same techniques and methods, based upon some of the same theoretical assumptions, as bonafide change agents – especially those who work with groups rather than with individuals – and although they may seek to change individuals and/or groups within the system, change is not their main function. Indeed, their functions are many, but the most important ones are usually concerned with the creation and maintenance of a system and structure within which it should be possible to maximise the creation of the organisation's end product, whether this be the outcome of an industrial process, a commercial venture or a service system.

Such changes as are made managerially are basically directed at maintaining or increasing the functional efficiency of the organisation and are more often than not occasioned by a perception of changes taking place outside the organisation itself, such as social changes in living conditions, methods of working, competition, innovation in the production and use of new ideas and technology, new institutions, changes in policy, in law, in prosperity, consumer changes and changes in the habits of communities.

Certainly the changes managers can make are 'intended' in the sense in which the term is employed here, and they do affect the individual members of organisations in which they are introduced – indeed in some organisations vast changes are brought about by changes induced in one or two key personnel. But, in essence, the intended change is directed almost exclusively at securing change in the organisation itself, and the change in individuals is a step in the process. This is often compared with a somewhat similar process in groups, where the small organisation is deliberately changed with the absolute intent of creating clearly desirable and beneficial change in the individual members of those groups. The basic theory about the link between individual and system may be the same, but the ends to which it is put in practice are significantly different.

However, some organisations are managed along group lines where small component units have a degree of autonomy within the system and bear the same relationship to it as that which exists between the individual members and their group.

In large organisations, one problem for managers who wish to bring about change consists of the differences of allegiance and perception about the functions of the organisation which exist in different parts of the organisation, and which often are manifested as different levels of commitment and an inability to see a common aim.

It must be noted that the role of management consultant equates closest to that of change agent, as it is directly an intervention with intent to change in the selected organisation. Once again the theoretical background, and indeed many of the techniques used by such consultants, are based upon the same understandings of group behaviour as those used in the world of group work and therapy.

I think the point about management responding to outside pressures can be amply demonstrated by taking a brief look at some of the latest texts on such management in the Health Service; in education; in voluntary organisations, and in other organisational systems. In almost all of them, the starting point is establishing what changes are necessary because of the change in pressures from without – usually a direct reference to resources, both human and material. In many of these organisations, traditional management was provided by professional members of the organisation taking up the role of management on the valid assumption that the professional would actually understand what it was that would be required for other professionals to function effectively in the organisation.

This tended to ignore that management required special skills, amongst which knowledge of the professional needs of organisational members was only a part. So much more stress now being placed upon the need for all organisations to be efficient, in the sense that they offer value for money, has brought into stark contrast the professional caring ethic and the efficiency demanded by the realisation that in such organisations as the Health Service there is actually no foreseeable limit to what could be employed in the way of resources to meet what looks like an ever growing and probably insatiable demand for services. The static nature of much early management is not able to cope with demands and changes which, in Tofler's (1970) eyes, are occurring with greater rapidity than ever before in our history.

The literature is full of such items as *Managing Scarcity* (Klein, Day and Redmayne, 1996); concepts like 'managing the internal market' and understanding the process of contracts; the development of strategies and holistic approaches (Preedy, Glatter and Levacic, 1996).

If some similarity between management and intended change as performed by change agents is to be found, it resides in the fact that management in organisations occupies much the same position vis-a-vis intended change as the individual or group–recognising that something is wrong and that survival changes are needed.

Thus we can argue that intervention in organisations has two main approaches:

1. A structural logical approach – which involves the rational planning of organisational change based upon some concept of the function of an organisation. It is usually an imposed change, though varying degrees of consultation are employed ranging all the way from 'apparent' consultation – in which the process is actually a placatory facade designed to act as an emollient to the expected response to decisions already taken – to full consultation – which implies a total involvement in the consideration of all decision-making processes of all those directly and indirectly involved.

   Such changes are regarded as structural in that they tend to allocate roles whose chief function is to meet the assessed needs of the organisation, thus the occupants of such roles will perform in ways expected of them by those with power to control the way the organisation functions.

2. An approach which may be termed 'interrelational', in that it considers the humanity and needs of the human elements in the organisational structure as being as fundamental to the successful performance of an organisation as its structure. Organisation Development is a prime example of this kind of approach. It has some of the purpose of intervention in special groups in that its main task is one of exposure of practice based upon the assumption that the individual components of an organisation may hold and operate to quite different strategies – which are divergent one from another and from the overall purposes of the total organisation – while remaining wholly unaware that this is so. It is claimed that the exposure of these differences will lead to their diminution or removal, thus increasing the functional efficiency of the organisation.

In smaller groups, like families, work groups, gangs, committees, friendship groups, teams, etc., because they have all been created or grown to achieve ends which are, or were at the point of origin, very clearly defined, the same factors of use and habit often obliterate the consequences for their members and the group as a whole of their actions. Such practices are frequently described as constituting the 'norms' of the group. Once established, often for very practical and pressing reasons, they are seldom reconsidered, although they may be the very factors which are handicapping the group's efficiency. Argyle (1972) once described the process of the function of norms as being established as the approved way of doing things and referring to matters which are the group's main activities.

Because such groups have reasonably well-defined goals, what the change agent has to work with are the precise ways in which the group functions in attempting to achieve them. Crucial to this process is the technique of exposing what is actually already taking place, so that comparisons can be made with what the group members believe is happening. This often reveals such discrepancy of belief and practice that most of the functional deficiencies of a group can be laid at its door. The option has now been created for action to be taken to change to a greater consonance between belief and function. In essence, the change agent's principal theme is that a clear understanding of what is actually happening in a situation offers the choice of what to do next, whether such an option is actually taken or not.

The difference between groups which are specifically created for the purpose of examining the problems of the members of those groups, and those groups which were created or which arose to achieve other ends, dictates the approaches which are used. If an organisation or group is not functioning well, it can be restructured in ways which are deemed to be more functionally effective for its end (that is, its end product), which is its reason for existence. But it is still the individuals who comprise that organisation or group who have to change if the group itself is to change. Where, because of the function and structure of the organisation or group, structural change cannot take place, the alteration of the attitudes and behaviour of the component members has to be the focus of organisational and group change.

One of the mainstays of the arguments in this book has been that intended change, directed or worked at with an individual or group, has much of the quality of working in the dark unless rather more can be known of the context in which the individual or group resides. This is particularly true of those contextual elements which initiate support and maintain those behavioural patterns to which change efforts are to be directed. An inexact analogy is with the treatment of plants designated as weeds. Their visible manifestation can be removed or changed quite easily, but if the whole of the non-visible supportive system of roots and nourishment is not also dealt with, the 'weed' will very quickly re-establish itself.

The initiating, supporting and maintaining functions of context are most visible in small created groups, for the simple reason that it is exactly the influence of these elements which the group has been established to use to procure the intended change desired by both group members and group convenors. The purpose of creating a group with a specific membership and goals is precisely to be able to exercise some greater element of control over the effects and intensity of operation of those self-same elements of initiation, support and maintenance, plus the extra elements of exposure to scrutiny which do not exist in ordinary social milieux. If the processes which maintain behaviour can be made visible, some element of choice is possible over the effects they produce which was not possible when their existence may not even have been suspected.

This poses the question that, if these elements of control – when exposed – can be used to change behavioural patterns, how can something similar in terms of revealing them be employed when a group is not created for precisely that purpose but exists in its own right for what is often defined as 'natural' purposes – that is, for long established and traditional reasons?

In the large sphere of national politics, a prime example of these maintaining factors – which in this case constantly frustrate the process of change – can be seen in Northern Ireland, where traditional ideas and the power of history hold the separate groups in a constant state of inability to work together for the general good. Though in many senses typical of the resistant effect of the maintaining elements, what is particularly illuminating here is the clarity with which they have been exposed over many years and the immense difficulty which still exists in effecting change.

The three major elements involved are the republicans, the unionists and the British government. This simple tripartite arrangement is complicated by two other very powerful maintaining factors – namely belief and history. The ideas held, cherished in fact, by the two sides in Ulster are based upon idiosyncratic interpretations of their history. Which of these views of the history of Ulster and its relationship with the rest of Ireland and with Britain is true is of little or no consequence, for, essentially, all history, as we have seen, is an interpretation of whatever facts and events are available for scrutiny. What is fundamental here is that different, in some cases vastly different, and opposed views of the events of the past are not only held by the different parties, but are implicitly believed to be the truth. What is more, they are passed from generation to generation within the lives of families and in social institutions and, moreover, are used as the basis for the interpretation of current events – thus compounding and intensifying widely differing viewpoints.

Such a tradition fosters and maintains a series of attitudes, not just to the past, but also to the present. Thus the standards and values against which events in the present, and those proposed for the future, are assessed are radically different and, because change of any lasting value has to be based to an enormous extent upon agreement and acceptance of agreement by those involved, a position of deadlock and ascerbation of the situation is the most likely outcome.

There is nothing particularly exceptional about a situation like this, it is a world-wide phenomenon – holding as true in the relationship between individuals and between small groups as it does between nations and communities. Such attitudes have amazing force and are maintained by powerful emotions including fear, hatred, suspicion and almost always an extremely strong and pervading sense of injustice both past and present, and to come. Thus all events, intents and purposes, behaviours, suggestions, ideas and actions are interpreted in this light. To the uninvolved observer, such interpretations appear at best to be illogical and at worst deliberately destructive and malevolent. This often provokes a reaction from such observers of condemnation and criticism, which usually seems to confirm to those holding the attitudes under attack that they are eminently justified and correct in believing that they are unjustly treated, little understood and also right to maintain their hostile behaviour.

As we have noted earlier, the two main forms of intervention, in very bold and simple terms, involve either some form of force to effect change or some form of facilitation; the latter involving some kind of agreed change of those situational factors amenable to change, or a change of the ways in which the situation is perceived. In many national situations, due to the apparently intractable nature of the differences in perception which already exist and which, as we have seen, are of long standing and are very powerfully backed – being an essential part of every child's background while growing up – force in the form of physical violence, ranging from individual attacks to all-out war, is almost always inevitable. The purpose, like ethnic cleansing, is to remove those with different views, or to conquer or subjugate them.

The alternative of the use of logic, of the gradual perception that other views of the same situations may be equally valid, or that a third or other view might even be better than any of those traditionally held, is a very difficult process to establish. But, like all such processes, it has to start from some element of willingness to try, which in most cases implies that the change agent must come from outside the factions involved and must have some degree of credibility with them. This in itself is the well-known, much tried and often maligned process of arbitration – which is in essence an attempt to turn away from those elements which maintain conflict to any elements where some degree of agreement is possible. The assumption of the change agent must always be that some such area of possible agreement exists, and if it does not it must be created. The assumption must also be that in the process of negotiating the small area of agreement, the opposing factions will assume different positions, status and value in each other's context. It is known that con-textual invasions can generate a change in perception of those involved, which may either add extra material to that which already exists and maintain hostility, or may reduce and redirect such perceptions. The change agent's purpose is to attempt to ensure that more of the latter occurs than the former.

The other elements involved which have a strong supportive and nurturing role for a particular outlook are pride, belief, identity, justice and tradition. In themselves such elements are neither right nor wrong, it is the use to which they are put in individual situa-tions which may turn them into supporters of hostility and main-tainers of intransigence. But it has to be kept in mind by change agents that initiating change can, in certain circumstances, clearly be seen as an attack upon such elements; thus the problem for the change agents is one of being able to initiate change which appears neither to diminish pride, nor to reduce the security of identity, nor add to the sense of grievance and injustice. Equally, changes which, if used, would tend to enhance the supportive nature of these elements would be self-defeating, for they would essentially serve to reinforce that which they sought to change.

Essentially, therefore, the methods of intervention in organisa-tions are usually largely concerned with exposure. By that I mean that the processes by which the organisation functions, the beliefs it espouses, its history, current and future development have to be brought from a situation of uncritical acceptance (which may well be reinforced by very powerful emotions), into a relatively unbiased scrutiny and, moreover, related to the consequences continuing acceptance produces, preferably designated by those wholly un-involved with the organisation in the usual course of its life.

The important first step in this particular process has always to be one of acquiring acceptance by the organisation that there is some need for an enquiry into its processes, to be undertaken by someone who has no vested interest in either the organisation itself, or those with whom it may be in conflict or competition. The opportunity for this initial step to occur tends to arise when the organisation, or some powerful part of it, has reason to believe that it is not performing as well as might have been expected. If internal investigation has also discovered no ascertainable or acceptable cause for this falling off in performance, the request for outside assessment may easily follow.

The strength of the supporting and maintaining elements and of their emotional back-up will be directly related to the degree of resistance to exposure which will inevitably arise. Two things will then present as possibilities:

- It may become clear that what parts of the organisation actually do and what they and other parts of the organisation believe they are doing are poles apart.

- It may subject the organisation to an interpretation of its own behaviour in the terms of an unbiased observer.

Inevitably this kind of process involves threat; not least because it may assail beliefs which are illogically founded, but which form the basis of an identity and of security within the organisation; as well as from the perception that change will involve some considerable expenditure of energy and time. In other words, the perceived costs will be high. As I have already shown, in whatever social situation change agents operate, if perceived costs, as assessed by those who are to pay them, are higher than perceived gains, unless there are hidden gains which can be set against those costs under consideration, they will not be incurred.

Thus involved with the process of exposure has to come some evaluation of the future gains which can be made from the changes which appear to be necessary. The estimate of gain and reward is a very difficult business because, as there is no common evaluative standard, the perception of some rewards is essentially idiosyncratic and usually not very visible. What actually constitutes a high level of satisfaction for one group may have little or even negative value for another.

Like all change situations where force or compulsion producing public conformity for the duration of the compulsion is not an essential element, organisational change appears to require some level of commitment to the process which is not given and sustained by external duress.

17 Issues and Problems

> Experience teaches us that almost all methods are helpful for a
> short time in some way or other.
>
> Jaspers (1963: 830)

This section on the processes and theories of intervention raises
more questions than it provides answers; in fact it would be true to
say that it is a chapter of questions.

For instance, if we ask the question, why do people need to be
changed?, the answers may well cover the facts of suffering which
has to be relieved; of the poor use of resources; of not conforming
to the essential rules of socially accepted behaviour; of personal
dissatisfaction such as a feeling of having missed out in some way
– the list is possibly endless.

Again, the question can be asked why is it essential that the
nature and quality of those theories which have consistently been
used to underpin change efforts should be explored?, the answer
may well be because the need to change individuals is so important
and universal (see the answer given above), then the process of
change needs to be guided and underwritten by as good an understanding of human behaviour as it is possible to achieve. It is
possible that in the complexities of human behaviour the ineffi-
ciency of change efforts can be masked, and if they have been,
then it would be as well to know.

A great problem lies in the next question. Does logic necessarily
posit that if an intended change process within the context of
human experience actually works, its mechanisms are susceptible
of analysis and of understanding? If this is true do we then have to
accept that a process which is claimed to work must be based upon
concepts which are valid? But we know that the concepts upon
which much change effort is based are unprovable by the direct
application of logic. We also know that the follow-up studies of the
effects of intervention have been very erratic and bedevilled by a
large number of factors, not the least of which is the non-objective
nature of most of the available evidence.

But essentially it cannot be logical to think that it is possible to deliberately change something like human behaviour in defined and relatively precise directions when it is not clear how such behaviour arrived at its present state nor what has maintained its existence.

The difficulty of verifying assertions about human relations gives wide scope to ulterior motives,and provides immunity for the purveyors of false information.

Andreski (1974: 39)

What emerges from any consideration of interventive action is the substantial connection between the change agent's theoretical conceptions and the way in which change efforts are formulated. For instance, if the change agent believes that human behaviour is largely determined genetically, then he or she is compelled by logic to direct his or her interventive actions to explicit areas of behaviour in the here and now.

Such a domination of action by theoretical ideas has the effect of making interventive actions more conditioned by ideas than by what might be described as the actuality of human situations. Thus if theory is so powerful a conditioner of action, it is only proper that the nature of the ideas which comprise it should be considered very carefully. Are we in the process of performing the extremely serious task of interfering in other people's lives on the basis of an understanding of the elements of human behaviour which are not as substantial as they seem or, indeed, as many would have us believe?

Are we right to put trust in interventive behaviour based in ideas which, while they may have an essentially logical structure once a basic premise is accepted as true, have no way of proving that the basic premise is itself true or able to be validated? Is this a complaint which is unnecessary because the basic premises are really only 'as if' propositions and the essential elements of human behaviour are in fact unknowable? It may well be that in the present state of knowledge these essentially very powerful conditioning theories are all that we can expect and that what we can achieve by using them is the best that is available.

One of the problems facing change agents concerns the way in which information about the processes of intervention is correlated and accepted. Ideas about intervention processes are promulgated, refined, added to; some pieces are accepted and others rejected; sections from entirely different sources are eclectically combined on a pragmatic basis. But the evidence of factual and provable data appears to remain at a roughly constant level.

This 'evidence', though lacking statistical validity, comprises one main area of concern, which is that successive generations of potential and intending change agents in all disciplines make the same mistakes as their predecessors, produce roughly the same kind of successes and failures and suffer precisely the same kinds of frustrations.

In the search for 'new' ideas which will make either a 'breakthrough' or at least introduce some increment of certainty about what they do, change agents accept statements of 'findings' and 'experience' relatively uncritically and use them as the basis upon which to build further ideas. By 'uncritically accepting', I refer to the use of ideas, which, while very relevant in the context in which they originated, which may be unsuitable when applied in other situations where the context is different.

There appears to be little consideration of the fact that even minimal differences in initial conditions in the practical application of theoretical ideas may produce huge variations in outcome, and indeed initial conditions may often not be just different but actually alien.

Take, for example, one of the few widely accepted and often repeated paradigms of groups, that groups 'develop' in an organic way demonstrating recognisable sequential stages in the process.

The very use of the word 'development' implies a process, and in the writings of individuals working with and theorising about groups there has appeared a remarkable similarity of presentation over many years. If we examine this phenomenon of similarity three possible explanations occur.

1. Groups of all kinds actually develop and change organically in a recognisable sequence of stages in the same way that plants and other vital organisms do.

2. Observed growth patterns occur as part of a process of familiarisation of the individual members of a group to each other in a manner which is common to all human societies though with different emphases; the observed differences in sequence and stress then being due to the differences in the communities and societies from which the members come.

3. The ideas and beliefs, not just of the group members, but also, and perhaps more strongly, of those who take on the leadership

roles, impress and mould the group's processes in particular ways, quite a large number of which will be influences which are not directly under the conscious control of those leaders. There may also be an element of pressure from the organisation of which the group is part.

Yet most, if not all, of the writing about group development wittingly or otherwise cites only the concept of organic growth. But this is not surprising when it is realised that such a stress is entirely compatible with the widely held concept that a group comprised of individuals gradually becomes an entity in its own right in which the dynamics are of a different order from what could be expected of a collection of individuals merely operating in each other's presence. Admittedly in the more complex forms of statement about group development, sequences are no longer presented as a straight lineal process but one which can be beset by reverse sequences, stagnation and even deterioration. Nevertheless group workers are led to expect that a sequence, complex or simple, will actually occur if a group stays in existence long enough. Thus a strong basis for a self-fulfilling prophecy will occur.

Organic sequence is common in group-work literature but it occurs in other forms of intervention also. There is a considerable difference between propounding the certainty that a sequence of steps will occur and stating that there is a probability that certain events are likely to occur, or even that there is a reasonable expectation of their occurrence. For instance, to assert that the experience of grief over loss of a loved one will follow a sequence of events as a probability is one thing but it cannot be affirmed that it is either a certainty in either occurrence or, if it does, in the sequence that will be followed. There are so many influencing factors involved that the sequence which is usually quoted may not even be a statistical probability.

The problem which arises from this lack of the 'real' or probable nature of the developmental sequence is that change processes are based on it as if the sequence was a reality, a property as it were, of a distinct entity called a group. The concept that a group 'grows' naturally is thus important because intervention in what is believed to be a growth or developmental process is intervention which attempts to mould and guide based on a false assumption. The processes which are being used are not the essential and unique processes of an entity called a group but merely the production of societal habits and social relationship behaviour in a group context.

If there is no predictive theory of change processes but merely a collection of experiences elegantly refined, what can we adduce as the value of experience? What is the value of intuitive understanding – those flashes of insight? Even if such things are effective, what value can any form of theory have for them? If history is not governed by inexorable laws, what standing has the history of the individual – especially in predicting both the future uninterfered with and the future involved with intended change processes?

Why is it that the most permanent and durable changes in behaviour occur to those people whose circumstances change and who are compelled of necessity to bring about adaptive change in their behaviour patterns by themselves? Why is it that even with great motivation sometimes individuals cannot make the necessary change? It may be that the willingness is there but not the knowledge of how to achieve change. So perhaps the most fundamental role that a change agent may employ is not to initiate change as such but to know a great deal about the ways in which it can be achieved.

It is not that it is necessary to reject inductive theory because of the way in which it is constructed, but merely that it is essential that the nature of its pronouncements should receive their due weight relative to theories with a predictive and provable base. Much can be done on the basis of belief, but belief cannot be argued as a rational basis for action by virtue of the essential nature of all beliefs as forms of acceptance that require no logical proof.

If a change agent sets out to change the behaviour of an individual or a group by changing the information and knowledge base upon which they are operating, he or she can be reasonably certain that:

- If they accept and understand the changes to their knowledge base then changes to their behaviour are possible but never inevitable.

- They may deliberately choose not to use the new knowledge – they may not have the opportunity as other factors may weigh more heavily – which all comes down to the fact that change becomes a possibility which may not have existed before but it is not inevitable.

- There is no necessary and inevitable connection between acquiring a new and different explanatory and informational data base and a change of behaviour founded on that base.

Another approach which involves the creation of insight into behaviour patterns also contains the same problem, i.e. that insight may not lead to any desire to change what has been revealed.

Effective change based on new and different data may need an intermediary step to be effective, which could be related to how to put into practice what the new information has made possible. Change may be forced by virtue of consciously attempting to achieve something; for example, safety, freedom from punishment, etc. This is controlled change where the control is vested in the target and not the change agent, but there is little evidence that such changes are very durable except where the circumstances which enforce the change remain in existence unchanged for very long periods of time.

Given the strictures noted about theories of human behaviour, why do change agents appear to assert in their written material the universality of such theorising and its parity with truly scientific and predictive theory? Prestige may provide one answer and acceptability may provide another. The history of agents purporting to be able to change human behaviour in intended ways and directions is littered with practitioners whose quotients of success were related to ignorance, fear, magic and mystery. Out of this melange of practices, only learning and training have acquired a degree of theoretical validity, and that is largely due to the fact that they are mainly concerned with a continuation of a natural programme of development in the individual which was and is related to survival.

Indeed, the whole idea of behavioural change is still frequently regarded as abnormal. Since the decline in religious belief this is less strong than it was; change is no longer seen as interfering with the creations of God, but is still something markedly more unnatural than learning. Punishment for unacceptable behaviour has always existed and appears to be founded on the trenchant idea that an individual was in control of his or her behaviour and thus responsible for the consequences. Now that it is widely accepted that such control is not as complete as was originally believed, the concept of change based largely on establishing control over those areas and precipitating factors which lie outside the area of 'natural' control, has a recognised and legitimate base. It is believed that the revelation of the unknown sources of action and belief will bring them under conscious control.

But there is little empirical evidence of a testable kind of the nature and development of these unknown factors. What we have is a series of elegant explanations which appear to describe the processes and outcomes with admirable exactitude, none of which can be proved. In a sense it is a little like the Aztecs believing that the sun would rise every morning only if a blood sacrifice was

offered at the appropriate time. Because it would be extremely catastrophic if the sun did not rise each day, the sacrifice was never
missed. The connection between action and phenomenon was thus
established – one brought about the other. It appeared to be a
wholly satisfactory explanation, it appeared to work – but it was
not true, as the Aztecs discovered when the Spaniards forbade
blood sacrifices and the sun continued to rise. The population were
then faced with the need to find other explanations.

But explanations are all we have got, whether they define the
actuality or even some part of it we do not know. This means that
all change efforts have no basis of certainty. The fact that many
change efforts produce some, if not all, of the outcomes which they
intend is no valid argument for asserting that they are based on
provable fact.

The matter is complicated, as Eysenck noted, by an element of
pseudo-predictability. If a good degree of predictability exists then it
can be claimed that a theory is reasonably close to being based upon
factual data. But the predictions of change efforts have no such high
degree of predictability except in the development of expected symp-
tom formation. This is a difficult area and one in which practitioners
can be maligned for what is a very common experience.

There is no value-free contact between human beings. All close
contacts and change situations are highly sensitive. Individuals pick
up signals which were never consciously emitted as to the nature of
expected behaviour. In simple terms the expectations of the change
agent based on the theoretical constructs he or she is using to bring
about intended change, become part of a self-fulfilling prophecy and
the expected behaviour becomes part of the response pattern of the
target. There are many instances of individuals displaying different
expected behavioural responses when under the guidance of change
agents with different theoretical orientations.

This leads to the much discussed problem of interpretation.

Interpretation implies the conversion of one thing into another
deemed to be its equivalent for the purpose of increasing understanding. But in many change situations the observed or reported behaviour of an individual is translated or described in verbal terms which
are part of a series of theoretical constructs held by the change agent.
If this process of translation was one of clarification of the use of
different and probably unfamiliar terminology with the express purpose of generating understanding of what was being discussed, then
the process of interpretation would be an innocent process and probably beneficial. But interpretation actually goes beyond clarification to
what can only be described as the allocation of meaning.

Consider where this now leads us.

The theoretical constructs which the change agent holds are an explanation of apparently unknowable processes – they are not and cannot have any basis in provable fact nor can they possess any high predictive value as in true scientific theories. Thus the interpretation of behaviour by the change agent in terms derived from these constructs and imbued with the idea of meaning places a value of reality upon the interpretation which cannot under any circumstances be true except by an astronomically improbable chance.

A 'possible' explanation has become an assertion of fact.

Providing the distinction between possible and actual are never lost sight of, then the possible can be a working instrument; particularly if the relationship between its parts mirrors in some way the unknowable processes it was produced to represent. There is no way of knowing this relationship actually exists except in two simple senses:

• that it nowhere contradicts the observable and recorded facts;

• that, in the process of using it as an instrument of change, it works pragmatically.

Each change effort, wherever or whatever its theoretical base may be, is never a wholly charted and known journey. There are so many unforeseen probable events on the way that one journey ostensibly in the same direction, under the same rules of procedure and heading for the same destination, is likely to have only a very general likeness to another.

Psychology and the other 'sciences' of human behaviour are not exact in the sense that physics or chemistry is exact, even in the realm of the theories which are proposed. This lack of exactness becomes even more pronounced when the theories are applied in practice to deal with individual problems when the gap between the general nature of the theory and the eccentric individuality of a human being becomes glaringly obvious.

There are two ways in practice of dealing with this lack of fit:

• to try to force the individual to fit the generalities of the theory;

• to realise that the theory provides nothing more than extremely wide and general guidance – a kind of sketch of what are probably some of the more remarkable features of relatively unexplored terrain.

This last approach then becomes empirical and is dependent for any success on the ability of the change agent to utilise the factors with which the change situation presents him or her. Thus the differences between the general and the particular are liable to owe a great deal more to the experience and personality of the change agent and of his or her clients than to any foreseen adaptations of change theory.

In astronomy the presence of unseen and unknowable entities and forces can be reasonably predicted because of the effects known as perturbation which they appear to have on known forces and presences. It is known that certain kinds of forces and presences produce effects which have been observed and recorded on other elements within their field, even when that field is immense. Thus when similar effects are observed without apparently visible cause it is assumed that the forces and presences which cause them, although not visible, are the same as those which cause the visible effects.

Even this is a risky business because it is possible that like effects can arise from different causes. Thus to predicate the existence of an invisible element on the basis of perturbation must stay in the realms of probability until further evidence of a different kind is available to substantiate the apparent relationship of effect.

In the world of the physical sciences, perturbation effects are treated with caution. In human behaviour, perturbation is also a factor. Frequently, behaviour is produced and observed, but for which reasons cannot be established. Therefore such behaviour is assumed to have arisen as the result of some function or malfunction of unknowable elements. But the process of deciding what these causative elements may be does not even have the evidence of similar events occurring elsewhere in a visible and observable state. So even the probability available to astronomers, which they tend to regard with great caution, is not available to students of human behaviour.

Certainly where there are chemical or physical causes for behaviour then the connection becomes closely one of cause and effect – the difference, for instance, between the causes of GPI and those of schizophrenia. What are the causes of criminal behaviour? Social conditions, as some maintain, or genetic endowment? Is intelligence a genetic or a social factor, or do we hedge our bets and say both in varying proportions? As long as causes are obscure then what tends to be available for use by change agents are the current behaviour patterns and, less effectively, the collected data of a historical sequence of observed patterns.

Serious questions about the effectiveness of procedures, the limits of knowledge, and the uncertainty of accomplishments must be acknowledged. These matters can neither be obscured or ignored.

Vinter (1974: 7)

But the point is that having stated there are limitations, Vinter and other writers then go on to produce a procedural approach to intervention in human behaviour which is as tightly precise as a legal document, which would seem to indicate that if one follows the correct procedures, unfailing results can be obtained. The statement quoted above is an example of a common form of a nod towards accepting that human behaviour is untidy and that what knowledge and techniques we possess for changing it, while stated here in highly specific and logical terms, are in effect crude and unpredictable.

One of the greatest deterrents to the assessment of effective intervention after the extreme difficulty of measuring the change is created by what amounts to a camouflage of accuracy in the phraseology used to describe the processes of intervention. Whereas most verbal camouflage is effected by deliberate vagueness, the language of change agents is of an almost mathematical precision. 'Strategies of intervention', in itself a formidable phrase, is defined by various 'means of influence', also defined in detail. For instance, Vinter, who wrote the words quoted above about not forgetting limitations, also wrote:

The kinds of change sought, as defined by treatment goals, range from acquiring new relationship skills, to changes in self-images and attitudes towards others, to behavioral modifications or integration into conventional structures.

This is calling both sides of the spun coin at the same time. Blumberg and Golembiewski (1976), writing about experiential learning in groups, said:

However, experience does not necessarily lead to *productive* learning nor, indeed, to any learning. Merely to put people in groups so that they may experience each other can have good results, no results, or damaging results.

The most important word here is 'productive'. Change – in this instance, learning – is very likely to occur. But out of three possibilities referred to above only one is positive, that is, productive.

What this means I have clearly defined as 'intended' change, that is change which is effected along preconceived lines and with some end-point in view.

But even this simplistic one-in-three positive outcome is not factually true. Consider that one of the outcomes is listed as 'no change'. Can this be true? What the authors are saying in effect is that literally no visible or recorded change takes place over the period of contact within the group. But what they probably meant was that no change in which they were interested occurred. This highlights another of the problems connected with change: few, if any, follow-up studies of the effects of change efforts have been undertaken. If they had, would the 'no change' element still have been recorded as such? And, indeed, how would anyone know? So many factors impinge upon an individual's life that the possibility of ascribing any of them with certainty to a given causative element is remote.

So what intended change is apparently about is not attempting to bring about a clear-cut change in whatever area of an individual is targeted which can exist independently as a new and altered element, but it would appear to be an attempt at change which has a large element of chance about its possibility of success. A reduction of these chance elements may be brought about by controlling as far as possible some of the known influences which affect outcomes. The hospitalisation of an individual is a good example of such a control exercise which creates a situation in which limits are placed upon the incidence of contacts with others and by controlling the environment. But even in such circumstances random and unpredictable elements can still intrude and dramatically affect the outcome.

What seems to emerge from the brief summary of intervention ideas and practice here is that there is a level of explanation which has not to my knowledge been widely explored, but which might serve to place most of these ideas and procedures within one overall concept.

If we look for a moment at a process which affects quite amazing changes in human behaviour, religious conversion, while apparently having little connection with other change processes, it may reveal matter of some moment. Religious conversion is concerned with the belief system of the individual. In some cases this system amounts to not having a belief, that is a religious belief, at all. Nevertheless it is logical to assert that non-belief is still a belief system. The process of conversion, however, achieved is one in which the individual becomes imbued with the belief system to which he or she is being exposed.

There is little which is logical about belief. Indeed, belief can be defined by its absence of rational proof. If an individual believes something, then he or she accepts it as true and will continue to do so in the face of any denial and in the absence of any rational validation of its truth.

If we now go back a step, it will be remembered that at an absolutely fundamental level there are only two possible forms of change which can be applied to human behaviour. In essence these are:

1. to change the situation in which the behaviour occurs;

2. to change the perception of the individual producing the behaviour, as to its nature, benefit and consequence.

In the first instance, changing the situation, while it may and often does produce different behavioural patterns, offers no guarantee that the original patterns will not eventually be re-established in the new setting. In the second, while a different perception of the nature of behaviour arises, its manifestation and maintenance may well provide the basis for changing it, but, like the first option, there is no cast-iron guarantee that such change will take place.

The ultimate factor in either of the change approaches – which may, incidentally, be applied in combination – is the co-operation of the individual in actually choosing to produce the changed behaviour.

Ignoring for the moment the first of the two basic options mentioned above, it would appear that all change agents make some attempt at converting their clients. Believing that all human beings appear to do is to act in what they believe to be their best interests, is, of course, an assumption, but to believe otherwise would run counter to most people's experience which is to survive and to make the most of things except in some very exceptional circumstances. In essence this is a part of most individuals' belief systems about themselves and about the nature of the world in which they live.

It may be somewhat begging the question to assert that parts of an individual's belief system are not eminently conscious and available. Nevertheless, those parts often encompassed by a sense of what is 'natural' and 'normal' still operate to control and produce behavioural patterns.

Conversion then comes into focus when an attempt is made to alter an individual's belief system, by adding to, subtracting from, substituting or replacing parts of it. Indeed, conversion to a belief system which the change agent, acting on behalf of his or her society, holds may be one which will be 'better' in that society's eyes for the target. The concept of alienation, which, at different times in our recent history has been described as the root cause of behaviour that is self- and socially destructive, implies that alienated individuals have a belief system about themselves and about society which is dramatically at odds with the belief systems of the majority of citizens.

Of course, the idea of belief systems, both conscious and of which individuals are largely unaware, is an assumption in the same way that all other approaches to intended change are based upon assumption. But in all of them there is a strong element which can be described as attempted conversion. For instance insight creation and understanding are both exercises in converting individuals from belief systems which produced inappropriate, maladaptive or asocial behaviour, to systems where such products would be diminished or altered.

If the process of conversion were more widely accepted as a basic process then the need to claim as true what are essentially assumptions would be considerably diminished and the scepticism which such obviously fallacious claims generate might be removed. Of course, this exposes the whole ethical problem of conversion to 'what' and 'by what right', but that would be an advance over conversion which at present takes place under the guise of treatment or care.

Part Four:
The Consequences of Intervention

18 Consequences, Probability and Prediction

Things and actions are what they are, and the consequences of them will be what they will be: why then should we desire to be deceived?

Joseph Butler (1692–1752)

... But, to judge from the heated arguments of philosophers, no extension of vocabulary or ingenuity in definition ever seems to clear away all the difficulties attached to this perfectly common notion of probability.

Moroney (1951: 4)

This chapter is not so much a study of probabilities in the actuarial sense, though some of that kind of material is appropriate, it is more a look at how change agents can be alerted to the fact that multiple probabilities exist in any social situation, and to attempt to show to what factors in the establishment of priorities attention must necessarily be given. Of course such a choice can only be based upon the nature and quality of the data available, plus the skill and experience of the assessor in recognising the potential influence of different variables. Methods deriving from the physical sciences are relatively useless in this field because of the operation of human intelligence and the factors of imagination and established thought patterns in the targets with an awareness of what is taking place – even if that awareness is not accompanied by understanding.

The outcomes – the consequences of intervention – predicted by change agents almost always refer exclusively to those results which they have striven to achieve. Thus the predicted success of intended change efforts seems to be based purely upon whether the original and/or subsequent revisions of the stated goals have been achieved in some recognisable way. This ignores the simple fact that, in most circumstances, there is no known method by which the target behaviours can be isolated from all the other behavioural variables which exist.

- The nub of intended change efforts is that they should bring about specific consequences.

- The efficacy of this process should be what determines the reputation of the change processes.

But it is already clear that while change efforts do appear to produce the intended consequences, there is little enough evidence that they are solely responsible for what often occurs. The consequences of intervention are most usually the product of intended change efforts plus the effects of the context in which they are applied.

To recapitulate a little let us reassert the simple facts of change, any change. Change is what occurs to the state of an object, individual or situation between two sequential points in time when the second state is different in some form from the first. Change takes place whether it is observed as such or not, but change cannot certainly be said to have occurred if there is not a base point to which the later points can be compared.

One of the major difficulties for change agents arises not with the perception of change as described above but with any attempt to decide how the observed changes were brought about. In some circumstances this difficulty is not a great one, such as, for instance, where the influences operating on an object are limited to one, then unless unknown factors are present the cause of any change can be safely ascribed to the solitary influence. But the isolation of possible causes is the main problem in measuring change because influences are seldom easily identified. To try to eliminate or make allowance for other factors than the one to be measured poses insuperable problems in controlled experiments and results in statements with degrees of probability rather than certainty.

Thus any intended change effort feeds into such a complex of interacting factors that to ascribe a causal effect to such an effort cannot often be justified, let alone proven. Again, most intended change efforts are not in themselves comprised of a simple or single element, so multiplicity of possible causes is compounded by multiple approach elements.

The observation of change is simple; knowing with a reasonable degree of certainty what actually caused it is not.

When change efforts are applied to individuals, groups and organisations another complicating factor, that of choice, enters the equation. It can occur that an intended change effort can be based upon an accurate assessment of what needs to change about, say, an individual, and upon a correct understanding that the required potential to accept change efforts and implement them exists, and yet it can fail for reasons which lie wholly within the decision-making behaviour of the individual concerned.

Newton and his followers believed that the universe was of a precise mathematical nature and that to understand how it functioned required only the discovery and enumeration of the laws which governed everything. Hence it was considered possible to construct a model of the solar system in which the constituent planets pursued orbits in relation to one another which were totally invariable.

In any very general overview, of which this is one, next must come the contribution deriving from the laws of thermodynamics which tended to show that systems, far from being stable and invariable, were actually subject to decay and the loss of energy which had to be replaced in some way if they were to keep going. The myth of perpetual motion can only be entertained on the basis of a belief that systems do not lose energy.

Systems theory applied to human systems was a good example of the use of machine technology based on the analysis of the universe and its forces. It is mechanistic in the Newtonian sense only in that it assumed that human behaviour is governed by universally applicable laws like everything else, which is not meant to imply that people are machines but that some human behaviour patterns possess a striking resemblance to the functions of machines.

More recently, modern chaos theorists say that the ancients were perhaps nearer the truth than the deterministic Newtonians. Their ideas start from speculation about the revealed inaccuracies of systems believed to be mathematical. An early and basic idea was that complete accuracy is a myth. For instance Bronowski, in *The Ascent of Man* (1973), stated Heisenberg's principle of uncertainty thus:

All knowledge, all information between human beings can only be exchanged within a play of tolerance.

But he preferred to call the idea the principle of tolerance. He assumed that it meant we can never be exact – whichever direction we pursue it, measurement is held within limits and an act of judgement is built in (the area of tolerance or uncertainty) – it is never possible to obtain zero tolerance.

Thus arrived a general realisation that even with the number-crunching ability of modern computers, the results of predictions about natural events (e.g. the weather), were nothing like as accurate as might have been expected.

Even in such loose structures as human organisations, the continued appearance of unforeseen consequences fuelled despair about the possibility of achieving any increase in the accuracy of prediction. Researchers realised that when interventions are made to social systems in order to bring about some intended change, whether such a change was eventually achieved or not, the major consequences of intervention tended to be different from those intended and, moreover, were nearly always unforeseen and unexpected.

Chaos theorists have recorded what they call the 'sensitive dependence on initial conditions' – that is the slight differences which occur at the beginning of similar systems which were usually so small that they were ignored, but which proved to be crucial in affecting the accuracy of prediction of the development and performance of a system. Indeed they proved to be the source of overwhelming differences between so-called similar systems as they developed. All such systems seemed to possess inherent instability at all points and any chain of events seemed infallibly to have points of crisis which would magnify small differences.

For most people, perhaps the most visible manifestations of chaos theory have been the Mandelbrot sets and the beautiful patterns of fractals – endless similarities that are never quite identical. But the message from these theories for the change agents is rather more serious than beautiful images. We have, for a considerable period of time now, attempted to identify patterns in human groups which were stable enough to be recognised and described and which could be taught to aspiring group workers. It is not too brutal a statement to say that this attempt has met with little success and the best which has emerged are some very general statements of a sequential nature, like the stages of group development.

The reasons for this palpable failure are not difficult to find and fall into two very distinct categories. The first relates backwards to the residual determinism in our perspectives; the second is concerned with the conscious state of the elements of human systems.

Group dynamics is a relatively new field of study in the academic sense. In order that such a study should be able to obtain academic validity it needed laws and statistics to back its assertions, and the model of the physical sciences was followed to achieve this. But, as the Chaos theorists have now shown, the vaunted precision of measurements even in the physical sciences are not as infallible as previously thought, even in those areas of study which are extremely susceptible to measurement. How, therefore, is it to be expected that measurement which is dependent upon stability, can serve to delineate human systems which are seldom stable and essentially only crudely measurable? How much more impossible to predict? We have fallen into the basic deterministic error of believing that true understanding relates purely to measurement and thence to prediction, when what we are working with are systems which have never been truly susceptible to such forms of understanding.

Chaos theorists have shown that material systems are subject to perturbations and turbulences which are wholly unpredictable because they are not dependent upon predisposing factors which would make them gradual and cumulative, but they are most frequently discontinuities – precipitous and unexpected.

Our understanding of human systems is in reality much more tacit than deterministic, that is, there are certain general expectations which may be more or less fulfilled but which can never have the certainty of prediction.

The second element which ensures a level of failure in our attempts to predict group outcomes is much more obvious. The properties of the elements of physical systems are ultimately what decides the ways in which they function. But the properties of the elements of human systems are not so clearly definable and include the factors of conscious awareness of the situation, and the ability to effect change by an effort of will and by taking action.

Thus once again, the argument that human systems can be understood in terms of the deterministic laws of physical systems cannot be correct. This would imply that all the regularities which we believe we observe in such systems, like development and interactive states, roles, and so on, are not determined by the nature of the group system itself.

As we have seen, the attempt to impose order on chaos has a long history and its manifestations in the process of working with groups are clear enough. Any order, any regularities which can be observed in such systems, must be those which are largely imposed by the intervention of human intelligence, the environment, expectations and beliefs upon the elements of which it is composed (i.e. the group members and their leaders). Thus it can be said that the process of group work is to convert the perceptions that the members have of their system to conform to and adopt a preconceived patterning, which, by altering the actual elements of the system, change the probable outcomes in selected directions.

Most elements of observed order in a group left entirely to its own devices will come from whatever analysis the individual members can make of the situation, and then from any relevant past experience which could serve to indicate ways to respond. This would include their expectations of being in the group situation and their perception of what might/should be expected of them by others.

The problem is essentially one of control. In any form of intended change operation there is the fact that a great deal of the context in which the target exists is unknown and probably unknowable. This means that the change efforts are being directed into a system or series of maintaining systems which are largely unknown and for which little predictive ability exists. Where possible, change agents attempt to reduce the number and power of such contextual elements by decreasing or changing the environment in which the change efforts take place.

Some years ago, a young mother complained bitterly that the hospital who had taken her autistic son in for several weeks of respite care had reported to her that during his time in the hospital he had behaved in an exemplary manner. At home he was extremely difficult, indeed almost unmanageable. His mother was distressed because she thought that the hospital were implying that she had exaggerated her son's behaviour problems in order to get him admitted. In fact what had occurred was that in the hospital her son had received a much greater degree of control than he had been able to receive from his single mother who also had other children. His context had been changed in such a way that there was much less freedom for his behaviour to expand into areas which could not be covered by his mother working on her own.

Similarly John Rous' problem (see Chapter 19) was that he had come to realise that he could not cope with life in its normal uncontrolled state, but others insisted on continually discharging him from controlled situations into the kind of life he greatly feared. Eventually he had to kill someone before he was finally given the control which made his life bearable.

One thing which emerges relatively clearly from any detailed examination of a long-term contact between change agent and subject, is the different quality which can be assigned to events over the period when they are viewed retrospectively and in sequence. The factor of hindsight and the different perspective which it accords has already been mentioned, but we must look at it here in some detail.

Mel Gussov (1994: A4) writing about Tom Stoppard's plays and, in particular, the revival of *Rosencrantz and Guildenstern are Dead* at the National Theatre, summed up the major problems of prediction when he wrote:

> Stoppard shows us these two peripheral characters in Hamlet baffled as Shakespeare's play sweeps past. As they discover, it is impossible to know life's plot even if one is at the vortex. *No matter how much one prepares, the unknowable awaits,* subjecting the unwary to the vagaries of fortune.

I would regard this statement as a remarkably succinct and apposite comment on the situation of all human beings, but most particularly on those, like change agents, who need to have some large element of the ability to predict behaviour and the consequences of behaviour as a central part of their professional competence.

Deterministic approaches to the understanding of human behaviour are founded on the assumption that what occurs earlier in an individual's life not only conditions and, in effect, produces the current behaviour, but will also condition and produce the behaviour of the future. Thus the pattern, or at least its larger elements, is established in the early stages of human development. While it would be ridiculous to assert that this is not true, for indeed we can see the elements of such patterns operating all around us, it would be equally ridiculous to accept that the nature and quality of the contexts either side of the immediate present are in no way identical.

The determining past has already occurred. The problem for change agents is not one of guessing the probability of an occurrence and its effect, but actually of finding what has already happened and fitting it into the historical sequence. This problem is very well known and is complicated by the effects of the passage of time upon the availability of data, which can be marred by the inaccuracies and bias of all forms of recall and the obvious inability of all historians to assess with correctness the actual value that any event held for those involved at the time of its occurrence. Much historical material may thus be extremely difficult to acquire and, when obtained, be biased and wrongly valued, but at least it exists or existed.

The future side of the current present which is continually approaching and becoming that present but has not yet occurred, and the assumptions that can be made about it, tend to be based upon the probability of the continuance of patterns which existed in the past and which exist currently. In terms of human behaviour this poses many problems.

Where the number of influencing factors, social contacts, and so on, are few, the probability of more accurate prediction of outcome must obviously increase. For instance, the predictability of the behaviour of babies, the very old and isolates can be more accurately made than those of the rest of us with vast numbers of social contacts, freedom to move, and living in circumstances which are in a constant state of flux. The patterns of the past can be overwhelmed, if not in essential but in peripheral form, by unforeseen events in the future. Reducing the probability that unforeseen events will occur means, essentially, diminishing the multiplicity of sources of such events to a very few which may then be subject to some degree of control.

Even then there is the distinct possibility that an individual, apparently 'out of the blue', will decide to do something different. It may be that if all the antecedents were known (i.e. had been available to observers), the apparent surprise element would have been shown to be a possibility, and the indications that the observed change might occur were all there.

What faces change agents is the simple fact that in most cases they enter into the context of their clients at a particular time at a particular place and are mandated to deal with a particular aspect of behaviour. In whatever way they assess that position and their own relationship to it, they must know that whatever changes they can effect have to slot into a whole mass of client context about some of which they may know nothing, and about other aspects of which they may have only an inkling.

At the point of entry into the subject's context, its apparent state may look dramatically different from the way it will appear later. The whole value of any particular incident can, and does, change dramatically as its position in the sequence of events becomes one of being part of a longer perspective. Thus what was designed as an intervention to achieve a particular outcome may well, over time, produce an entirely different sequence of events from that originally intended.

One way to avoid the worst effects of this sequence is that

used by behaviourist change agents. In order to be reasonably sure of the cause/effect relationship, they select as the focus for change behavioural patterns which are essentially small parts of larger constellations of behaviour. Two very important facts stem from this process:

1. Because the pattern of behaviour chosen is small, the number and quality of influence processes which affect it is also small and, as we have seen earlier, where this occurs naturally it can be accompanied by a significant rise in the ability to predict outcomes.

2. Because the areas chosen are small, their antecedents and consequences are visible in the current and recent present, which gives the behaviourist change agent a clear opportunity (a) to note them; and (b) to use the close connection with the target behaviour to change it. The success of behaviourist change efforts is directly limited to the size of the areas dealt with and the visibility of the precipitating and reinforcing factors.

Only subjective phenomena and objective data are directly accessible. The meaningful connections are still clear and distinct to us. The question of cause arises when meaning has ceased. Once a causal connection has been established theory comes in to cope.

Jaspers (1963: 530)

19 The Effects of the Quality of Data

Introduction

Chapter 12 presented the forms of information which could be available to a change agent and upon which he or she could then formulate a rational programme for effecting change in those areas where it was recognised as being necessary in an individual or group. I now attempt to show the inherent weaknesses and problems of those particular informational forms, and also the possible outcomes of the idiosyncratic nature both of their formulation and presentation and also of their reception and interpretation.

Although such a process sounds somewhat dramatic, all the possibilities I will describe exist in nearly all forms of human communication. The fact that this brings about far fewer communicational catastrophes than might be expected can probably be explained in that the deficits in communication produce really dramatic outcomes only when the degree of precision and accuracy of the process is crucial to the situation and the tolerance of the deficit, which is normal in everyday communication, is drastically reduced.

Such precision and accuracy of communication is what is required most often in exchanges between individuals and groups and change agents when the express purpose of the exchange is that of generating intended beneficial change.

The terms 'accuracy' and 'precision' are to be understood in this context as relative, for in most human interactions there can be no question of a total understanding between individuals. But in a professional relationship where the change agent's purpose is both beneficial (mainly) and moral, there must be an assumption that to work on the basis of less than the most accurate information which is available, or can be obtained, is both unethical and, most likely, ineffective as well – if not downright damaging.

The most effective way of ensuring that the best possible standards of informational quality available are used lies in two factors: (1) the willingness to spend time and energy to collect and check information, and (2) to be wholly aware of how and why distortion and other forms of inaccuracy are liable to occur. Ultimately this should lead to an estimate of the quality of the available data and thus, also, of the limits and boundaries of how such information may be used.

Of course from the data available at the beginning of an intervention process, that process itself will produce further information, both new and possibly a reformulation of what was originally available. Thus constant monitoring of information and the use of conscious updating is necessary to maintain the original standards.

Many of the problems which relate to the quality of data and the consequences of that quality can be illustrated by the case of John Rous – serving a life sentence in Broadmoor for the murder of Jonathan Newby in 1993. Rous' life shows a fairly typical pattern of almost aimless wandering and contact with the law, psychiatry and social work over a 30-year period after a diagnosis of schizophrenia had been made when he was 16. The details of this life, presented extremely briefly here, are instructive.

John Rous was born in 1949. When he was 3 years old he was fostered with his baby brother to the Townsend family who had two children of their own. He is described during the time of his fostering as being a bright imaginative little boy with a talent for painting, history and carpentry.

At 12 he stole his foster brother's wallet and disappeared for several days, ending up in the local hospital. There followed a period of erratic wanderings, drug and alcohol abuse, petty crimes, living on the streets and, at various times, in prison and in psychiatric hospital. It was while in hospital, then aged 16, he was diagnosed as a schizophrenic.

During the 1960s and 1970s Rous appeared in the Oxford area. He was now about six feet tall and the records show that he made numerous court appearances in connection with drugs, petty crime and bizarre behaviour. He was said at this time to 'find difficulty in rationalising at crucial times'.

In 1972 he smashed windows at Littlemore hospital and demanded to be admitted, for which he was put on probation with a condition of outpatient attendance. There followed a 10-year period in which he was homeless and wandering, until, in 1992, he was offered a place by the Oxford Cyrenian community. He was described by staff and other residents as flamboyant, dependent, selfish and attention-seeking, showing bizarre behaviour, but also good fun to be with.

In 1993 he stabbed Jonathan Newby to death. Newby was 22 years old – a volunteer left in sole charge of the hostel, though he lacked professional training and was not supervised. At the time of the attack Rous was drunk, but he had rung the police to tell them he had a knife and was going to kill someone. The call was not acted upon. A newspaper report on the incident said: 'Rous quite clearly killed him [Newby] because he wanted to be in a secure hospital. He couldn't cope with the community. He wanted to be in a secure environment.'

With hindsight it is easy to see the recurring patterns of evidence that Rous was very fearful of an insecure environment. The evidence was cumulative, but it was not collected or passed on. The decisions about his disposal were taken on the evidence available locally and at the time, but biased by the current 'rules of the game'. The nature of the decisions taken and the quality of the data are not compatible. All of Rous' behaviour patterns were either self-damaging or attention-seeking. He probably knew that what he required was to be held in a safe and secure environment – indeed he is on record as saying so during periods of lucidity. But he must eventually have realised that the only way he would achieve safety was to be locked up for life, and for that he would have to kill someone.

It is not so much that people make misjudgements – they may be valid in the state of their knowledge at the time, but they are not adequate for the demands that society expects. General criticism has been levelled at the Cyrenians for leaving Newby, an untrained volunteer, in charge on the night that he was killed. But it is debatable that the quality of carers would have mattered all that much, given the apparent central drive of Rous' behaviour. If, and it is a large if, he had worked out in his own particular way that 30 years of transient care had served to demonstrate that the only way to activate the system in order to get the long-term security he so desperately felt he needed was to kill, then maybe someone else might have been chosen as the victim, but indubitably a victim there would have been.

Kinds of Data

There are two main classifications of information which a change agent can acquire, which, for the sake of brevity, I will call 'direct' and 'indirect'. In the former category is all the material which the change agent elicits by direct contact with the sources and, in the second, that material which is available but which the change agent was not personally responsible for eliciting.

The distinction is simple but has to be made for the simple reason that, in the second category – which consists mainly of recorded material – the process of recording and of selection, and of establishing priorities was done by others and may have been obtained by those with different interests and priorities from the change agent, and for different reasons. This is an important issue because in using such material a change agent has no way of checking either the quality of what has been recorded or its suitability for the current purpose.

For instance, a child in a residential system may at one time have created a considerable amount of disturbance and distress. If this is recorded in the child's notes and the exact nature of the event is not recorded, when these notes are used at a later stage in that child's career by people with no access to a witness account of the original and subsequent behaviour – the label of 'troublemaker' will appear, out of context. Thus a relatively gross injustice could be perpetuated in good faith, and expectations based on such records could succeed in generating confirmatory behaviour in the child involved.

Sequential behaviour, repetitive behaviour, number of events and frequency of occurrence are all important factors in recorded material which are essential if the material has to bear some relatively real connection with the behaviour of the recorded individual.

Witness Data

Witness data comprises directly elicited information and consists mainly of information obtained by the change agent from the target of the intended change effort, and from those in contact with that target. Otherwise the information comes from the change agent operating as witness in his or her own right by noting, observing and recording his or her direct contact with those involved. Of course the change agent is ultimately responsible for assessing all forms of evidence and information, but there is a distinct difference between the assessment of information which is received from others and the personal assessment which is made of the agent's own perceptions of situation and people.

Observational Data

One of the essential problems with data derived from direct observation relates to the status of the observer vis-a-vis the incident being observed. In essence this may be regarded as part of the general process of attribution and the ubiquitous search for acceptable meanings for observed behavioural events. In the crudest form the description of an event given by an individual with the status of non-participant observer is usually biased towards the attribution of the causes of behaviour of the others involved as residing in their individual personality characteristics. The description of the same situation given by those actively engaged in the event, however, would be biased in favour of the causes of their behaviour arising as a response to their perception of the needs of the situation in which they believe themselves to be.

In the position of change agent and target, an interesting complication occurs in that both are simultaneously actor and observer, though the former will no doubt be more exacting in his or her observation than the target and even the latter, in a situation with large elements of the unusual about it, will be seeking for clues as to how best to deal with it with minimal risk and maximum benefit. So it is feasible to treat both change agent and target individual in direct contact as both actor and observer.

As observers in such situations, both will have considerable ignorance of the ways in which the other will act, but each will have cast the other in a role or roles according to their understanding and, in each case, this is liable to consist of a very confined range which may be expanded by extended contact. It is possible that the responses each produces to the other will be set in terms of expectations defined by a limited knowledge of role, and even those responses may be seen as emanating from personality factors.

The most important visual cue one individual has about another is that individual's appearance, and secondly his or her behaviour. If appearance is consistent in its major aspects, there is a tendency to associate it with a similar consistency of behaviour and disposition. Likewise, a noted behavioural pattern can also be assumed to be consistent and an expectation developed of its appearance in situations other than that of its original production.

An actor – that is, an active participant in a situation – tends to emphasise that his or her responses were largely dictated by, not only what were seen as the environmental factors, but also by a need to justify the actions which eventually emerged. The predominant need for there to be an acceptable explanation of events propels participants into causative explanations, even where confusion may well have made any logical explanation wellnigh impossible (see the example of confabulation later). An actor may well have knowledge of intent to inform his or her explanation of behaviour which the observer does not have in the same direct form, but instead only as an inference derived from knowledge of the actor and from observation of his or her behaviour in the past.

As perception of risk, personal security, advantage and a whole host of other survival elements are based in our ability to assess what we can see, hear and feel about situations, it is a process well established in all individuals, but it contains elements of difference, of bias and deficits which are related to ability, environment and learning. So when an individual, in our case a change agent, seeks to obtain information about another individual in order that the change process can be effectively based and pursued, the process – which all too often is regarded as being relatively simple – is beset by problems of difference. Such differences as exist naturally may well be complicated further by the need to categorise. This occurs in any case, but the change agent's need is backed by his or her professional training, which requires observations to be classified into a structure which will eventually produce a meaning for the behaviour which is different, deeper and more 'significant' than the disparate behavioural elements, without the defining theoretical assumptions of a categorising process, would permit.

Into the process of observed behaviour come all the factors of gesture, non-verbal speech, facial expressions, movement, contact and posture – all assumed to communicate something about an individual. Some conscious use is made of forms of bodily communication; much is involuntary, but in either case the data provided by the individual has to be 'read' or interpreted by the observer. Some such signals are wellnigh unmistakable, but others have such a plethora of possible causes that the choice of one 'reading' rather than another must be based upon a large element of personal preference, which itself may be based upon experience, or otherwise supported.

Even when familiarity between participants in a change situation has developed, and the validity of observational data and the intervention processes established, the problems can still continue to emerge. Perception of behaviour may now be limited to confirmation of an existing thesis. It often occurs that mistakes in the intended change process arise more easily from failure to note elements which emerge outside the established area of concentration. Concrete reality is infinite and it is essential, in order to be able to work, that choices have to be made about what data to use, what to accept as essential and what to ignore. But, given this necessarily pragmatic approach, it is not essentially logical to promulgate it as a process with the high probability of success – which could only reside in a process which had access to a much wider and deeper range of data and a more efficient basis of selection of what was essential.

Verbal Data

Verbal usage is stable because the objects and situations with which people are confronted and which they need to describe, discern and alter, are also fairly stable. They resemble one another in many ways and tend to resemble themselves at different times. There is, however, very seldom any single element in such resemblances which is identical as between different individuals or in the same individuals at different times.

Weldon (1953: 28–9)

Weldon was affirming that, apart from lexical definitions, words have no meanings – only uses. But, even given the usage of words in a verbal exchange between change agent and those he or she is working with is stable and similar, there are still all the problems of communication failure which are brought about in the form of hindrances to the communication process of one sort or another.

For instance, the environment in which the verbal exchange takes place can provide any number of possible distractions which diminish the possibility of effective communication. If the participants in the exchange are operating in conditions of excessive noise or vibration, or if the quality of the atmosphere is poor – too hot, too cold, with not enough fresh air – or the humidity is high, their ability to concentrate on the exchange becomes diminished. Likewise, the condition of the participants themselves in terms of stress, ill health or lack of sleep, can affect the quality of the communication. Indeed mood-swings and the effect of drugs or alcohol can contribute to the diminution of quality. Even if the participants are aware of the distracting elements in the environment, unless they remove themselves from it there is little chance that the effects can be efficiently countered.

One of the most common distractions occurs when a verbal exchange for the purpose of eliciting information has to be made in the context of other verbal exchanges taking place simultaneously. It is because distractions diminish the quality of the data received that the sacrifice of context is deemed a risk worth taking in order that verbal exchanges can take place in less distracting environments like interview rooms and clinics.

Individuals vary quite considerably in the amount of information they can take in. This may be due simply to some deficiencies of sensory receptors, but it can also relate to the fact that individuals have widely different rates of processing power. Added to this is the problem of quite different attention spans.

A problem of great significance for change agents is that which arises when the participants in a verbal exchange are operating with very different and unacknowledged reference bases. When systems of knowledge are significantly different and the processes of encoding and decoding information are also different, the possibility of misinterpretation and lack of understanding must become quite great. Allied to the possibility that such a lack of connection may not be noticed, and the assumption of full understanding made, the quality of the data obtained from such an interaction can scarcely be expected to be of a good standard.

The world of the change agent and of his or her clients may be quite different, and visibly so, but their psychological worlds may be even more different because the personal constructs which each uses to make sense of that world are founded on different kinds of experience, disposition and environment. Of course incongruities of outlook fostered by different constructs are allowed for in the training of change agents, but the level of practising objectivity may still be quite low in some areas of difference.

In all interactive situations, factors of which the participants may be unaware will usually be operating. Some of these, like fear, anxiety, mistrust, defences and the attitudes of the individuals, can have constricting and biasing effects on communication, even to the point of blotting out some things and heightening or diminishing others.

A series of problems which verbal material has in common with written data is based in the fact of presentation and will be dealt with later.

It must be obvious from this brief survey that messages about the ordinary and familiar events of life need, for their accurate transmission, what is eventually a closed system in which words have clear-cut and unalterable meanings. But a great deal of the material which has to be transmitted between change agent and his or her clients does not concern the well known and the familiar, but the new and perhaps frightening experiences which no ordered and stereotyped form of words can serve to convey adequately. But when language is adapted and extended to attempt to portray this kind of experience, it tends to become personal, idiosyncratic and a form of communication subject to ambiguity and to misunderstanding.

We live in a verbally oriented society and we tend to think that all human experience can be adequately conveyed in words. Perhaps it can – the problems arise not just in the process of encoding experience in words but also in the decoding process at the receiving end. The gap between sender and receiver can be huge, and for the change agent who is hoping to discover what requires to be changed and to find ways of effecting that change in the information contained in verbal interaction with his or her client, this is an extremely serious problem. The quality and effectiveness of intervention is essentially based on both the quality of the data and the nature of its interpretation.

Some problems in the acquisition of information are concerned with the difference between what we know and what we take for granted; part of our construction of our existence comprises large quantities of data which has seldom been updated, or even reviewed, but is still in active use as a standard against which new information is judged. There is always some difficulty in distinguishing between what we may reasonably believe and what we should actually question. Let us look for a moment at distortion – both involuntary and otherwise.

The concept of the distortion of verbal data must be founded on the idea of an absolute truth. This has to be regarded as an unobtainable ideal, but one which sets a standard of veracity for verbal transactions. But even before the idea of relative truth is broached, the constraints of language ensure that in many exchanges what is said bears little relationship to what was intended to be expressed. Bateson and others have argued that experience is circular and language linear, and the latter certainly not capable of expressing the complexities of the former.

Then there is distortion. This can occur in an involuntary manner where the intent of the speaker is to convey an exact record of salient life events and the distortions are imparted to the information by processes over which the speaker has no control, or of which he or she is unaware. Of these factors, memory and recall are very important, as are selectivity in the acceptance and grading processes.

Distortion can also occur because of varying degrees of conscious influence ranging all the way from deliberate lying, to evasion based on fear; or on a peculiar perception of a particular situation; belief systems; the need to impress, and so on. Even a sense of humour or mischief must have a place in this list. The implication of this deliberate form of distortion for the change agent is that the veracity basis of the interaction between the change agent and the target has to be pragmatically established probably by a process either of compromise or by the submission of one set of perceptions to the other.

Illustration of a form of involuntary distortion
A young single mother of two was a confirmed alcoholic. Her children were in the care of their grandmother while mother received treatment on a daily basis. Her husband had deserted the family some years earlier, supposedly because of his wife's heavy drinking. During the period of treatment this young woman was missing for four days. Her neighbours did not know she was at home – they thought she had been admitted to hospital, a fairly frequent occurrence. The hospital thought she had forgotten to come to the clinic – also a frequent occurrence.

She had in fact drunk herself into complete unconsciousness and for three days had been 'out' or asleep, interspersed with bouts of continued drinking.

When she had been dried out it was obvious that there was a three-day gap in her life about which she could remember nothing. But when asked what she had done and where she had been on the days she had been unconscious, she gave a detailed account of her activities. These included collecting her children from school, taking them to her mother, shopping, visiting friends, tidying the home, and so on – none of which was actually true.

A few months later the pseudo-memory of those missing days was so fully established as part of her past that, in an interview with a social worker, she described the three activity-full days as part of the amazing success of the hospital's treatment programme.

It would seem that even for an individual for whom inexplicable gaps in the memory of her life must have been a fairly frequent occurrence, three whole days was too big a gap not to be filled and, once filled, the confabulation became an actual part of her memory and was accepted as a true recall. Such false memories incorporated in this way can then be offered, along with relatively true memories, as an actual part of their life to anyone requiring knowledge of an individual's past.

One of the important and unintended effects of change efforts is to produce data from clients on which future parts of that change effort will be based, but that information is impaired and contaminated by various factors – there being very little that can be done to validate or corroborate such information except under very unusual circumstances.

Recovered Memory Syndrome

A major concept of determinist intervention is that, in order to change current behaviour, it is necessary to seek in the target's past to find the causes and maintenance factors of this particular target behaviour. For such a process to be at all viable there has also to be a further belief – which is that some part of the human brain stores every event of an individual's existence, from the moment of birth (some believe from the moment of conception). There is little in the way of conscious direct access to this phenomenal feat of memory, and only by an approach through symbolism or by associative chains can memories of long-past experiences be brought to consciousness and used to demonstrate the possible origins of current behaviour.

Lately, where these processes of recall have been employed, some long-forgotten instances of sexual and physical abuse experienced as a child have been brought to light, and, as a result, charges in courts of law have been filed against the 'perpetrators'. In many cases these have been the child's parent. When such cases have been exposed to legal procedures which depend for their prosecution on the production of verifiable evidence, several faults have been seen to emerge.

It immediately becomes apparent that memories recalled in the process of therapy have all the deficiencies of memories of a more conscious and everyday kind. In short, they combine elements of factual accuracy with selectivity and confusion. The latter is usually concerned with the overlay of impressions which have occurred since the event being recalled. For instance, confusion often arises from information about the recalled event in the form of discussion about it, reading about it and seeing photographs of the people involved – which, after a period of time, can no longer be clearly separated from the actual occurrence. Selectivity and emphasis occur because certain facts about the event recalled have a personal loading of interest or of aversion for the individual concerned, and so events are given undue emphasis, the sequence of their appearance becomes changed and they are left in or omitted on this basis.

But the memories of childhood are often a long way in the past, and the likelihood of possible contamination by events occurring since is correspondingly greater than for more recent events. Thus, subject to the need for corroborative evidence, many of these recovered memories failed to prove either their accuracy or, indeed, that they had ever had any basis in actual fact. This of course caused considerable distress to those accused on the basis of the memories being true.

Other factors involved, apart from the process of contamination in the current crop of sexual abuse recall cases and the inability to distinguish memories which originate in actual events and memories which arose from subsequent events, relate to the currency of sexual and physical abuse of children as a topic of immense interest and concern. There is also the direct and indirect imposition of the therapist's beliefs and expectations, amounting in some cases to a directive to the client to search for such memories in the apparent belief that they are there to be found. In other circumstances there is an equally strong belief that such memories would be found, but the pressure to search for them is indirect – usually taking the form of the selection and use of words and of incidents to emphasise.

Because memory is an essential part of many approaches to change practices – which are not therapies in the strict meaning of that term, but rather attempts to improve the quality of life of clients and to support or create new behaviour patterns – it is clear that the nature of recall needs to be understood in a somewhat different way from that which is usually found in the 'caring' professions. Client memories, and those of others who have contact with them, form a large part of the information basis upon which change efforts are formulated.

While the belief that long-term memory is permanent may be quite legitimate and have some evidence to support it, there is little or no support for access to it being free of contamination.

> Normally, memory may be faulty with constant limitations and fluctuations as regards fidelity (reliability), duration, readiness and serviceability.
>
> Jaspers (1963: 173)

Part of that impairment, particularly of historical memories, may consist of the contamination of the recall process by simultaneous evocation of other associations, or by the intrusion of other psychic processes. Apart from this, falsified memories contain large elements of new creation, whereas recall is defined as the retrieval of stored information without change. It is interesting that when evidence of some past event is summoned up in a court of law, the judge is extremely likely to give his or her opinion of what occurred in terms of the 'most likely' form – which implies that it is composed of the most often repeated and confirmed episodes from a number of different sources.

When people in groups are asked to recall their previous group session, the fact which is most noticeable is that, in combination, their responses can incorporate the selectively remembered individual contributions into a much more comprehensive picture.

There is also the problem of the accuracy of the basic information upon which planned intervention is founded. Two factors, *quality* and *probability* are of importance here. With the former it is not possible to know every detail – even of that information which is required for the proposed intervention. This inevitable limitation is well demonstrated in that, even when time is available to collect considerable amounts of data – to the point of being swamped by facts – large gaps in essential knowledge will still exist.

This factor is compounded by the use of various forms of selectivity, often based upon personal factors like preference, prioritisation based on theoretical conceptions, the time available, situational and system priorities, and so on.

Hindsight

In the Rous case, one of the major effects of not just the quality of data but its availability and its priority at the point of need becomes apparent. Given the assumption that Rous deliberately killed – not out of any malice or rage, but deliberately, and in reasonable certainty of the outcome – to activate the system, that 'fact' immediately highlights earlier situations which clearly had the same intent, but at the time were not, or could not be, related in terms of that intent.

The recorded behaviour of someone like Rous, in this case over some 30 years, is bedevilled by two facts: the early diagnosis of schizophrenia; and the isolation of each incident from the others when he came into contact with authority. The diagnosis at 16 may well have been a correct one, but the effect of it would be to follow him wherever he went, not so much as a clinical entity but almost as folklore. So, whatever he did, all who dealt with him were given a logical and acceptable explanation of his otherwise bizarre and sometimes self-destructive behaviour.

Again, as he was dealt with over those 30 years by many different social agencies, each may have had access to the notes of previous dealings, but each was also conditioned and constrained by its own determined purposes and approaches. Thus, despite such records, each would deal with Rous in terms of their own remit; as a criminal; a patient, and so on, though of course modified by knowledge of past behaviour. The essential point here is that there seems to have been no focal point at which all the recorded information on Rous could have been examined dispassionately and free of professional slant so that patterns over time could emerge.

Indeed it is more than possible that, had such a dispassionate appraisal been available, the central theme of Rous' behaviour – as proven by his final act while at liberty – may still not have been noted. The central and pivotal drives of human behaviour are frequently only to be seen as such when the bright light generated by some late event picks them out and a sequence emerges clearly from the background of much other behaviour which, before this point, had seemed equally, if not more, consequential.

It has been stated many times that decisions cannot often be of a superior quality to that of the data upon which they are based. Indeed I have made that comment here. But I have also argued that the quality of data is not the sole determinant of the quality of the decisions made. Rous' case shows quite clearly another major factor – probably even more clearly demonstrated in the case of Kay in Chapter 11 – which hinges on the incompatibility of the standards of precision required by two interacting systems. In the cases of Rous and Kay, those two systems were a diagnostic system, both social and medical, and a legal and justice system. The former are compelled to make decisions on evidence of changes of behaviour, which they know from experience has quite a low probability of being correct, in order to satisfy a system of legal rights which has been defined with a much greater precision and an assumption of a higher degree of the probability of being correct.

Thus the law tends to assume that it is reasonably possible to define the differences between a state when a person can be legally detained as requiring treatment and one in which the same person is capable of existing within the community as an independent person. The medical profession do not have and cannot have either that kind of precision in terms of mental and behavioural conditions, or that kind of precision of prediction. So, in many instances, the demands of the systems are essentially in conflict, and their demands incompatible.

The whole process of decision-making is also complicated by moral and ethical standards – the rights of individuals – which tend to result in individuals, like Kay for instance, being given rights and privileges to which it is assumed they are entitled, and for these to be abused, frequently with tragic consequences.

Without doubt this highlights major dilemmas for change agents. They know that the nature of the evidence (data) they have about the individuals with whom they work is actually inadequate to make the kind of decisions that, legally and morally, they are expected to make. The whole system of data on human behaviour may have high levels of accuracy in assessment and diagnosis, and also even in the change process when some large elements of the situation may be controllable, but the predictive element tends to be poor. Largely, I suspect, because we have very little ability to assess the quality of the changes which have been introduced, but are compelled by other social and moral systems to offer a spurious certainty about them.

20 The Effects of Change Agents

> The consequences of our actions take hold of us quite indifferent
> to our claim that meanwhile we have 'improved'.
>
> Nietzsche (1886)

As most of this book is about the effects which change agents
produce, it may seem that a chapter specifically about 'effects' is
superfluous. But the effects considered here are mainly those which
are in a sense peripheral to the agent's intervention in a situation.
This is not to say that they are wholly unintentional, far from it,
factors like charisma are often consciously exploited and the making and likewise the maintenance of a particular kind of relationship with a target is a central tenet of most approaches.

But whereas a relationship may, for instance, be deliberately
structured in order to forward the process of the change effort, as
with most other factors in this area there is not a great deal of
control over either those elements of such a relationship which are
unforeseen (how could there be?), or its ultimate consequences.

Apart from anything else, developing what is often and euphe-
mistically called a 'relationship of trust' is essentially the preparation of a channel of communication through which the actual
change process can flow in a relatively unobstructed fashion. If
such a channel is essential, and it is, then the probability of persuasive efforts becoming coercive abounds. The difference between
the change agent's intent and what actually occurs must be attributed by both parties to different perceptions, because they are different individuals and operate to different values.

It often appears to be forgotten that a 'change effort' between
agent and client is one which involves perceptions on both sides of
the people engaged in the situations as they arise. There is little
which is concrete, factual and measurable about this process, but
much which is about feeling, experience, perception, and all those
factors which are notoriously idiosyncratic. For instance, comparisons of the perceptions that group members have of their leaders or

therapists with the self-perceptions of those leaders invariably yield wide discrepancies. Even if part of the change process has been an attempt to match perceptions so that agents and targets are on the same wavelength, so to speak, about their areas of mutual concern, there is no guarantee that such matching has actually taken place, or will yet affect outcomes. Indeed, the perception of targets of the power, skill and knowledge of change agents is such that it almost inevitably precludes a close match.

An Example of the Effects of Change Agents

A middle-aged woman came to a psychologist expressing feelings of being depressed, weepy and above all inadequate. After hearing her version of the major events of her life, which were many and of which a large number were bad and a few horrendous, the psychologist asked if she had ever thought of the cumulative effect of stress. The woman admitted that she had not, indeed she had not thought of what had happened to her in terms of stress at all – merely, and in keeping with her background, as the intolerable events of just being alive. So the psychologist explained that research had shown that major events in a person's life, good or bad, often induced stress; the amount varying according to the nature of the incident, and its effect varying according to the nature of the person experiencing it. He showed his client how stress-causing events occurring over a short period of time became cumulative, that is, the effect of one was added to another before the former had worked its way out the individual's system. In the case of his client, where so many events (including two major catastrophes) had occurred within the space of two years, he suggested that little if any of the effect of one event had been cleared before another occurred. He suggested that the woman should take some time to consider the matter and to compile a record of events in date order and, alongside that, what she could remember of the onset of the various problems of which she complained.

The effect of cumulative stress is a widely accepted thesis amongst change agents but, if we stop to examine the effects, some interesting points emerge.

The concept of cumulative stress was unknown to the woman so, when it was presented to her and she had no reason to reject it as fanciful, the idea was an intrusion into her way of thinking about herself. It eventually became integrated as a trace in her memory and started from the point of hearing and from her acceptance of it, to have an effect on her thinking about herself, and it also possessed the potential to ultimately change her behaviour.

There was also the possibility of adding another element to her thinking: if she accepted the idea of cumulative stress as having the force of reason behind it, and if it was significantly different from the previous thinking she had done about the causes of her current state, the idea would have become an event in her life – in the sense that it would precipitate a discontinuity in her thinking. She would now have what she could accept both as a rational and believable explanation of her behaviour, and one which was much less damning in her eyes. Her self-esteem could be raised by no longer thinking that she was unable to cope, weak and inadequate, but instead a victim of circumstances over which she did not have a large element of control. Her behaviour could change, and her sense of being a failure could diminish.

The psychologist who fitted the idea into her thinking also became an addition to her context, in the sense that an authoritative and powerful person who was not previously part of her milieu had now become a part of it; he also possessed the kudos of being the person who had changed her self-esteem and her behaviour.

Cumulative stress may not have been the cause of the problems presented by this woman. What the change agent had done was to offer, and have accepted, an explanation of those presenting problems which removed a large part of the woman's need to consider herself a failure. This is a prime example of the second of the two principal change operations – it changed the way that a situation was perceived rather than changing the situation itself.

If, however, the newly designed perception is not a true one, the possibility continues to exist that future events may prove it to have been false reassurance. For instance, if from now on this particular woman leads an almost crisis-free life and her symptoms return or intensify, she is essentially faced with having to acknowledge the fact that whatever relief she experienced may have been dependent upon some degree of self-deception.

The moral issues at stake here are quite considerable:

• Should the psychologist have offered such an interpretation or explanation when he was probably unable to offer better evidence of reality than inductive reasoning?

• Knowing the nature of the idea he was presenting and its possible effect and risk upon acceptance, was he justified in using the idea to produce what might have been quite long-term relief, but which also possessed the possibility of ultimate distress, and perhaps a large intensifying of problems?

• If he had actually told his client that the relationship of the idea he was presenting to reality was largely statistical, would this have diminished any relieving effect if it produced an expectation of future failure?

My personal answer to these questions has to be that most of the information that change agents work with has the same relationship to fact in terms of the causes of behaviour, as the idea of cumulative stress. If we cannot move to help without possessing unassailably correct causative data, there will be no attempts to relieve suffering and distress or to solve problems and help with difficulties other than from those approaches which are physiological in nature. But such a statement does serve to indicate the huge and essential element of belief which is present in all effective and ineffective change operations, and reveals the puzzling and worrying need of change agents to disguise this fact in a blaze of pseudo-scientific terminology. Perhaps Andreski (1974) was very close to the mark when he suggested the difficulty of verifying assertions about human relations increased the need for change agents to promote public credibility. No one can trust or believe a change agent who has no credibility because credibility is a major part of the change process.

The change agent frequently produces in his or her work the consequence of redefining the situation for the target in terms of his or her own observations and theoretical orientations. This effect may be wholly unintentional or deliberate, but essentially it could allow the target to see his or her situation in a different way and free him or her to deal with it – no longer tramlined by a particular, and probably habitual, perceptual set.

But such a translation, even if only in the terms used to describe situations, problems, attitudes, and so on, can also bring a shift from reality to a non-reality situation. One unhelpful spin-off in this area occurs when the process of dealing with a situation becomes an end in itself.

In such a situation the target has no inclination to proceed to the end point of the change process because, for whatever reason, the process of getting there has become more rewarding than achieving the original intended change. For example, some individuals when admitted to hospital or psychiatric units for treatment are very difficult to discharge, for the simple reason that their symptoms immediately recur when they are in the process of being discharged and they have to be re-admitted. Life in the unit or hospital and undergoing treatment is considerably more desirable than life outside, bereft of the support to which the patient has become accustomed.

With other change agents, the relationship with individuals and groups becomes more important than the change process for which the relationship was originally established, and contact is continued long past the point at which the intended change process should have been completed.

This all throws light on the difficult problem which I have mentioned before – change agents have to come to terms with the rather large discrepancy between the non-verifiable nature of their theoretical propositions and the essential need to appear as credible in the eyes of society. Their needed image is not really sustainable by the true nature of their knowledge.

For instance, in the public eye psychoanalysts tend to emerge with a very powerful public image and so there must be a vested interest in maintaining that image to enable it to withstand the failures which are publicly reported. Social workers are less effective than psychologists as change agents because the latter have managed to create a public image which inspires a certain amount of faith despite occasional public ridicule for some of their more bizarre utterances. The public's faith in social workers is quite low, for the simple reason that few really understand what social workers do and, therefore, they can conveniently be blamed for not doing what is sometimes beyond the scope of any human being to do.

The very fact of creating differences in an individual's situation by just the presence, behaviour, influence and performance of the change agent will almost inevitably bring some degree of change, which may remain after the withdrawal of the change agent and can form the basis of further change. This may have absolutely nothing to do with the change agent's attempts to deliberately change by his or her actions but be entirely due just to his or her presence. In groups, the introduction of a new member, whatever resources that person brings to the group, adds one more person and immediately the potential relationships change, both numerically and formationally; the size of the group, now increased, may alter the relationships of the individuals in it. All are changes which are concerned solely with individuals being in a place and are nothing to do with the actions taken there.

It appears to be the fate of change agents to be susceptible to and to get bogged down in target fads and fashions. Thus we get a considerable fuss made about particular and specific human problems, usually on the basis that they are problems which appear to have been grossly neglected. But in this process the heavy emphasis placed on the problem aspect more or less completely overshadows the fact that what is available to deal with the problem is still the same set of processes as were available for all the other problems. What is new is the problem itself, or at least the attention which is given to it. What generates the appearance of the use of new and specific approaches to that problem, and obfuscates the fact of their being common to all problems, is the investigation of the 'new' problem and the production of large quantities of information about it, both statistical and anecdotal.

This produces the 'specialist' change agent in, for instance, problems relating to gender or race problems. What these specialist change agents have which is different from non-specialist change agents is, it is to be hoped, greater and more detailed knowledge of their specific problem area. The techniques they will use are in essence no different from those which have been in continual use for a very long time. The effect is to increase the number of specialists, but also to obscure the development of methods for dealing with all behavioural problems in favour of an increase in information about specific problems – which, incidentally, also protects the role of the specialist.

> Charisma involves an intuitive awareness of what it is that causes the feeling of woundedness among a people.
>
> Myers (1986: 54)

In 1946 Weber produced the concept of 'the charismatic individual' in that he believed that such individuals had power over others because they were suffering. As Myers says, 'These gifted individuals embody and are able to articulate the emotions of others.'

The concept of charisma in relation to the ways in which change agents are able to influence the behaviour of targets poses some quite difficult problems. In the same way that French and Raven (1959) conceptualised power in terms, not so much of some quantifiable existing entity, but as the effect of the perception of involved individuals in attributing power to specific individuals, so it is with charisma. It appears to be an attribute with which those who are, as Weber maintained, 'suffering' endow certain individuals who appear to have some understanding of that suffering. It is feasible to argue that the perception of charisma arises because those who suffer have a great need to find some individuals of whom they can have some expectation of understanding and help. But, like the perception of power, it must also be subject to change. For instance, if the person who attributes a charismatic status to a change agent in the course of working together has reason to change his or her original evaluation of the change agent because of experience, the attribution of charisma may also change.

As part of the relationship which can be created between agent and target, it is subject to exposure. If relationships of this sort are not based upon the actual production of satisfactory outcomes (that is, from the client's point of view), the possibility of the relationship becoming seen as artificial and untrustworthy is quite large.

Finally, one of the major effects that change agents have upon the change process is the intrusion into it of their prejudices. These comprise philosophical prejudices of the order of speculation which involves seeking understanding without testing against experience and making value judgements and moralistic assessments. The problem of keeping opinion, in the form of judgement, separate from observation is extremely common.

Another problem lies at the heart of the main thesis presented here – the dependence upon a theoretical basis which, at its best, is a series of elegant speculative constructs. Interpretation based upon theory prejudices a genuine assessment of what factual data has been obtained. A third problem lies in considering human beings to be biological machines. Such a mechanistic approach, while often producing some quite interesting results, is also very liable to reduce understanding of the true nature of human behaviour. Equally, rationality plays only a small part in human behaviour and it is often exaggerated by change agents searching to explain such behaviour in rational terms. Other prejudices relate to using descriptive analogies as if they were actual existing entities, and accepting that quantification by itself grants existence to specific entities – especially if granting existence actually compromises the further collection and analysis of data.

What change agents have to bear in mind is that concrete reality is infinite – our ability to understand it, to quantify it and to use it is not.

21 Unforeseen Developments and Ripple Effect

Blessed is he who expects nothing, for he shall never be disappointed.

Alexander Pope (1727), in a letter to John Gay

It is only because we are ill informed that anything surprises us: and we are disappointed because we expect that for which we have not provided.

Charles Dudley Warner (1871)
'Eighteenth Week', *My Summer in a Garden*

The unexpected always happens.

Of course it does – it would be illogical to expect anything else. Warner was absolutely right, the element of surprise is related to the nature of the information we possess. What is unexpected is defined by what is expected. If it were possible for a conscious human being, as Pope suggested, to be able to expect nothing, that utterly remarkable individual would never find anything surprising or unexpected.

The unexpected is something of a statistical entity established by defining what is expected. Thus if a change agent defines a process or a goal by setting up a process of intended change, he or she has established a set of expectations. But, given what may be actually possible in such a relationship, and all the peripheral and involved factors of people and possible events, the creation of an intended change process is in effect establishing a ratio of desired outcomes to possible if largely unknown outcomes, which, numerically, is vastly in favour of the latter.

In gambling terms, the odds against knowing enough to prevent the unexpected occurring are very high.

So the unexpected always happens.

If we accept that fact, it would be essentially logical to make provision for this inability to predict with the requisite degree of accuracy.

There would appear to be two possible methods in use for dealing with this situation:

1. to be remarkably flexible in accommodating the unforeseen events when they occur; and

2. to redefine the extent of the influencing situation, and thus reduce the probable occurrence of unforeseen events.

The second is usually achieved or attempted by increasing the element of control over events and occurrences with a given situation. Events will occur in an individual's or group's situation whether there is intervention by a change agent or not. Intervention, which has a basic element of attempting to control parts of the situation or of redefining perceptions of it, must obviously regard some events which can and do occur as unwanted or pernicious.

For instance, in what Goffman called a 'total institution', an attempt is made to eliminate a considerable number of the influences which would normally be part of a resident's context, and to substitute others which may be considered to be more conducive of the required change of behaviour. It is assumed that, in such circumstances, an individual's behaviour can become more predictable. The problem, as has been much recorded, is that it is almost impossible to eliminate pernicious influences and that even total isolation still leaves the support of mental images and memories. These in themselves are sufficient to create unexpected responses and behaviour patterns to confound the change agent's intended outcomes.

In Chapter 3 when discussing intended change, I quoted the situation of Mrs Jones and her family as being illustrative of several of the forms of that type of change, of the data bases used, of the change efforts employed and of the kind of consequences which can ensue. The ultimate consequences of the break-up of the family and Mrs Jones' suicide are prime examples of unintended and unforeseen outcomes. Working in what was considered to be the best interests of the target client, Mrs Jones, to deal with her depression and to remove her from the source of personal violence, actually brought about not only her death but other dramatic consequences for the rest of the family.

244 CHANGE, INTERVENTION AND CONSEQUENCE

On a larger social scale, the fact of unforeseen consequences has been understood for a considerable length of time. For instance, the period of prohibition in the United States was originally intended to reduce the consumption of alcohol. It might have been expected that this could well bring about the illicit production and sale of liquor, but what was not foreseen was that this would in turn lead to organised syndicates and gang warfare on a huge scale, and to the consequent corruption and intrusion of the mobs into political life. Nor could it have been predicted that the most enduring consequence of prohibition has been the organised crime that arose to take advantage of the situation.

Direct intervention in society to bring about what may be absolutely desirable changes, notoriously throws up consequences which have the characteristics noted in the prohibition sequence; they are unanticipated, they are usually far greater in scope, intensity and force than the original changes and they are usually much more durable.

On an individual and small group level, while the effects are much the same very little attention has been given to the phenomenon of unforeseen consequences.

At a very simple level, a pertinent and telling example will serve to illustrate most of the characteristics of unforeseen consequences.

The concept of consequence is, as we have seen, something which logically follows some action or event. It is entailed by that event and, in some areas of social behaviour, has to be accepted. There has been a marked increase in our society of the evasion of responsibility for the consequences of actions. Indeed there has developed an apparently acceptable behavioural pattern of the transfer of blame on to anyone or anything that can be involved. There is no attempt to deny the consequences of behaviour, but an enormous increase in the refusal to accept that the incident which occasioned those consequences was the responsibility of the individual or group originally involved.

The process, as I have just suggested, is best described as one of the transfer of blame, and it creates problems for change agents.

For instance, a child may be admitted to hospital with every sign of having been physically abused. The parents do not deny that they were the abusers. Some years ago they would in all probability have attempted to excuse and explain their behaviour by claiming provocation, such as endless crying on the part of the child, or being extremely worried about their financial condition, and so on. These are all explanations which kept the responsibility for what had happened with them; they were in effect mitigations. Now the explanation is more likely to take the form of an accusation that the actual cause of their behaviour is to be laid at someone else's door. The social worker is blamed for not preventing their injuring their child; society is to blame because it has not given them the opportunities they felt were their right; and, ultimately, the government as the overall responsible institution for all society is to blame.

While all these claims often do have some justification, the overall effect is to remove much if not all of the responsibility for the parents' behaviour on to others. This then poses an essential problem for change agents: if his or her activities are directed at demonstrating the connections between the behaviour and responsibility of the parents, with what happened to the child being a consequence of that behaviour, the result of the agent's intervention is liable to be very different from what might have been expected.

This is but one example of pursuing an apparently logical connection of cause and effect in behaviour without knowledge of, or accepting as influential, the attitudes of those involved towards that apparently logical connection. The whole process of the transfer of blame is fraught with difficulties for the change agent and is a fertile producer of unforeseen consequences. In essence, what is important in the effort to effect change is not the accuracy of the belief of the causes of particular problems, but the pattern of the belief itself. It is a fact of the existence of the individual concerned and, right or wrong as it may be, the effect it has on behaviour has to be taken into consideration.

The transfer of blame is only part of a much larger producer of unintended consequences, which might be described as belonging to a religion, but which includes all the other beliefs which people may hold, such as about rights and duties, about justice, fairness, the social system, employment, and so on. Modern societies no longer have coherent and generally accepted belief systems – largely because the societies themselves are not coherent, in that they comprise so many different sections, most of which subscribe more fully to their own particular ideas than to any overall ideas which might be said to be those of the society as a whole. Indeed another problem to add to this immense variety is the factor of change itself, in that ideas which were prominent in guiding one section of a population are quickly replaced by others, and stable long-enduring values, where they exist, tend to get submerged in this plethora of rapid and often superficial change.

One of the relevant and unforeseen effects of this situation is that the theories of behavioural sources which change agents use tend to deal with the basics of human behaviour, which may well be constant, but when the environmental influences have a major effect on behaviour those theories can be less than helpful in predicting, not so much outcomes, but ways of dealing with behavioural manifestations. If, as appears most likely, there are considerable shifts in public values, then texts based on the values of even a few years ago may well be out of date.

Much of the evidence of unexpected outcomes has been discussed elsewhere in this text, it remains to state here some of the consequences of these unexpected factors – including, most prominently, the distortion of the whole change process. To reiterate, an action can only be as good as, and may be much worse than, the quality of the data upon which it is based. There is a belief on the part of change agents that the recall of past experience has a degree of accuracy which will allow it to be used as the basis of the construction of a change strategy. But that data can frequently be shown to be subject to invasion, contamination, simulation and impairment, and so some serious reassessment of its value is necessary.

I suppose that one of the most important factors to be considered here is that, when accepting verbal information, the change agent must be aware that what is offered – apart from any distortions caused by selective memory – must also contain at least a bias which is founded in the target's assumptions about what is required, and also what he or she believes may be in his or her best interests to deliver in the kind of situation that he or she thinks they may be in. The individual's context will have determined his or her interpretation of the situation, and provided the basis for the selection of material and the manner of its delivery.

There needs to be some consideration of what has been called the 'ripple effect' in producing unforeseen occurrences. In essence, this is what happens when the contacts between agent and target spread into the support system/networks of the target and produce effects there which may never have been considered. Indeed, this process goes both ways in that the change agent is also affected by it. Consider that most agents are working for an agency of some sort and have either a supervisor or at least the need to report back on the work that they are doing. The effects of this process can often be seen when the supervisor has offered an analytic comment on what the agent has been doing and this then feeds back into the change process with the client.

Thus the ripples flow backwards and forwards with the obvious potential of causing unforeseen effects for the main protagonists. Some of these effects are actually created by one side of the transaction as part of the process. But what is often overlooked is that ripple effects create reverse ripples which flow back towards the centre of the disturbance. These, in their turn, create for the agent and the client unlooked-for outcomes which offer still another possibility.

When such unlooked-for events occur there is a strong tendency to attempt to explain them. Because their origins are unknown, the ascription of causes has a strong inclination to be based in the wrong areas of the change experience. So the response produces even further possible unsought outcomes. The spiral effect of these consequences is well illustrated by Laing where he describes a conversation in which the two persons involved keep missing the point of each interaction and the whole encounter spirals further and further away from any form of real contact.

One of the problems in this area with the so-called 'talking therapies' is not so much that they operate on unprovable and unverifiable theoretical bases, but that when they achieve some measure of success, which they undoubtedly do, there is no way of being absolutely sure whether the success can be directly ascribed to the therapy, or that the target had a higher than chance probability of some similar change occurring anyway, or that some unintended by-product of the therapy had produced the outcome.

In some cases of addiction, it has been found appropriate to abandon any change efforts directed at the addiction per se, in favour of concentrating on, as it were, teaching addicts a vocabulary by which they could learn to describe what was happening to them without recourse to the junkie's or alcoholic's jargon. The semi-mystic belief that words have immense power and that the right words in the right place can bring about change may still be something which is deeply ingrained in the human brain. But it is evident that there is a great deal of truth in the idea that to be able to name something clearly and unequivocally, no matter how intangible it may be, can create a sense of power over that something and an enhanced ability to control it. In the case of the addicts, there was also the abandonment of the jargon associated with their scene, which contains a large element of bravado and of shoring-up of the individual addict. When this is clear, one major obstacle to a reality-based assessment of the problem has been removed. In other words, as I have commented earlier, it makes the process of conversion from one set of beliefs to another, in this case to those of the change agent supported by society, much easier to accomplish.

To follow this through, is it possible to assert that the talking therapies create a vocabulary as part of the process of interpretation which may in itself generate a greater ability to control behaviour than the intended process of therapy?

The answer may well be affirmative. But there is no way in which this can be proved for two very simple reasons:

- There is no base line against which to measure the effect of therapy. Because the explanatory nature of all the inductive theories of behaviour cannot demonstrate a direct cause/effect sequence between input of therapy and any consequent change of behaviour without turning proof into an act of faith, what actually occurs after therapy and during it can always be claimed as being caused by it. If there is no possibility of adducing evidence of the effect of therapy, there can equally be no evidence of the fact that it had no effect, or that any effects were brought about by factors other than the therapy.

- Because 'talking therapies' and their derivative forms rely so heavily on the formation of a relationship between the therapist and the client, and indeed use that relationship as a therapeutic tool, it would be almost impossible to adduce which parts of the relationship were consciously applied and took root and which did not and, more importantly, which parts took root without being consciously directed as part of the processes of contagion and imitation – processes strongly based in childhood learning experiences.

It has occurred to social work theorists in the past that clients of social work practices may have some clear personal understanding that the process involves a degree of bargaining in which rewards within the competence of the social workers to give can be procured by learning to say things and even, temporarily, to see things in a particular way. This is the reverse side of the conversion idea, and also part of the process of public conformity which we have dealt with earlier. Cynical this may be, but at least it shows some recognition of the fact that the process of social work, like that of therapy, is badly served by being described as a process of 'giving' – whether what is denoted as given is care or treatment. Clients, targets, what you will, have lives, minds, concerns and opinions of their own – if they seek change or are compelled to accept it, it can only be effective if, at many points of contact, it is credible and contains a great deal of the client's ideas and input.

What I hope to have shown by the brief presentation here of the many diversions which can occur in outcomes is that the whole process of the change of human behaviour is much nearer to our concept of chaos than it is to our concept of order. Our ability to predict, and our ability to control those factors which may influence outcomes is so uncertain; there is so much which is unknown and indeed unknowable that even the degree of success which is obtained is remarkable.

It is quite obvious that a true estimate of the degree of success in change operations is not one which the general public would accept as valid as it has such high expectations and need of an effective change effort system. It is not surprising, therefore, that no such true estimate exists, nor is there much likelihood that it will until change efforts can be presented with a much more certain success rate.

22 Resistance, Reversion Effects and Maintenance Processes

Change is the process by which the future invades our lives, and it is important to look at it closely, not merely from the grand perspectives of history, but also from the vantage point of the living, breathing individuals who experience it.

Tofler (1970: 11)

It is necessary to be very careful about the idea of 'resistance to change'. In many instances the term is used pejoratively by change agents about the behaviour of their target individuals. Usually the implication is that there is some unfortunate lack of perception by the client about the change processes involved being essentially beneficial. Indeed the term 'resistance' has come to have the connotation not just of a block to progress but of active defiance of it.

But it is the prerogative of all human beings to resist that which they either do not understand, or believe to have possible deleterious effects, or which generates fear or anger. That all these reasons for resistance may be incorrect or unnecessary as protective moves is irrelevant. Survival comes high on everyone's list of priorities and protective moves and attitudes can only be based upon the perceptions and information which are available at the time of their making. That much of the power behind these protective measures may stem from motivations which the individual producing them would find considerable difficulty in explaining rationally or at all, is also irrelevant. They can and do exist and, unless this fact is accepted and the possible nature and source of such resistive gambits is understood, the likelihood that change processes will be effective is greatly reduced.

Even more so, those change processes that do take place will have a level of quality which will be essentially dictated by the degree of power such resistive processes still possess. For instance,

acceptance of the necessity for change may be at the level of compliance rather than at that of whole-hearted acceptance. In fact
public conformity has always been regarded as a security gambit
which has, as an integral ingredient, the intention to revert to a
previous behaviour once the pressure to change has been removed.

Resistance may also be based upon factors of which the change
agent knows nothing, and which the target may have considerable
difficulty in explaining, but which I have variously referred to here
as context, networks or anchors. These are those factors of environment and relationships; of experience and support which maintain an individual in particular patterns of thought and behaviour.
Thus an individual may be aware that the changes in his or her
behaviour which are being suggested would run somewhat counter
to the pressures and influences of the network.

We must explore these factors and others, for the simple reason that resistance is often offered by change agents as an explanation of their relative failure. Is it true that change processes
actually fail because of hostile resistance or deliberate inertia on
the part of clients? Or could it be that the protective gambits
which we all need and use have been inadequately assessed, their
possible influences unforeseen, and thus the consequences inaccu-
rately attributed?

One factor which may be basic to resistance is the actual scope
for change which exists in individuals and groups and perhaps, just
as importantly, their ability to make use of it. If we insist on
changing people, we are bound to discover the extent of their ability to cope with change – which implies not just a calculation of
present capacity but also of future probability. Some schools of
thought actually would have us believe that the capacity of individuals to change is immense and largely untapped. This may be
true, though there is little enough hard evidence for it. There is
evidence, however, of the fact that there are limits to what individuals can do – whether these are genetic in origin or whether
they have arisen because of the process of maturation and what we
pay attention to and what we neglect.

Part of the change process has therefore to prepare people for
the process of change, to learn how to learn with the production of
anticipatory information. It is noticeable that, in groups which are
run by people who have been through the same process of change
as they are now offering to others, the element of trust is high. We
assume this is because there is some knowledge in the leaders of
the practical steps which have to be taken, and they are evident
proof of a successful outcome. The ability to predict outcomes with

some degree of accuracy certainly serves to increase the willingness of clients to co-operate with the change process.

However, people differ widely in the degree to which they can anticipate the future. Long-term change may therefore be mystifying and frightening, and may need to be split down into manageable bits which lead successively into that future. How many times do we hear people saying, when something dreadful has occurred, that we must learn all the possible lessons from the situation so that it never happens again? But in order to learn from mistakes we need to be able to project our learning, not just into the present, but also into the future, and thus anticipate what will be needed.

Tofler (1970) suggested that shock was the 'disease' of change. He felt this was so because transitional change, instead of being a step-by-step process, was often one in which the stabilities of the past state were almost wholly abandoned. This is very similar to the idea of 'the edge of chaos' theorists – who insist that effective change is only possible when there remains sufficient stability in conjunction with the necessary chaos to bear the fact of change. Many people have become aware of the shock that enforced and relatively sudden change brings about and that, for the most part, tends to be described as threat. By definition, threat implies that the current stability of behavioural patterns which forms the basis of an individual's existence is in some way being challenged.

It is possible to regard these behavioural patterns as stability zones, as Tofler does, consisting of enduring relationships, habits and daily routines. It is these which will form the basis of support for any change and if they are also threatened by proposed change, there will most certainly be resistance to that change.

Tofler also suggests that some change is necessary in order to prevent stagnation. But such change has to be at an appropriate level, and has to be made in the right areas. The changes which a change agent will seek to make may not conform to this pattern of safety. If that occurs, shielding processes will undoubtedly arise – to try to block out stimulation to change which is moving the process close to the adaptive limit of the client. In some ways this thesis of adaptive limits is paralleled by a more obvious limitation process which is that of energy use. Even in the most active people, as well as those whose energy levels are low, there is some need to prioritise energy use because its supply is not endless.

In Carolyn Sherif's (1976) book on Social Psychology, there is a theme of 'anchors' which runs all the way through. One of the strong arguments about resistance and about change can be founded on this theme. Anchors are those factors which hold people relatively stable in their social orbits. It would appear that no change which has any real effect can be achieved if the holding power of these anchors has not first been realised and allowed for. Indeed, these anchors may be sufficient to explain how individuals who achieve change in circumstances which are specially created to facilitate it are often unable to sustain that change, at least in any considerable degree, when they are free of those circumstances.

What would appear to happen is not so much that they revert because the sustaining effect of the specially created circumstances has been removed, but because the networks which held them in their particular position in the first place have been able to reassert their effect – either because they were never removed or because their presence was not even acknowledged. This would tend to explain why some changes which appear to be accepted by the targets never seem to become integrated, but remain superficial. They have in truth been accepted because the client deemed there was some pressing need to appear to conform.

Thus it would seem that any attempt to change an individual or group would need to be based upon some consideration of the anchors which hold and sustain their present behavioural patterns. Of course such anchors are not expected to be entirely a counter influence to change as, if they are truly understood, their use in the change process in terms of modifying existing anchors or even creating new ones which sustain the changes being made would undoubtedly be a wholly admirable and successful process. The process is, however, complicated when, as we have seen will eventually happen, the change agent becomes part of the context of the client and thus probably one of the anchors involved. The only approach to this of which I am aware is that any change agent must know that such a circumstance inevitably arises, and must not ignore it but accept it and work with it.

Another element in the process of apparent resistance can be that of inertia. In the material world, inertia is what causes a body to appear to resist movement when in a state of rest, and to resist being stopped when in a state of movement. The problem is essentially one of energy.

It takes the application of energy to any state in which an individual exists in order to bring about change to another state; except that of degeneration when the energy flow is outwards, not inwards. In physics this is external energy applied to what, in most instances, can be said to be inert material; that is, to material which has no innate energy of its own except that which holds its atoms together. In the case of human beings, a major part of the application of energy to effect change is internal, by which I mean that it has to come from an animate being who possesses energy and is already using some of that energy to pursue various ends.

It follows, therefore, that it is not possible to say with such simple directness that one of the major aspects of bringing about change in human beings is the requirement of the application of direct external energy. What has to be said, which is somewhat similar, is that resistance to change requires the use of energy to overcome it. But the main difference is that human resistance is not usually a physical fact which is constantly present (i.e. inertia), but tends to be largely composed of a relatively rational appreciation of the need to commit energy; a need that is assessed on the basis of a series of priorities. The general tenor of such an assessment appears to be based upon the assumed cost such a use of energy would involve. Whereas in physics, therefore, the application of the right amount of energy, at the right place, at the right time and in the right direction will always overcome inertia, to overcome human inertia requires the application of the added factor of the internal energy of the client. This is under rational control, which is based upon the idea that only a given amount of energy exists and is thus a scarce resource which has to be allocated according to the individual's idiosyncratic priorities.

It is this cost/reward thesis of human behaviour which would seem to indicate that true change, as far as human beings is concerned, can only be brought about by the individual him or herself. Help and guidance may assist in this process but, unless that initial energy is committed to the process – even if the required change is well within the capability of the individual to achieve – it will not take place, or if it does it will scarcely be a durable change.

If learning which takes place in a change situation is to become a permanent feature, it has to be capable of being transferred from the situation in which it was acquired to the general life of the individual. For instance, if an individual goes through a good training group experience, the immediate effect is one of emotional and spiritual change and, while the group is in existence and the individual is a member of it, this emotional high is sustainable. The effect might well be to alter an individual's perception of what is possible in terms of his or her own social behaviour and reactions to others; or it may open up different levels of awareness, of thoughts; it may actually develop, change, supplant or implant important beliefs. But when the group no longer exists, either because it literally ceases to be or because the individual no longer attends, whatever was gained or changed, in whatever form, has to be sustained by something other than the support which was readily available within the confines of the initiating group. Usually there are two sources of support available: the memories of what the individual believed occurred within the group; and the individual's determination to act according to those recalled experiences. In other words, if what may have started as an emotional experience coupled with a source of learning is to exist divorced from the sustenance of its origins, it has to become an almost entirely rational process by which the individual conducts him or herself on the basis of his or her understanding of what occurred in the group situation.

Now whether or not this group process can be called one which instigates an increase in sincerity and honesty or an increment of insight is debatable. But these are the words frequently used to describe the outcome of group training sessions. It can, however, also be described as a process of selective programming which, usually with the individual's consent, is presented as a coherent, morally sound form of social existence which has the value of possessing a seemingly less maladaptive nature than the life-style of the individual in place before the group experience.

One factor that appears to be fundamentally important in this process is the element of loss; which seems to be a universal experience of all group members when they leave such a group. This holds true if there has been an emotional catastrophe which has forced the withdrawal of a group member before the completion of the group programme. The descriptions of parting from training and sensitivity training groups frequently use terminology which could equally be used in grief at the death of a loved one. It seems inconceivable that such universal recognition of loss would be one of the most significant response patterns of participants if what the individual had gained from being a member of the group was not perceived as being of inestimable value, and could change the major patterns of his or her life outside the group.

Such a response is indeed much more compatible with the realisation that what the individual gained most as a member of the group was almost wholly dependent on *being* a member, and that any appearance of change is/was largely sustained by being continually present amongst those who have had, or are having, similar experiences, and offer similar commitment to the group's aims.

Thus the adaptation needed to transfer from the group experience to the ordinary social processes of life without access to the group, necessitates the establishment of that experience as a memory model and the exercise of conscious, rational action to implement the learning and change which may have been embodied by it. It at this point when the supportive nature of the group has to be replaced, and in the face of the indifferent and sometimes hostile nature of ordinary existence, that a second important factor emerges.

Most of the research into the continuing effect of having been a member of a group is, at best, equivocal about the way originally accepted change is sustained over a period of time and of absence from the founding group, or substitute. Indeed, as most such research is based upon subjective responses by participants to questionnaires, there is much to question in the evaluative reports which emerge. But, even so, their tenor would seem to indicate a rapid decline of the acquired change patterns unless, within the everyday life of the ex-group member, there is some system which actually reinforces and supports the change patterns induced during the period of group membership.

Thus, what is at issue here is whether the consequences of group experiences are in reality somewhat different from the expectations of those who programme them and of those who receive the programming, and whether it would be more realistic to suggest to potential group members that the percentage of change which will probably remain without the advent of largely propitious supportive circumstances, is relatively small.

One final point on this theme is that one of the main supportive factors of group membership is the ongoing possibility of using the group as a reference on how to cope with new life problems, some of which may well have been brought about by the early changes induced and supported by the group. Without the group, such developments would have to be dealt with by the individual and such support as he or she may have available. The only viable alternative would occur if the changes which had happened were not entirely experiential but were related to a formal system of understanding, so that new developments – while unknown and unexperienced – could be dealt with on the basis of their being recognised as fitting somewhere in the formal system.

The explanation of the relatively large percentage of training group members who are actually damaged by attending such groups may be due as much to this particular problem as to the one usually offered, which is that such members were emotionally damaged before they became members.

The process of the memory of the change experience taking

over, through recall and retrieval of stored and learned impressions from the support element of the intervention system – individual or group – is dependent firstly upon the quality and quantity of the initial filing, subsequently upon retention, then upon effective recall; and finally upon being able to act on it. Thus the whole process of social learning, which has been externally stimulated and encouraged, has to be transferred to an internal process dependent upon recall and energised by an act of will. The movement is from 'other directed' to 'inner directed'. It may not be possible for some people to achieve this kind of change in any circumstances – a matter of personality, ability or experience – for it is one which, in most cases, needs constant support from others to achieve anything.

Having maintained that change is a universal of human existence, it is somewhat paradoxical to also state that a common element of the failure of change processes is the relative lack of permanence of their intended results. But the paradox is easily resolved when the time-scale over which the criticism is lodged is taken into account.

Many change efforts are directed to only a relatively small part of an individual's total existence. Despite this, such induced change may still filter effects through the whole of the individual's existence. Alternatively, they may remain small and proportionally insignificant. So, when permanence or durability of change efforts is under discussion, the concept must be related to the time in which such a change could become an integral part of an individual's or system's behaviour, and not to some long-term and distant point. Indeed, permanence of such a long-term nature would be counter to the constant state of change, which we know to be the natural order of things.

If a change effort is successful, and the individual or system accommodates it so that it becomes not an addition or an accretion but an integral part, then not only has the behaviour of the individual or system been changed, but the elements of the change must also be changed. They are no longer elements introduced from outside the individual or system (whether they are digital or analogue changes is irrelevant); by being part of the new and different system they are inevitably adapted from their original form in order to become a functioning part of the system. This may well be the essential criterion of the success of any change effort, i.e. not only in that it is accepted, but that it is changed by that process of adaptation.

For example, the process of desensitisation is taught as a technique to overcome particular phobias. The fact that the phobic individual progressively learns that by a formulaic procedure he or she can overcome the effects of the phobia means that, in many instances, the process is successful in freeing individuals from what may have been a severely limiting and handicapping process. Whatever it is that has generated the phobic state undoubtedly remains in place but the individual has learned how to cope with its effects.

The process is formulaic – which means the individual learns how to perform several routines and procedures which reduce the handicapping effect of the phobia and make the handicapping pressure manageable. The change element is essentially the formula which has been learned. Without doubt, the encouragement and support which the phobic individual has received from the change agent during the process of learning to apply it was largely instrumental in achieving this end. What is interesting is that when that support is withdrawn, as it inevitably must be – usually upon sufficient evidence of the individual's ability to handle the formula reasonably successfully – it is often found that the formula has itself been changed; adapted from the original state. It has been personalised; not just accommodated and adapted but redefined, probably only in minor ways, but it has become an instrument of the individual.

Such changes as these have the reputation of being durable in the sense that they continue to function in their personalised form for as long as the individual may need to use them, or until their use is overtaken by other factors of a pathological nature which change the priorities of the individual concerned.

Desensitisation techniques tend to work for several interesting reasons which, when compared with other change efforts, may serve to highlight some of the problems.

1. The area of behaviour chosen to be dealt with is both clearly defined and, while undoubtedly significant in the distress and difficulty it may entail, is still small in relation to the individual's total behaviour pattern. It is this smallness which allows for the continuation of the major stable patterns of behaviour upon which the changes will rest.

2. The intervention is directed not at the cause of the phobic state but at the emergent behaviour.

3. The process of learning is one with which all are familiar, and the instruments of control are usually extremely simple.

4. Success is related to the degree of determination with which the individual is prepared to pursue the implementation of the control elements.

5. It appears essentially logical.

Few of these elements are present in change efforts applied to other aspects of human behaviour.

Initially, induced changes tend to have no very deep root in the life of the individual. They are relatively fragile growths, and thus easily displaced. The sheer pressure that can be exerted by those social factors which most likely were partly responsible for generating the behaviour which was subjected to the change process, is almost irresistible. Given the fact that these influences were often in place for very long periods of time without challenge, and probably started when the individual had least reason and ability to resist them, this is quite logical. Indeed it may not be too strong to maintain that the behavioural patterns which developed under this kind of pressure did so because in some way they were deemed to be useful. Perhaps a better way of describing the process would be to say that, however bizarre and illogical the produced patterns may appear, they were at the time of production and development preferable to anything else within the knowledge of the individual. They may have had a survival value; been used to block out other patterns; or to achieve some particular ends, and so on.

As long as the patterns of behaviour were successful, what they cost the individual to maintain them was an acceptable expense. Even if that expense was unacceptable in one sense it would have been preferable to any known and available alternatives. In other words, the individual could see no other way of dealing with the situation, at whatever cost. The fact remains that such behaviour patterns draw their support, not just from the individual who produces them, but also from others within his or her social ambit who come to have some expectations that such are part of the individual's life-style.

Indeed, as Laing and others have shown quite clearly, individuals may be held in patterns of behaviour which serve the needs of others much more efficiently than they do the individual performing such patterns.

How clever has one to be to be stupid? The others told her she was stupid. So she made herself stupid in order not to see how stupid they were to think she was stupid, because it was bad to think they were stupid. She preferred to be stupid and good, rather than bad and clever.

Laing (1971: 23)

One of the major problems of change agents has always been quite simply, that an individual's manifest behaviour is sustained by the networks in which that individual has his or her being; any change in those patterns of behaviour has to include some element of at least cognisance and, preferably, use of those influence factors. The end result can be reduced to which influence proves the stronger and, indeed, to which the individual as target actually gives most credence.

Planned intervention aims to effect change in selected areas of behaviour, perception, insight, understanding, and so on, as well as in the environmental situation. But by virtue of focusing on target areas, such intervention cannot equally focus on other areas of an individual's existence which are inextricably linked with, and interdependent upon, those target areas. What compels change agents to ignore such areas is that there are so many of them and they are largely unknown even to the target individual. In some instances having to ignore large areas of the network does not matter, but in others it does – and then it becomes a very prominent candidate as the cause of the quick extinction of newly acquired changes such as skills, attitudes, etc.

It is commonly assumed that if an individual is 'opened up' (that is 'unfrozen' in Kurt Lewin's phrase) to receive an intended change process, then before he or she is released from the confines of the change situation, he or she should be 'refrozen'. That this process seals in the changes which have been induced is the somewhat pious hope of the change agents. In essence, what is being attempted is the turnover from an assisted change process to one of individual control of and responsibility for what has been acquired, while at the same time trying to reduce the degree of vulnerability created when the opening-up process started. In some terminology this would be described as a process of integration and adaptation. It is axiomatic that the opening-up processes are essentially easy to achieve and the sealing-off processes very difficult. If clients are thus left relatively exposed, whatever changes have taken place are subject to influences which are at the very best non-supportive and the individual because of the process of acquiring them, may be more vulnerable than previously.

With all the processes of preparation and information which may be provided, there is no guarantee that they will work for the same reason that all the change processes are vulnerable – namely lack of any validated information about how the system of integration of change actually works.

23 Issues and Problems

In the previous five chapters I have attempted to detail the effects of most of the main situational factors, beliefs and actions involved in the process of intended change. The reasons for this attempt are quite simple:

• In pursuit of a spurious image of certainty, such factors are consistently minimised by practitioners, with the obvious result that – although ignored – such factors continue to produce effects upon practice which are then often attributed to other influences.

• Until such effects are considered as realities affecting practice, and are not evaded, there is small chance that practice can be adapted to take cognisance of such factors and, indeed, used constructively so that a large element of reality can be introduced into the process.

It may dent professional images somewhat to have to accept the reality of what changes can be effectively pursued and to what level, but at least it will avoid the unethical process of overestimating the possible, and the subsequent levels of disappointment and, in some cases, damage which can ensue. Indeed if, as seems increasingly likely in the light of genetic research such as that into the probability that male homosexuality is at least partially brought about by genetic factors, more and more evidence accumulates of the genetic and biochemical sources of behaviour, a great deal of our intended change processes will be shown to have been tinkering with methods of controlling outcomes, rather than of changing essential sources.

What seems to emerge clearly from our look at the consequences of intervention in intended change processes are the effects (most of them largely unintended) that the kind of information available to change agents can produce in the change process. There are the problems relating to language – most change agents operate through the medium of speech and they are immediately faced with the impossibility of defining and explaining ideas, theories, insights and intentions because of the restrictive nature of language. At the best, theoretical attempts to explain behaviour are, and can only be, crude approximations to what actually happens. No change agent can go into a situation without not only having expectations of what he or she might find, but also some system of ordering the information he or she expects to discover. Without doubt, even with the greatest care being taken that these factors shall not influence the situation, there is a strong, even irresistible, force for this process to generate a self-fulfilling prophecy.

Consequence

Because the major consequences of intervention may turn out to be those which were least expected and unforeseen, there is a need not just to note immediate consequences but to track those consequences through the system.

On Wednesday 8 May 1996 Celia Beckett was jailed for 5 years by Mr Justice Garland in the High Court for poisoning two of her daughters and killing one. Beckett, diagnosed as suffering from a compulsive personality disorder – Munchausen's syndrome by proxy – had also originally been charged with grievous bodily harm to a third daughter, Clare, who had died at the age of 7 after a mysterious brain injury, but this case had been dropped.

The interesting fact of this case is not so much that it took 8 years from the first attempt on the children's lives for it to be realised that this woman was wholly capable of killing her own children, but that it highlights once again the enormous gap which exists between what the public expect of change agents and what those agents have the capacity to deliver. During the proceedings, evidence was offered of the way that social workers had allowed one child back into the care of her mother after she had been hospitalised as the result of a massive overdose of anti-depressants administered by her mother.

David Graves (1996: 90) quoting from the Nottinghamshire Child Protection Committee wrote:

It said: What the analysis reveals is that as years went by and worrying evidence mounted there was a kind of mental rigidity which prevented workers from thinking the unthinkable and taking hold of this tragic situation. The records are dotted with comments from social services, health and police to the effect that Celia Beckett would not harm her child. It is difficult for us to see why there was such misplaced confidence.

The gap in expectations which led to the unforeseen consequences in this case is frequently explained by reference to the assessment of the available information. This usually includes:

• There was insufficient information.

• There was sufficient information to make a correct assessment, but it was not available at the time to those who needed it.

• The assessment of the available information was wrong because
  – the information was inadequate for a true assessment to be made; or
  – there was a lack of skill in making assessments; or
  – there was a distortion of the information to fit preconceived theories or ideas; or
  – there was tramline thinking which obviated the possibility of thinking being extended beyond the apparently normal range.

In the case of Beckett, what she did was entirely compatible with the known evidence of her behaviour patterns, and yet she was consistently held to be incapable of exactly that behaviour.

What reason can there be for change agents not to see evidence which should cause them to be suspicious and to postulate outcomes well outside the ordinary?

Here, the consequences of such a lack of imagination led not to the caring family situation towards which the change agents were working, but to the death of two of the three children; to the attempted murder of the third; and to a 5-year prison sentence for a woman who, as the judge admitted, required treatment and help rather than a custodial sentence. The gap referred to above is clear evidence of the lack of effective understanding of the potential of human behaviour patterns and of any validated methods of bringing about change.

There is a complex relationship between individual elements of a behavioural pattern and time. The exact nature of individual behavioural events is frequently revealed by the passage of time to be contextual; that is, they are only parts of a larger behavioural pattern and, in this embedded form, can be seen to possess a somewhat different nature and focus from that which could be attributed to them when considered as unitary events.

They are in fact steady states in a stochastic whole, and their true value can only be adjudged in relation to the larger context in which they occur.

The case of Rous quoted earlier is eloquent in this respect. The individual elements of his behaviour, as they were perceived by those charged with dealing with them, were almost always not related to the larger context in which they appeared. This was for a variety of reasons, one of which was the non-availability of previous assessments, and, as a result, each incident was dealt with on its own current merit, as appeared fitting at the time. In retrospect, each of those individual episodes appeared as part of the urgent need by which Rous was consumed, which was to be removed from the terrifying responsibility of controlling his own behaviour.

It is the acceptance of these individual events non-contextually which causes change agents to make decisions based on information and assessment which are only partially relevant, and thus almost certain to ensure that unforeseen consequences will be of greater ultimate significance than those which could be adduced from the individual events taken in isolation.

It is only when a unitary event embodies most of the characteristics of the larger stochastic pattern that such an assessment can come near to proving to be effective, by being closely related to the whole.

However, it must be stated that unintended outcomes can produce good results as well as bad. For instance, it must be ethically acceptable for targets to change for the better for the wrong reasons when they arise from effects which are wholly peripheral to the intended change process. But, nevertheless, it must also be maintained that intervention strategies that do not consider the ecology of the problems they attempt to alter will tend to breed a higher order of pathology. The reality of the client's situation is the primary reality, and this dictates what is possible – not what the change agent or other agency might consider desirable.

Probability

In all the many possible outcomes of a situation over a period of time, the process of intended change, by definition, causes its practitioners to select one or two as being preferable to all those which are known. This has two immediate effects:

1. Although any change agent is aware that a considerable number of possible outcomes are unknown and may exist only as potential, there is nothing which can be done about it.

2. It also creates a situation which is new, in the sense that before the choice was made it did not exist, and in which those involved were indifferent to the outcome, whereas they now become committed to expecting and indeed working to achieve a specifically defined outcome. That this will alter the possible outcome is without question, but the odds on a particular outcome – the selected one – occurring have only changed slightly due to the attention directed to achieving it, but have deteriorated hugely because of being one in many possible.

The process of intended change is, by definition, a process based on choice.

For instance, in a case written up by a probation officer, this selection process was an essential part of the change process. He highlighted those characteristics, motives and circumstances which made his client different from the criminal society in which he lived. Thus although he was guilty of a criminal act (helping his friends in a robbery), the probation officer believed that the 'meaningful' connections that he made about his client's behaviour were what lay at the root of this criminal act.

The point is, how could the probation officer be sure? What he had done was to select; he chose those factors of which he was made aware as being those which determined the difference between his client and the rest of the criminal element with whom he had been involved. How could he know that the factors he chose to stress were those which were crucially responsible for his client's behaviour? There were of course many others probably present, like susceptibility to persuasion by his colleagues, greed, and so on, which might have been selected, but which were hidden. There is a considerable element of faith in the choices that were made by the probation officer.

Effects of the Quality of Data

Each of the ways by which information can be collected about persons and situations carries with it the possibility of bias, contamination and distortion. But this imprecision, distortion and over-simplification has to occur because, otherwise, no change agent would be able to take any action. Essentially, complex ideas have to be reduced to a pragmatic form in order to be useful and, above everything else, changing human behaviour is an activity. The problem is one of the difference of logical types between what is said in the offer of information and the context in which it is said.

To repeat what has been said many times here; without context, words and actions have no meanings; so that the data with which the change agent has to work relates specifically to the context in which it occurs. The alternatives to understanding the data in the context of its origin are to change the environment or to destroy the target's connection with it. People are shaped by context and to move them to a new context is to bring about change.

Most change efforts are directed through the medium of talking, and there arise all the problems connected with the use of language. Language is symbolic and descriptive, static and linear, and it has to be used to describe systems which are dynamic and circular. There are very definite limits to the verbal communication of behaviour, as anyone in deep emotional distress often discovers. Against this is the fact that change agents tend to use approaches which derive from a lineal causation thesis in an area where there are no absolute truths and any causation is quite difficult to establish.

When dealing with written data, the manner of its writing becomes important. Most information culled in this way has been written for a specific purpose, and a large element of selectivity has thus been introduced both in the quantity and type of material used and the emphases which it has been given. Behaviour is so complex that, for fear of missing out something which may prove to be significant, many reports on behaviour contain masses of material which are largely irrelevant to the problem. On paper, also, many apparent links between parts of the material are apt to emerge, and are passed on as direct causal links.

Of course all these factors are those which bedevil communication in general, but in the process of intended change their inclusion has the possibility of materially affecting the quality of life of the persons engaged in the change process. The major problem lies in the fact that this may not even be recognised. The process of checking through feedback, while an improvement on uncritical acceptance of the value of any communication, is itself no guarantee that messages between participants will be congruent.

Effects of Change Agents

It is seldom that a reference can be found in the literature of change to the fact that change agents may themselves become part of the problem which has to be dealt with. Before the arrival of the change agent into the scene of an individual's or group's existence, the factors available for dealing with any problem were there and in place. However, any change agent tends to be seen as a powerful person with knowledge and expertise in dealing with problems and there is a strong possibility that this perception will create a new situation which is rather unbalanced and which generates expectations that are often counter to the process of establishing lasting and effective change.

There is always the idea that intervention, by definition, is something which comes from outside but, as I have tried to show, change agents become part of the system once they engage with clients; they do not remain outside. This idea is somewhat in conflict with the way in which change agents tend to label their approaches as being based on scientific principles, and to regard their work as being one of solving 'problems'. There is no objective truth in human relational systems, but change agents have to do something because that is their job. They have to make sense of a mass of data and they use as a 'sense-making' system some hypothesis about human behaviour which is founded in generalities.

Amongst other problems is the failure which sometimes occurs when change agents cannot distinguish between patterns of behaviour; thus they often choose to tackle behaviour which does not relate to the essential difficulty. It has often been stated that intervention should be restrained to the minimum required to bring about acceptable change – underlying problems may remain unresolved, but at least a particular issue has been dealt with constructively, and without damage.

Most change agents work inside organisations of some sort and, like all organisations, there is a need to label entrants into the system so that they can be allocated a proper place within it. This process is quite recognisable by any industrialist and is concerned with defining which part of the system shall have responsibility for the new acquisition. But as we have seen in some of the cases listed here, one result of such a labelling process is to pass on an individual in the system by defining him or her out of a particular part of it, and in the worst scenario this can become a process of constant movement without any static points. Sometimes this is referred to as 'reframing' – which means redefining the 'problem' so that it can be seen in a different, more constructive and workable way without actually changing any real part of it. Such reclassification can however cause the obliteration of a 'problem' in one part of the system, only for it to reappear in another in a changed form.

Ethics

For change agents there is always the problem that what appears to work in the change process may be unethical, usually in the sense that if the target actually understood what was happening he or she might conceivably refuse to co-operate. This contains the issue of power and of powerlessness. which is currently a much-debated issue in all human relationships.

There is some need for change agents to be aware of the reasons for compliance other than that of whole-hearted co-operation, for, where this latter is not given and based upon a real understanding of what is involved, the bases of later resistance and drop-out have already been forged.

An illustration which contains almost all of the ethical problems involved can be discovered in the use of drugs to bring about change.

The problem with performance drugs (e.g. Prozac, Ritalin, Retinova, HRT and steroids) is that they produce changes in those to whom they are administered which constitute an improvement over and above what the natural limits of the organism would normally permit.

There is a very complex argument involved here. If drugs are administered to overcome a handicap, a disability, a deficiency or an ailment, they are being used to repair or restore something which previously existed. In other words, there is no attempt to produce a higher level of functioning than the client's individual genetic endowment would have permitted. With performance drugs something entirely different is envisaged. They are generally employed by those who, for one reason or another, are dissatisfied with their 'natural' performance levels and are taken with the express purpose not of repairing damage but of improving 'artificially' their normal performance level.

The argument goes that if people can improve their performance, feel happier, increase their attention spans and improve their ability to learn, why should this not happen? Why should the natural limitations imposed by genetic endowment be regarded as inviolate?

Probably one of the main counter arguments here is that we do not fully know what the costs of interfering with normal functioning levels in this way may turn out to be in the long term. Especially, as in the case of Ritalin, where the drug is administered to inattentive and hyperactive children. There is always the possibility that, in children, the application of performance drugs may mask what the true (that is, the natural) performance levels may be and, indeed, natural states may come to be regarded not as naturally deficient in some area or other but as some kind of disorder which can be remedied by the appropriate medication.

There are no concise answers to these matters, for they are of a moral nature; but they are matters for consideration in the processes of change because the simple fact about performance drugs is that their availability may be not just a matter of desire, but of an ability to pay, and of a need to gain advantage over others.

Resistance

It is logical that the same factors which hold individuals in their social positions – that is, the networks of relationships and experience – also form an essential part of any resistance to change. As we have seen, these networks or contexts are what give meaning to an individual's life. They may be real in the sense of their current existence, stored, or even fantasy, but all serve roughly the same purpose and can to some extent replace one another when some part of the net is lost; for example, when the individual moves to a new location or suffers enforced change of living conditions, or isolation.

Children have bigger fantasy nets; old people who become physically isolated have smaller real nets but larger and more vivid stored nets. Change implies the need to break into some part of these nets, or at least to change them by substitution, or a different emphasis, or the addition of a new and different part of the system. It follows that there is a need to know the strength of the links of these nets, and also the possible consequences of trying to change them. Unless there is a clear recognition on the part of the target that what is being offered is as good as, if not better than, what it is suggested should be replaced, resistance is an obvious consequence. This inevitably brings into focus the possibly quite different perceptions of what is beneficial between change agent and client.

It is not possible to programme people to behave differently.

Fear of change is related often enough to anxiety about the unknown. Change tends to threaten security; it appears to require costs which can seem to be quite out of keeping with what is on offer; for instance, the realignment of support systems to hold the new behaviour patterns in place. Even the transfer of learning from the situation of its origin to the general existence of the individual is fraught with problems, because learning in one situation does not necessarily become decontextualised and thus the basis for change in other contexts. Clients may have already attempted to sort out their problems and discovered that learning does not always readily transfer, and this experience may again form the basis for resistance.

Maintenance

Keeping a change working is another great problem. For instance, change which is possible and sustainable in a specifically selected context may be unsupportable in others. Many patients in psychiatric treatment are able to function very well indeed but on discharge, with the supportive system of the unit no longer available, the pressures of their 'normal' system can quickly reassert their power. Thus, the essential fact of the maintenance of changed behaviour lies with the system in which the client has to exist.

If, instead of looking at this from the point of view of the change agent, we stand the process on its head, it can be seen that resistance and reversion are the maintenance processes of the system. That is, changed individuals do not function well within the system and the system then brings pressure to bear on them to revert. It is possible that changes which are not too great stand a better chance of being maintained than those which are larger, and thus much more likely to be in conflict with the social system. The alternative, which has long been recognised of course, is removal of the client to an entirely different system for long periods of time.

24 Conclusions

Much of the material I have presented in this book can be divided into two main areas:

- a discussion of the commonly used ideas and processes of intended change; and

- an attempt to show where those ideas and the processes which derive from them run into difficulties.

It is easy to pick holes in the theories and practice of a profession which is dependent for its existence upon an order of facts which a physical scientist would tend to reject as unworkable because of their unprovable and largely unknowable nature. But, perhaps because of this fact – and because of the need to develop some sense of possibility in those they work with and, to a large extent, to protect themselves – change agents have consistently over-elaborated and certainly over-stated the certainties of their processes, and it has always seemed to me that this illusion of certainty has been unnecessarily over-done.

If the truth of the matter is that the probability of change efforts being successful is far less than is broadcast, then I for one believe that the truth should be told. For in the end what actually emerges will always be less than was expected, and the final result will be that the very disillusionment which the agents were trying to prevent will have emerged anyway, and with the extra force of disappointment.

Thus my first aim has been to try to introduce an added element of reality into the whole process of intended change. This may be condemned as unduly pragmatic and lacking in the imaginative insights which have so often proved to be the precursor of some splendid new addition to knowledge. I don't agree; for the simple reason that I have always accepted that such insights will occur, because practitioners faced with unforeseen problems will think on their feet in order to find some kind of acceptable solu-

tion. But I have also always argued that insights need to prove
their value in the marketplace, otherwise they have to be classed
with flights of fancy.

It must be better to be reasonably certain about the ideas and
practices one is using and to seek to add to them whatever
insights arise than to extend one's range without calling their
validity into question.

There is little need to review the kind of information that we
have available about human behaviour. All that needs to be said
here is that new knowledge is being added in the realm of physical
causation of behavioural patterns. Because this field of exploration
is the nearest that behavioural scientists can come to the physical
sciences, the standards of accuracy and replication of information
are high. For the rest we have elegant explanations by the score
but, as has been said many times, explanations are endless, facts
are extremely limited; but we do have speculation, and we have
intuitive and other forms of understanding. But let us start from
the beginning and assess what we actually do have, then perhaps it
might be possible, when the mists of obfuscation have been somewhat cleared away, to see what there really is to work with, and
what kinds of outcome we might reliably expect to achieve.

To start with the obvious – there are only two major areas of
intended change: firstly the situation in which individuals exist can
be changed; and secondly their perception of and thus their response to that situation can be changed. The first is not always
possible and the second depends largely upon finding out how
individuals see a situation, what it means to them and, finally,
whether they can actually handle whatever changes may be deemed
to be necessary.

Training

One of the problems of intended change agents is how future
generations of agents may be taught. It has always seemed to me
that what we have attempted to teach in the past has consisted
largely of material which is peripheral to the actual face-to-face
practice of intervention. Also we seem to have assumed that
effective 'change' work is an art or a skill, which may or may
not be dependent upon what Jaspers (1963: 830) called, 'a mastery of natural causes for practical ends', but is in any case
usually part of the natural talent of potential agents before they
actually become engaged in the practice. If not, it is a skill

acquired by practice over long periods of time, backed by the peripheral areas of knowledge mentioned earlier and, if fortune is present, by experienced supervision. The opposite end of the spectrum from natural talent would then appear to be the operator whose approach is all, or mainly, acquired techniques and information, and where the tendency then almost inevitably becomes one of attempting to compress their change targets into the confines of those techniques and information.

What this must convey to any critical observer is that the main process of change efforts cannot be isolated sufficiently to be taught in any systematic way. This, in turn, implies that the kind of understanding which enables change agents to be even as successful as they are is one which is based not so much in data, information and knowledge, but in a sensitivity to indefinable elements of human behaviour which can only be acquired by exposure and by testing outcomes – in effect, to use computer terminology, by long-term programming, which in the case of change agents must be essentially idiosyncratic and personal.

Jaspers, referring to psychotherapy – which is one of the major change processes – wrote:

This therapy, however, so far as it can be taught, is not derived from such knowledge alone to any major extent but remains an art that uses science as one of its instruments. The art can indeed be developed and enriched and transmitted through personal contact but it can only be learned in its technical aspects and reapplied to a limited degree. (1963: 380)

Contextual Collision

For most of my professional working life I have argued that human behaviour has meaning only in the context in which it is produced. This argument is accepted in biological circles, where it is understood that living organisms can only be truly understood in the context of their environment. Equally, in linguistics, words are seen to have no meaning other than a lexical one out of the context in which they are spoken or written.

This argument has been accepted in the sense that the environment in which an individual lives is seen as greatly affecting, conditioning, influencing and maintaining his or her behaviour. But 'environment', in most cases, is taken to mean the social milieu in which an individual exists. Ecologists have suggested another term which can easily be seen as being even more inclusive than 'environment' and that term is 'context'. In my terms 'context' means the totality of those features in which an individual is embedded and which he or she carries around – for instance, thoughts, ideas, physical presence, experience, fantasies, and so on – as well as the situations and people with whom the individual has contact.

In working with groups, for instance, there have been two major forms of operation which have been variously defined, but essentially, are differentiated by the use to which a group of people may be put.

- There is use of the group as an instrument, where the process is one of welding the disparate individuals into a group unit, which is usually characterised by an acceptance by the members of groups rules and norms, and to which each member has committed energy, belief and trust. In simple terms, this is an attempt to create a group as a separate unit, with an easily recognised identity, and which is thus believed to operate as a system deriving its energy from its members, and producing goods for those members and probably for significant others as well.

- Then there is the use of the group as a background; a specifically assembled environment which brings into play all the known effects that the presence of others has on individual behaviour. This is, in essence, a created context which gradually becomes part of the background in the sense defined above. Each member of a group operates within this context in essentially idiosyncratic ways, but these become more like those of other members the longer he or she stays with the group and the greater the group's meaning for the individual becomes. Each member can learn something new about themselves, perhaps redesign part of their context, and partially merge with the context of the group. This process, which most often takes its initial impetus from a skilled group leader who guides the individuals in the learning and recontextualising process, is usually referred to as that of the 'group as context'.

What I have attempted to show in this book is that most forms of change efforts concentrate on a decontextualised individual; either by regarding him or her as being principally the victim of their genetic endowment, which may well be true; or as the end product of their history, which may also be true, but essentially the process is one of regarding the living organism as something which can be dealt with wholly out of context or, at best, in only part of it.

Consider the methods of change which are related to the idea that human predicaments are problems. Without doubt such an approach can yield benefits because many human predicaments contain a problem element within their complexity. But the essential result of casting a predicament as a problem is that, logically, it may then be supposed to have an answer. If it has an answer, the problem no longer exists – unless the answer is one which can not be pursued. I for one would regard such an answer as not constituting a real answer in any pragmatic sense.

But the nature of many human predicaments is such that they are the manifest consequences of decisions and choices taken at earlier stages in the individual's life, and many are indeed unforeseen and unexpected consequences which currently present, as Laing suggested, as 'knots' from which the individual has little or no chance of untying him or herself.

Essentially, it does not matter a great deal why such choices and decisions were made; whether, for instance, they were made in clear sober situations, or under duress either of circumstances, individuals, mental or physical states. These sources are indicators of the probability of such choices being repeated, and may show also something of the nature of the intensity of their fulfilment. What is essential is that they were made in order to achieve what appeared to be some desirable end, however minimal. As I have tried to show, virtually no such choice or decision made by an individual in whatever circumstances – whether it succeeds in promoting the desired outcome or not – is free of entailed consequences which were either ignored, not known about, or in other ways not allowed for. It is also most likely that these unforeseen consequences actually have an impact status which is considerably higher or of greater magnitude than the original intended outcome.

If this sounds rather incredible, it is only necessary to concentrate on the process of decision-making in order to discover ample logical reasons why it occurs. When choices and decisions have to be made, whatever the pressures which are present (small or great), the process of decision-making is one which causes thought process to concentrate: firstly, on defining what it is that has to be decided upon; and secondly, on assessing what is available in order to deal with it. As some forms of game playing, particularly predictive games like chess, tend to show, even when the prediction of the consequences of making any move is (or could be) a known element, the ability of an individual to raise his or her predictive ability above the focus of the immediate problem is one which is possessed or developed by remarkably few people.

The difficulty lies in the fact that, from the processes of focusing down to the essentials of a problem and of deciding on a move to deal with them, there tends to occur an effective exclusion of those possibilities which are not immediately visible. The predictive ability of human beings is never very good except where the categories of choice are extremely well-defined and this, by definition, tends to preclude considering factors which lie outside those defined categories, and for which there is little existing evidence of the probability of their incursion into such consideration.

It is little wonder that the history of humankind is full of attempts to explain the effects of unforeseen consequences in terms of non-human agencies controlling events, or being the result of the intervention of luck, chance, fate, etc. One major characteristic of all these attempts at explanation has been an acceptance of their inevitability and also, therefore, of the puny nature of any attempt by individuals alone or en masse to control their emergence.

If we go back to the problem approach to human predicaments for a moment, it will be to note that one beneficial factor is that it is an approach to predicaments in terms of their current manifestations. The apparent antecedents of the predicament may be considered, but by seeking solutions it is in essence offering a minimal form of contextual change for those involved. What is itself problematical is that the so-called 'solutions' may not be within the contextual acceptability of the individuals concerned, for the simple reason that by regarding the predicament as a problem the actuality has become an abstraction, and thus the solution will contain large elements of abstraction also. By 'abstraction' in this case I mean that it will represent a formula which will be at some remove from the contextual situation of the individual or group to which it is applied.

Herein lies the root of the problem of acceptance of solutions, which is related to neatness of fit in the perception of the target individual. Rationally, what is posed as a solution to a problem may well have all the appearances of an acceptable reality. But given the complexity of any individual's context, if it does not mesh at an adequate number of salient points with that context, its level of abstraction and of difference may well preclude its absorption into that context in sufficient strength to become a permanent part and an element of change.

Maslow believed that human predicaments could only be dealt with by an extension of the choices which were open to human beings. But he realised that the ability to make choices was dependent first of all upon what he called the 'hierarchy of needs' – with survival needs taking priority over others – and also upon the clear recognition of what choice involved. Indeed, most of what appears to be presented to people in difficulty are logically non-choices, for the simple reason that they are offered by those whose understanding of the choice may indeed be clear and some of the entailed consequences known from past experience, but they are offered to those to whom they appear as abstractions – ideas which only very lightly touch their reality as they know and experience it. If they are then accepted as choices, that acceptance is more likely to be based not so much on a true evaluation of them as choices but more on the kind of presence which the acceptor believes is represented by the offerer, or by the circumstances in which he or she finds him or herself. That pressure is just as likely to take the form of trust, affection, acceptance of expertise, desperation or fear as it is of a clear understanding of the benefits of what is being offered.

Ellis (1971) produced an approach to dealing with human problems which contained a large element of behaviourist ideas. The two main concepts were 'childish demandingness' and 'perennial disturbability', by which Ellis thought to convey the idea that disturbed people are characterised firstly by their demands to be well, to be treated fairly, and for the world to be a place in which they can live easily; and secondly by the ease with which they can be upset.

> When the individual importantly or mainly chooses an irrational way of life, and significantly keeps defeating his own best interests and/or keeps antisocially sabotaging the interests of others, he is usually doing so because of some kind of childish demandingness. (p. 101)

Ellis' rational-emotive therapy has always been regarded as a very tough approach, its author consistently refers to puerile whining on the part of disturbed individuals. But I find it relevant to look at his work briefly here because of its insistence on the factor of choice. Like cognitive therapists, Ellis believes that the predicaments of human beings are largely brought about by the nature and consequences of the choices they make.

> Human demandingness or disturbability, in other words, may be transiently short-circuited and sidetracked by a vast number of

psychotherapeutic methods which are variously labeled psychoanalysis, encounter therapy, hypnosis, meditation, decondition-
ing, Christian Science, Scientology, Voodoo, witch-doctoring,
religious faith etc. All these methods work to some extent but
the vast majority of them seem to be palliative. This is because
they tend to concentrate on doing something about the individual's demands and the symptoms he is plagued with when
these are not gratified to his liking; but they rarely help him
effectively to minimize the demandingness itself and thereby
once and for all to undercut the roots of his propensity to
disturb or upset himself.

Ellis (1971: 102–3)

Ignoring Ellis' obvious contempt for less 'robust' methods, it is
clear that he has latched on to two central facts about change
efforts: the partial nature of the main approaches to the contextual
nature of human behaviour; and the essential responsibility of the
individual, for the production of predicament status, its maintenance, and its change through the process of choice. There is an
understanding that if an individual can rationally accept new ideas
about his or her behaviour, there can be little or no real change
from these ideas unless they become instrumental in changing
some of that individual's personal constructs. Kelly's (1955) thesis
of personal constructs implied that individuals make sense of their
world by creating a series of schema against which external and
internal events are measured. In essence this is a description of a
value system which is personally adapted to an individual's needs.

At this point we must consider some of the effects of choice. In
colloquial language people are said to 'paste themselves into corners'
by virtue of making a sequence of choices. By this is meant that they
arrive at a time in their lives where they are faced with the realisation
that they have reached a predicament which is usually characterised
by the need to make more choices in order to extricate themselves,
all of which can be seen to entail more or less unpleasant consequences. At this stage it tends to become clear that, if they had not
done what they did based upon decisions made at the time, they
would not now be faced with what looks like an inescapable dilemma. Anger, consternation, anxiety, depression, illness, bizarre behaviour, retreat, blame-laying, frustration, despair, guilt, and many
other corrosive human emotions arise from such a situation and,
because they are manifest in behaviour patterns which are eminently
recognisable, they tend to be presented as the major difficulty, and to
some extent accepted as such by change agents.

The theoretical assumptions of the sources of behaviour presented here seem to me only to tackle parts of this manifestation of disturbed behaviour. Obviously those elements of behaviour which are directly and explicitly traceable to genetic, physical and biochemical sources can be dealt with appropriately. But there is often no clear distinction between such explicit causes and the manifest behaviour; indeed, the close effects produced by the elements of an integral emotional/physical system can be extremely confusing as one element manifests patterns initiated or originated in other elements. The complexities of hysteria and other psychosomatic manifestations are clear examples of this factor, as is the control which some individuals can exercise mentally over physical states.

For the most part, the predicaments in which human beings find themselves are the consequences of making choices. Now if the choice-making ability of an individual is defective or deficient, either because it was genetically so determined or because it has been damaged in some way and has not adequately developed, the decisions can be expected to be different in some ways from what would be logically appropriate. But, nevertheless, the choices are and will be made, with or without assistance, and consequences will ensue.

When intervention is set in motion by a change agent what actually appears to happen is that one person with the express intention of bringing about beneficial change comes into contact with others. This is the essence of intended change as I defined it earlier. But now we are in a position to say that this apparently simple insertion of one person into the lives of others with intent is much more complex than it would appear. What actually occurs could more appropriately be described as a contextual collision and a probable partial amalgamation all of which tends to be ignored.

The concept of the powerlessness of some of those who are on the receiving end of the attentions of change agents and the description of their methods as exploitative or discriminatory can be seen to refer only very inexactly as crude approximations of a process which draws individuals out of their context and into that of the change agent.

Take, for instance, any one of the psychiatric interviews which were part of Mrs Jones' story in Chapter 3. Without exception, they were all held in a clinic which was almost totally the environmental context of the psychiatrist. But if they had been held in Mrs Jones' house, there would then have been a situation in which her context had been altered by the presence of the psychiatrist – a person who was well versed in creating extensions of his context which could, and did, define large areas of Mrs Jones' existence for her in ways and along lines of which she had no experience.

Of course, such contextual interference is a common enough experience. The crunch comes when it occurs not in everyday and thus expected experience, but in terms of some essentially crucial and important aspect of life.

References

Andreski, S. (1974) *Social Sciences as Sorcery.* Harmondsworth, England: Penguin Books.

Applebaum, A. (1995) *Daily Telegraph* (3 Oct): 24.

Argyle, M. (1972) *The Social Psychology of Work.* Harmondsworth, England: Penguin Books.

Argyle, M. (1973) *Social Interaction.* London: Tavistock Publications.

Bales, R.F. (1950) 'A set of categories for the analysis of small group interactions'. *American Soc. Review* 15: 257–63.

Bateson, G. (1973) *Steps to an Ecology of Mind.* St Albans: Chandler.

Bennis, W. G. (1970) 'Change Agents', in Golembiewski, R. T. and Blumberg, A. (eds) *Sensitivity Training & the Laboratory Approach*, pp. 306–20. Illinois: F. E. Peacock Publishers.

Blau, P. M. and Scott, W. R. (1980) 'Who Benefits?', in Etzioni, A. and Lehman, E. W. (eds) *A Sociological Reader on Complex Organisations*, 3rd edn, pp. 101–15. NY: Holt, Rinehart & Winston.

Blumberg, A. and Golembiewski, R. T. (1976) *Learning and Change in Groups.* Harmondsworth, England: Penguin Books.

Bolton, N. (1972) *The Psychology of Thinking.* London: Methuen.

Bonner, H. (1959) *Group Dynamics: Principles and Applications.* NY: The Ronald Press.

Bronowski, J. (1973) *The Ascent of Man.* London: BBC Books.

Campbell, J. (1973) *Myths to Live By.* London: Souvenir Press (Educational & Academic).

Cartwright, D. (1966) 'Achieving Change in People: some applications of group dynamics theory'. *Human Relations* 4 pp. 381–93, NY: Plenum.

Chapple, E. D. and Coon, C. S. (1955) 'The Equilibrium of Groups' in Hare, A.P., Borgatta, E.F. and Bales, R.F. (eds) *Small Groups.* New York: Knopf.

Cochrane, P. (1996) 'Allowing your Computer to Forget, Connected', *Daily Telegraph* (25 June): 12.

284   CHANGE, INTERVENTION AND CONSEQUENCE

Ellis, A. (1971) *A Casebook of Rational-emotive Therapy.* Palo Alto, CA: Science & Behavior Books.
Erikson, B. A. and Erikson, C. W. (1972) *Perception & Personality.* Morristown, NJ: General Learning Press.
Etzioni, A. (1980) 'Compliance Structures', in Etzioni, A. and Lehman, E. W. (eds) *A Sociological Reader on Complex Organisations.* NY: Holt, Rinehart & Winston.
Eysenck, H. J. (1953) *Uses and Abuses of Psychology.* Harmondsworth, England: Penguin Books.
Eysenck, H. and Eysenck, M. (1981) *Mindwatching.* London: Michael Joseph.
Frankel, A. J. and Glasser, P. H. (1974) 'Behavioral Approaches to Groupwork', *Social Work USA* (March).
French, J. R. P. and Raven, B. (1959) 'The Bases of Social Power', in Cartwright, M. D. (ed.) *Studies in Social Power*, pp. 150–67. Ann Arbor: Institute for Social Research, University of Michigan.
Glasser, P., Sarri, R. and Vinter, R. (1974) *Individual Change Through Small Groups.* NY: The Free Press.
Gleick, J. (1988) *Chaos: Making a New Science.* Harmondsworth, England: Penguin Books.
Golembiewski, R. T. and Blumberg, A. (1970). *Sensitivity Training & the Laboratory Approach.* Illinois: F. E. Peacock Publishers.
Graves, D. (1996) 'Woman Who Fed Daughter Drug Overdose is Jailed', *Daily Telegraph* (9 May).
Gussov, M. (1994) 'Wits in Hamlet's Wings', *Daily Telegraph* (23 Dec): A4.
Hampden-Turner, C. (1966) 'An Existential "Learning Theory" and the Integration of T-group Research', *Journal of Applied Behavioral Science*, 2: 367–86.
Hampden-Turner, C. (1970) *Radical Man.* Cambridge. MA: Schenkman.
Hawking, S. (1995) *A Brief History of Time.* London: Bantam Books.
Highfield, R. (1994) 'Santa Fe Showdown at the Edge of Chaos', *Daily Telegraph* (9 Mar): 12.
Hill, W. F. (1974) 'Systematic Group Development (SGD) Therapy', in Jacobs, A. and Spradlin, W. W. (eds) *The Group as Agent of Change*, pp. 252–76. NY: Behavioral Publications.
Jaspers, K. (1963) *General Psychopathology.* Manchester: Manchester University Press.
Jenkins, D. H. (1964) 'Some Assumptions About Learning and Training', unpublished MS, Temple University, Philadelphia.
Kelly, G.A. (1955) *The Psychology of Personal Constructs* 1 and 2. NY: W.W. Norton.

Klein, R., Day, P. and Redmayne, S. (1996) *Managing Scarcity*. Buckingham: Open University Press.

Laing, R. D. (1971) *Knots*. Harmondsworth, England: Penguin Books.

Leighton, N. (1973) 'The Act of Understanding', *The British Journal of Social Work* 3(iv): 509–24.

Lewin, K. (1951) *Field Theory in Social Science*. NY: Harper.

Long, S. (1992) *A Structural Analysis of Small Groups*. London: Routledge.

Mechl, P. E. (1954) *Clinical & Statistical Prediction*. Minneapolis: University of Minnesota Press.

Medcof, J. and Roth, J. (1979) *Approaches to Psychology*. Buckingham: Open University Press.

Miller, G.A. (1966) *Psychology: The Science of Mental Life*. Harmondsworth: Penguin Books.

Moroney, M. J. (1951) *Facts from Figures*. Harmondsworth: Penguin Books.

Mowrer, O. H. (1964) *The New Group Therapy*. NY: Van Nostrand Reinhold.

Myers, J. G. (1986) 'Grief Work as a Critical Condition for Small Group Phase Development', unpublished doctoral dissertation, University of Wisconsin, Madison.

Oakley, K. (1980) 'Theories of Personal Learning in Groups', in P. B. Smith (ed.) *Small Groups & Personal Change*, pp. 85–105. London: Methuen.

Ornstein, R. E. (1975) *The Psychology of Consciousness*. Harmondsworth, England: Pelican Books.

Perls, F. (1973) *The Gestalt Approach & Eye Witness to Therapy*. Palo Alto, CA: Science & Behavior Books.

Polyani, M. (1967) *The Tacit Dimension*. London: Routledge & Kegan Paul.

Popper, K. (1957) *The Poverty of Historicism*. London: Routledge & Kegan Paul.

Popper, K. (1959) *The Logic of Scientific Discovery*. London: Hutchinson.

Preedy, M., Glatter, R. and Levacic, R. (eds) *Educational Management*. Buckingham: Open University Press.

Reisman, D. (1950) *The Lonely Crowd*. New Haven: Yale University Press.

Rogers, C. R. (1961) 'The Process Equation of Psychotherapy', *American Journal of Psychotherapy* 15: pp. 22–45.

Russell, B. (1950) *Philosophy and Politics. Unpopular Essays*. Harmondsworth: Penguin.

Schneider, K. (1931) 'Pathopsychologie im Grundriss', *Handworter-buch der psychischen Hygiene* (Berlin).

Schutz, W. C. (1959) *F.I.R.O.* NY: Holt, Rinehart & Winston.

Sherif, C. W. (1976) *Orientation in Social Psychology.* NY: Harper & Row.

Stevenson, R. L. (1882) *Familiar Studies of Men and Books.* London: Cassell.

Sundel, M., Radin, N. and Churchill, S. E. (1974) 'Diagnosis in Groupwork' in Glasser, P., Sarri, R. and Vinter, R. (eds) *Individual Change Through Small Groups*, pp. 105–25. NY: The Free Press.

Tofler, A. (1970) *Future Shock.* London: Pan Books.

Vinter, R. D. (1974) 'The Essential Components of Social Group Work Practice', in Glasser, P., Sarri, R. and Vinter, R. (eds) *Individual Change Through Small Groups*, pp. 9–33. NY: The Free Press.

Vinter, R. D. and Galinsky, M. J. (1974) 'Extragroup Relations and Approaches', in Glasser, P., Sarri, R. and Vinter, R. (eds) *Individual Change Through Small Groups*, pp. 281–91. NY: The Free Press.

Weldon, T. D. (1953) *The Vocabulary of Politics.* Harmondsworth, England: Pelican Books.

Wilden, A. (1980) *System & Structure; Essays in Communication and Exchange*, 2nd edn. London: Tavistock Publications.

Wilmont, J. Earl of Rochester (1926) *Works. A Dialogue Between Strephon and Daphne 1:31.*

Index

Index by Sue Carlton